T0418602

* *

RITUALS OF MIGRATION

**GLUCKSMAN
IRISH DIASPORA**

* *

Rituals of Migration

Italians and Irish on the Move

Edited by

Kevin Kenny *and* Maddalena Marinari

* * *

NEW YORK UNIVERSITY PRESS

New York

* *

NEW YORK UNIVERSITY PRESS
New York
www.nyupress.org

Please contact the Library of Congress for Cataloging-in-Publication data.

ISBN: 9781479825134 (hardback)
ISBN: 9781479825189 (library ebook)
ISBN: 9781479825141 (consumer ebook)

This book is printed on acid-free paper, and its binding materials are chosen for strength and durability. We strive to use environmentally responsible suppliers and materials to the greatest extent possible in publishing our books.

The manufacturer's authorized representative in the EU for product safety is
Mare Nostrum Group B.V., Mauritskade 21D, 1091 GC Amsterdam, The Netherlands.
Email: gpsr@mare-nostrum.co.uk.

Manufactured in the United States of America

10 9 8 7 6 5 4 3 2 1

Also available as an ebook

CONTENTS

Introduction

Rituals of Migration

KEVIN KENNY AND MADDALENA MARINARI

The idea for this book emerged when we began to notice and compare some of the customs surrounding emigration from Italy and Ireland. In Ireland, local communities said farewell to emigrants they would never see again by holding an "American wake," an all-night ceremony with drinking, music, and dancing punctuated by bitter lamentations called a *caoin* (keen). In southern Italy, even if the chances of emigrants returning were much higher than in Ireland, departure rites also featured lamentations, silent processions, and weeping elderly women dressed in black. Young women whose husbands left the Italian South became known as "white widows" (*vedove bianche*). In both Italy and Ireland, family, friends, and neighbors gathered to read the "American letter," learning the news from abroad and, just as important, checking to see if the envelope contained money or prepaid passage tickets.

In thinking about these aspects of migration, we drew inspiration from literature and film as well as historical scholarship. Maria Messina's short stories, published and set in early twentieth-century Sicily, capture the dilemmas of women left behind by their emigrant husbands as well as the challenges these men faced when they returned. Stories by the Irish-language writer Máirtín Ó Cadhain, published and set in the west of Ireland during the first half of the twentieth century, mix stark realism with magical elements in portraying a culture disappearing in the face of relentless emigration. In planning this book, we also thought about the opening scene of the movie *Rocco e i suoi fratelli* (1960), when the widow Rosario Parondi arrives in industrial Milan from the remote southern region of Basilicata with four of her sons; the Ellis Island scene in *Nuovomondo* (2006), when Fortunata Mancuso and her grandson

Pietro deliberately fail an inspection test so they can return to Sicily; and the scenes in *The Field* (1990) when a returnee known simply as "the American" rides roughshod over customary norms of Irish land use embodied by the tragic figure of Bull McCabe. All these works encapsulate key moments of transition for migrants at home and abroad.[1]

In a series of vivid historical essays, the contributors to *Rituals of Migration* offer snapshots of Italian and Irish migrants who embarked on overseas journeys that changed their lives. To capture these experiences, the book approaches migration from the perspective of rituals. The authors focus on particular moments, actions, sentiments, and material objects at the point of departure, in transit, and in the process of return. They tell the stories of Italian and Irish people on the move, the dilemmas they faced, the decisions they made, and the contexts in which they made them. Previous scholars of migration have examined rituals concerning food and religion in considerable detail. Aspects of these two well-studied topics feature in this book, but we adopt a more expansive approach, examining a broader range of actions and sentiments that occurred during moments of preparation, departure, travel, and return.[2]

In this respect, we find the idea of rites of passage especially helpful. At various points during their lives, individuals experience moments of separation, transition, and reincorporation—including birth, puberty, marriage, and death. They mark these special occasions with particular words, actions, sentiments, and objects. Emigration involves a particular kind of rite of passage: separation from the homeland, a journey to a new society, incorporation into that society, and the possibility of return. Grappling with the decision of whether to leave or stay was an expected part of the Irish and Italian life cycle. Then, as now, migrants and their families paused to mark the moment of departure and arrival, found the strength to embark upon unpredictable adventures, and went on to build new lives abroad in the face of adversity. *Rituals of Migration* tells some of their stories.[3]

* * *

The scale of both Italian and Irish migration is extraordinary. Whereas the United States is known for attracting immigrants, Italy and Ireland are among the classic nations of emigrants. Both countries experienced remarkably high levels of departure, which had enormous social,

1	Abruzzo
2	Basilicata
3	Calabria
4	Campania
5	Emilia-Romagna
6	Friuli-Venezia Giulia
7	Lazio
8	Liguria
9	Lombardia
10	Marche
11	Molise
12	Piemonte
13	Puglia
14	Sardegna
15	Sicilia
16	Trentino-Alto Adige
17	Toscana
18	Umbria
19	Valle d'Aosta
20	Veneto

Figure 1.1. Regional map of Italy. Matt Kania Map Illustrations.

economic, political, and cultural ramifications at home and abroad. *Rituals of Migration* focuses on the most intensive period of emigration from both countries, from the mid-nineteenth through the mid-twentieth centuries. During this period, more than 13 million people left Italy for overseas destinations and roughly the same number left for other countries in Europe. About 8 million people left Ireland in the same era, though Ireland's emigration rate was considerably higher than Italy's because the population was much smaller. The population of Ireland peaked at 8.5 million in 1845, on the eve of the Great Famine; fell to only 4.5 million by 1901; and was still only 7 million in 2024 (5.1 million in the Republic of Ireland and 1.9 million in Northern Ireland). Italy's population, despite mass emigration, rose from about 22 million in 1861, when most of the peninsula was united into a single kingdom, to 32.5 million in 1901 and 47 million in 1951, and it currently stands at 60 million. Both countries sent about the same number of emigrants—5 million—to the United States, the largest single destination. Italians also moved in large numbers to Argentina, Brazil, Venezuela, Uruguay, Canada, and Australia, while Irish emigrants settled in Canada, Australia, New Zealand, South Africa, and Argentina. Closer to home, England and Scotland were major destinations for the Irish, and continental European countries attracted half of the total Italian emigration.

Shortly after Italy unified as a country in 1861, it emerged as one of the major senders of emigrants around the world. The territory that eventually became Italy had a long tradition of seasonal, mostly male migration across the peninsula and to Europe. Long before 1861, Italian agriculture was based on seasonal migration. For centuries, peasants from Umbria, Abruzzo, and Calabria left the Apennine Mountains to harvest cereals in the Roman countryside. Nomad shepherds from Abruzzo led their flocks to the Roman countryside and Puglia during winter. During harvest season, the fertile lands in Puglia also drew temporary migrant workers from the surrounding areas. The Po Valley in the northwest of Italy, particularly the rice fields in the province of Vercelli, attracted peasants from the Alps as well as from the coasts of Toscana. Sicilians migrated to North Africa in search of work, land, or political refuge, a well-established pattern by the early nineteenth century. A small number of emigrants, mostly from northern Italy, also left the Italian peninsula for Argentina, Brazil, and the United States before 1861 because of political upheaval or to find work as sculptors, woodworkers, and glassblowers. Migration to South America, especially to Buenos Aires, emerged from the special role that Genoese merchants played in the Spanish Empire. The number of Italians living in the Americas remained insignificant until the late nineteenth century, however, with only about 25,000, mostly from northern Italy, arriving in the United States between 1820 and 1870.[4]

Figure 1.2. "Emigranti," 1894. Oil on canvas by Raffaello Gambogi (1874–1943). Courtesy of Museo Civico Giovanni Fattori, Livorno, Italy.

The first and most significant wave of large-scale emigration from Italy occurred from the early 1880s through the late 1920s. Some of these migrants were workers, artisans, or professionals, but most were peasants accustomed to migrating in search of work. Mainly single men from southern Italy, they stayed abroad only for a short time. Most of them were Catholic, but they often had an ambivalent relationship with the Catholic Church, partly because of the large, landed estates (*latifundia*) that institution owned. This ambivalence sometimes developed into outright rejection of Catholicism or in the embrace of radical ideologies like socialism, anarchism, and communism. Between 1880 and 1900, about 7 million people left Italy, mostly moving from northern regions of the country to other European countries. From 1900 to 1914, almost 9 million emigrants left, largely from the South and mostly for Argentina, Brazil, and the United States. By 1914, nearly a million Italians lived in Argentina and a million and a half in the United States. In each country, Italian immigrants settled primarily in urban centers, especially in the rapidly growing commercial and industrial port cities of Buenos Aires and New York but also in mining camps and, to a lesser extent, agricultural settings. At the beginning of the twentieth century, when the Italian government began to build a more centralized emigration bureaucracy, Italian officials discouraged emigration to Brazil and Argentina because of the exploitative labor agreements under which many Italians were brought to these countries. This development made the United States the primary destination for Italian migrants. The 1924 Immigration Act, however, introduced a national origins quota system that discriminated sharply against immigrants from Eastern and Southern Europe. The passage of the act—combined with emigration restrictions introduced by the Italian government after Mussolini came to power and the impact of the Great Depression—reduced Italian emigration to the United States significantly. From 1928 to 1940, only 1.3 million Italians departed, the majority leaving northern Italy for other European countries or for fascist Italy's colonies in Northern Africa.[5]

Mass emigration revived after World War II, mostly from the central and southern regions of Italy. While much of the migration to the United States in the postwar era stemmed from family reunification, the movement within Europe occurred almost entirely through bilateral temporary worker agreements (Belgium, Germany, and Switzerland) or was undocumented (France). Italians also went in significant numbers to Canada and, to a lesser extent, Australia. The rapid postwar recovery of Western European nations—facilitated by financial assistance from the US-funded European Recovery Program (Marshall Plan)—reduced the compulsion to emigrate, and the exploitative conditions in Belgium and Germany were a further disincentive. Nonetheless, from 1946 to 1970, the peak of Italian emigration after World War II, 6,712,000 people left Italy (3,572,000 of whom eventually returned home). Among those who moved abroad permanently, about half settled in European countries and the other half outside of Europe. Since the 1990s, Italy has become a major receiving country for immigrants from Eastern Europe, southeast Asia, and northern Africa, even as the country continues to experience ongoing emigration, primarily by well-educated young people seeking opportunity elsewhere because of socioeconomic problems and political instability at home. The number of Italian citizens living abroad increased by almost 50 per cent between 2006 and

1	Antrim
2	Armagh
3	Carlow
4	Cavan
5	Clare
6	Cork
7	Derry
8	Donegal
9	Down
10	Dublin
11	Fermanagh
12	Galway
13	Kerry
14	Kildare
15	Kilkenny
16	Laois
17	Leitrim
18	Limerick
19	Longford
20	Louth
21	Mayo
22	Meath
23	Monaghan
24	Offaly
25	Roscommon
26	Sligo
27	Tipperary
28	Tyrone
29	Waterford
30	Westmeath
31	Wexford
32	Wicklow

Figure 1.3. Regional map of Ireland. Matt Kania Map Illustrations.

2015, to almost 5 million. As of 2020, an estimated 80 million people around the world claimed full or partial Italian ancestry—about 27 million of them in Brazil and 20 million in Argentina, compared to 18 million in the United States.[6]

The Irish diaspora, meanwhile, includes an estimated 70 million people, half of them in the United States. As in Italy, Irish herders in the early modern era migrated with their animals, moving dairy cattle to upland pastures in the summer, a practice known as "booleying" (from the Irish word *buaile*). In the early nineteenth century, agricultural laborers migrated seasonally in search of work, both within Ireland and to Scotland and England, setting the stage for overseas emigration. Mass overseas emigration from Ireland began and peaked earlier than in the Italian case. In the seventeenth century, a small number of Irish servants, soldiers, and merchants—perhaps 50,000, nearly all of them men—settled in the Caribbean and the mainland colonies of British North America. Unable to form ethnic communities by marrying Irish women, and living short lives under brutal conditions, they left few traces in the historical record. In the eighteenth century, about 200,000 Irish people went to British North America, most of them Presbyterians from the northern province of Ulster who migrated in search of land and religious toleration. They and their descendants became the Scots Irish in the United States. In the generation from 1815 to 1845, almost 1 million people left Ireland for the United States and Canada, driven out by fierce competition for rental land in the context of rapid population growth and the commercialization of agriculture. Most of these emigrants, for the first time, were Catholics. Thereafter, Protestants accounted for only 10 percent of Irish emigrants to the United States, though they continued to dominate the smaller outflow to destinations within the British Empire.[7]

Irish transatlantic migration assumed massive dimensions between 1845 and 1921. In the decade following the onset of the potato blight in 1845, 2.1 million emigrants left famine-stricken Ireland—considerably more than in all Irish history up to that point. Another 1 million died of famine and disease, resulting in a population decline of one-third, a catastrophe without parallel in modern European history. Three-quarters of the famine emigrants (1.5 million) went directly to the United States, the remainder primarily to Britain and Australia; of the 300,000 who went to Canada, many also made their way south across the border. The Irish made up 35 percent of all immigrants to the United States in the 1830s and 45 percent in the 1850s. From 1855 to 1921, about 4 million emigrants left Ireland, three-quarters of them for the United States, where the Irish-born population reached its historical peak of 1.9 million in 1890. Even after southern Ireland secured independence from Britain in 1921, emigrants continued to leave in huge numbers, reaching rates in the 1950s comparable to those a century earlier. More than two million people left Ireland between 1921 and 2001, with Britain replacing the United States as the main destination. Emigrants continued to leave Ireland in the twenty-first century, mainly for Britain and Australia, even as Ireland—like Italy—for the first time attracted significant numbers of immigrants and refugees from Eastern Europe, Asia, and Africa.[8]

All areas of Ireland experienced exceptionally heavy emigration by European standards, with variations by region, chronology, religion, gender, and destination. The commercially developed north-central and south-central parts of the country had the highest rates of departure during the first half of the nineteenth century. Thereafter, emigration was proportionately (though not numerically) higher from the impoverished west, northwest, and southwest. All regions sent emigrants to North America, but Ulster, the most prosperous province, sent disproportionately high numbers to Canada and New Zealand; the western and southwestern provinces of Connacht and Munster sent emigrants overwhelmingly to America; and the south midlands of Leinster and Munster provided most of the Catholic emigrants to Australia. Male emigrants outnumbered females in the prefamine era, and they continued to dominate the relatively small outflow to Australia, New

Figure 1.4. Irish Emigrants Leaving Home—the Priest's Blessing. *Illustrated London News*, May 10, 1851, p. 387. *The Illustrated London News Historical Archive, 1842–2003*. Courtesy of the British Newspaper Archive (www.britishnewspaperarchive.co.uk) and British Library Board. Image © Illustrated London News Group.

Zealand, and South Africa throughout the nineteenth century. In the postfamine era, however, sex ratios among Irish emigrants to the United States were equal, and most of the women were young and single—a highly distinctive demographic profile that anticipated international migration patterns today.[9]

Irish and Italian migrations shared important similarities. Both groups left harsh economic circumstances and political systems that exploited and marginalized them, in search of better living conditions, economic opportunities, and social mobility abroad. At the same time, like today's transnational migrants, they worked hard to retain their ties to their families and their regions and countries of origin. Financial remittances from Italian and Irish migrants improved the conditions of their families at home. In both countries, politicians and government officials regarded emigration as a safety valve for defusing class tensions and raising the living standards of those who remained behind. The Italians and the Irish eventually came to wield significant influence abroad, working to strengthen relations between the governments of their new countries and their ancestral homes, advocating for their home countries' foreign policy priorities, and advancing bilateral economic relations and cultural initiatives.[10]

Irish and Italian migration also differed in significant ways. While members of both groups faced discrimination because of their religion, culture, and political ideas, Italians were directly targeted by restrictive immigration laws. The peak of Italian migration in the early twentieth century coincided with global efforts to establish gatekeeping immigration policies in response to the largest movement of people in world history up to that point. The United States pioneered much of the legislation and infrastructure to control global mobility as part of a backlash against all immigrants other than those from Northern Europe. By contrast, the once-despised Irish achieved respectability by default under the new immigration system implemented in the United States in the 1920s, receiving a relatively generous annual quota (though, with the onset of the Great Depression and World War II, Irish emigration shifted mostly to Britain). In addition to reducing the scale of Italian immigration, restrictive legislation transformed the demographic composition of Italian immigration. In contrast to the Irish case, Italian

Figure 1.5. Emigrants Leaving Queenstown, Ireland for New York, 1874. *Harper's Weekly*, September 26, 1874, pp. 796–97. Courtesy of the Library of Congress, https://lccn.loc. gov/92513178.

emigration had skewed heavily male before World War I, but the new immigration laws encouraged Italian men who secured admission to the United States to settle permanently and send for their families.

Different return rates also profoundly affected how Italian and Irish migrants related with their communities back home. About half of overseas Italian emigrants returned to Italy, along with two-thirds or more of those who went to European countries. Upon their return, they sometimes encountered hostility if they had failed to make money, stay in touch with family, or send back remittances. Yet because return was normal rather than exceptional, they generally faced much less estrangement than their Irish counterparts. Most Irish emigrants (with the partial exception of those who went to Britain) settled abroad permanently. Well under 10 percent of Irish emigrants who went to the United States returned to Ireland. Those who did so often encountered a mix of envy and

Figure 1.6. Landing at Ellis Island, 1902. *Quarantine Sketches: A Pamphlet Published as Advertising in 1902 by the Maltine Company for Distribution to Physicians* (New York: The Maltine Company, 1902). Courtesy of the Library of Congress, www.loc.gov/item/97501086/.

derision as "Returned Yanks" and found it difficult to adjust. The differences in return migration rates and sex ratios also affected naturalization. While Irish immigrants in the United States tended to become citizens quickly and in high numbers, Italians naturalized at much lower rates and later than most immigrant groups from Europe. This difference stemmed from the temporary nature of Italian migration and its mostly male composition. The fascist Italian government, particularly through the 1930s, also discouraged emigration because it needed men to work in agriculture, enlist in the military, or settle in Italian colonies.

Both migrant groups maintained strong regional identities after they moved abroad. They often identified more closely with their hometown or region of origin than with their country as a nation-state—the Italians even more so than the Irish. Because of the historical fragmentation of the Italian peninsula, the rigid social stratification of Italian society, and politicians' neglect, southern Italian villages tended to be isolated and insular, and immigrants preserved this isolation in their new countries. People from the same town often clustered together in enclaves abroad—on the same city block or, in some cases, in the same tenement building—and maintained many of the institutions, habits of worship, and social hierarchies from back home. In Italy, this notion of village cohesion was known as *campanilismo*—loyalty to those who live within the sound of the village church bells. Irish immigrants in the urban United States also clustered by place of origin and mobilized through county-based associations. Many immigrants, indeed, discovered a sense of national identity—Italian or Irish—only when they settled abroad.

* * *

Numbers and patterns, while impressive in their magnitude, can make the process of migration seem impersonal and abstract. How, then, might we capture this process at a more individual and intimate level? In this book, we propose the idea of ritual as one answer to that question. The origins of ritual as a concept lie in the anthropology of religion, featuring totems, celebrations, and highly stylized modes of behavior. We found nothing so formally structured in the history of modern migration, but we followed the lead of sociologists and anthropologists who use ritual to explain key moments in everyday life, from birthdays to New Year festivals, graduations, holiday parades, marriages, and funerals. To describe every social activity as ritualistic would drain the concept of meaning. Yet certain kinds of social activity convey meaning through their structure, form, and repetition. Rituals are communicative actions that must be performed to be effective.[11]

Approaching actions of this kind in the context of rites of passage holds considerable promise for the study of migration. Anthropologists at the turn of the twentieth century identified life events such as puberty, coming of age, marriage, reproduction, and death as rites of passage. Rites of this kind had three phases—separation, transition, and reincorporation—corresponding to, and indeed directly modeled on, a physical journey. These scholars, in the societies they studied, suggested that people who moved from one territory to another typically crossed a neutral zone marked by consecrated boundaries, whether natural or

Figure 1.7. A letter from Pat in America, Ireland, circa 1902. Meadville, PA: Keystone View Company, 1902. Courtesy of the Library of Congress, www.loc.gov/item/00651066/.

manmade. Local movement within communities featured similar dividing lines, such as the threshold of a door. Examples of rituals performed when leaving home, or when entering the home of another, included benedictions, physical contact, exchanges of gifts, eating and drinking, and smoking a pipe. Anthropologists began by studying the stages of such journeys and then used the journey itself as a metaphor for the transformations brought about by rites of passage. The transitional phase of moving across space came to represent the liminal stage—an intermediate period of uncertainty and growth, preceded by separation and followed by reintegration—at the heart of these rites.[12]

The original theory of rites of passage rested on Eurocentric and racialist assumptions that subsequent scholars have long since discarded. It assumed that human mobility in earlier European societies was constrained by a fundamental distinction between the sacred and the profane and that models of these earlier societies could still be found and studied in the aboriginal cultures of Australia and North America. Shorn of these imperialist trappings, however, the basic idea of rites through which individuals and communities negotiate the life cycle remains useful. Folklorists, historians, sociologists, and psychologists have applied this idea in a wide range of early modern, modern, and contemporary settings, and they continue to do so today.[13]

The idea of rites of passage, approached flexibly and with deference to the available historical evidence, can help us understand the process of human migration—with its elements of preparation, departure, transit, admission, exclusion, expulsion, and return—in new and powerful ways. It can also place the sentiments and voices of migrants and their families at the center of historical inquiry. Migration, moreover, sets norms and expectations not only for those who leave but also for those who remain at home, such as the *vedove bianche* of the Italian South. And funeral rites, through which members of a community come to terms with permanent loss, clearly provided a powerful template for emigration in both the Italian and the Irish cases.

The "American wake"—known in various parts of Ireland as a "live wake," "parting spree," or "American bottle night"—had well-defined ritual components. In the week leading up to departure, the soon-to-be emigrant called on friends and neighbors and invited them to the farewell ceremony. The women of the house prepared food; guests brought more food; and men brought beer and *poitín* (an illicit liquor distilled from potatoes). The "wake" started on the evening before departure and usually continued through the night, with dancing, drinking, and keening (wailing in grief). In the morning, the "convoy" began, as family, neighbors, and friends followed the emigrant along the road. The poorest emigrants walked with their belongings in a bundle; others traveled with a trunk in a cart or in a sidecar hauled by a donkey or mule. At an agreed-upon crossroads or turning point, the older members of the community said their last farewells, sometimes marked by more keening, and stood watching until their loved one disappeared from sight. In all these ways, the American wake slowed down and formalized the process of departure, binding the emigrants emotionally to their community and providing some degree of meaning and consolation to those who stayed behind.

Emigration from Italy featured similar funeral rituals that were offset by positive framing within local communities. As in Ireland, communities lamented departure and held formal processions. Government officials seemed all too eager to frame emigration in terms of death, an unavoidable part of the life cycle, as doing so made emigration seem inevitable rather than imposed. Yet rituals surrounding *la partenza*—family dinners, visits, packing, letters—featured excitement, anticipation, and joy as well as sorrow, just as Ireland's American wake had elements of merriment alongside grief. Moreover, because so many Italian men left as "birds of passage" with the intention of returning, they and their families could see migration as a temporary phase rather than a permanent loss. Italian emigration also came with the expectation that remittances would boost the economic and social standing of those who remained behind. The same was true in Ireland, with the significant difference that women were as likely as men to leave and more likely to send remittances.

Just as rituals involve nonverbal expression, scholars can study migration through physical objects as well as written sources. In all human societies, key transitional moments in the life cycle—births and birthdays, comings of age, weddings, and funerals—involve the transmission of objects. Most people in the past did not leave written records; nor did they use written language as their primary mode of expression. As historians have moved away from focusing on the history of elites to explore the history of ordinary people, they also have moved beyond textual sources to study the relationship between objects, meanings, and people. In doing so, they drew inspiration from the disciplines of archaeology, anthropology, art history, human geography, design, literary studies, and the work of museums and heritage organizations. "Material culture," as one guide to the subject puts it, "sheds light on our production and consumption of goods, our power relations, social bonds and networks, gender interactions, identities, cultural affiliations, and beliefs. Material culture communicates all kinds of human values from the economic to the political to the social and cultural." Studying material objects can break down the boundaries between academic historians, filmmakers, curators and exhibition organizers, and private individuals and families—all of whom preserve and investigate the past but do so in different ways. Material culture can also provide insights into intimate feelings, sensations, and experiences that leave no trace in written records.[14]

Migration history features a rich variety of material sources. These objects include trunks, suitcases, remittances, parcels, posters, clothing, and handwoven textiles, physical spaces and places (ruined cottages, pubs, ships, poor-law offices, consular offices, immigrant landing centers, hotels, and boarding houses), and nontextual cultural forms such as music, photographs, and film. Material objects can sometimes assume a spiritual or magical significance in emigrants' lives. Some Irish emigrants, for example, carried "frog bread," made by roasting and crushing a frog and mixing the powder with oaten meal, to ward off illness on the voyage. Similarly, Italian migrants often carried images of their town's patron saints in their steamship trunks to protect them during the trip and in their new life abroad. They also packed small charms against bad luck, swaddling clothes with amulets and embroidery that they believed protected infants from the evil eye, or cooking utensils passed down from generation to generation as a reminder of their connection to their family. Emigrants carried love charms, too, including pubic hair stitched into clothing or a drop of menstrual blood soaked in linen and sewn into a man's clothes to symbolize faithfulness.[15]

Material culture and ritual come together powerfully in Máirtín Ó Cadhain's short story, "An Bhliain 1912" (The Year 1912), told mainly from the anguished perspective of a mother whose daughter, Máirín, is about to leave Ireland for America. The story opens abruptly with two ominous words: "The trunk." Throughout Máirín's last week at home, her mother wants to move the trunk out of sight, for "it irked her like a white frost the way it had been perched up on the ledge of the kitchen dresser, adored like an idol. The children having great play with it, opening, closing, looking it all over." By the eve of her daughter's departure, with friends and relatives assembling for the American wake, the mother can take no more of the trunk and moves it to the bedroom: "It was like a burnt spot or a smallpox scar on the face of life, tonight especially since she seldom had a hearty gathering under her roof. It was useful and wellmade, but that was only a chimera, a ghost from the Otherworld come to snatch away the first conception of her womb and the spring of her daily life, just when the drinking, the high spirits, the music and merrymaking were in full spate." Its pale, yellow wood, lit by a guttering candle, reminds her of a color she had once seen but cannot remember at first—"the face of a corpse after a long wake in the sultry weather." She cannot bring herself to look inside the trunk, bound by "that same tabu which had kept her, though she had often tried, from looking at a corpse in a coffin."[16]

For Máirín, by contrast, the trunk and its contents provide a bond with the home she is leaving and the promise of a better life abroad. The items packed inside include "a sod of turf, a chip off the hearthstone, tresses of hair, a bunch of shamrock though it was autumn, stockings of homespun, a handful of dulse [seaweed], items of clothing, papers connected with the voyage across." Also inside the trunk is Máirín's new outfit: her shoes, coat, hat, and dress, which she lays out to admire many times during the week, though her mother— dreading the rituals of migration as much as Máirín looks forward to them—does not once encourage her to try the clothes on before the morning of her departure. Toward the end of the story, as the perspective shifts momentarily, Máirín realizes that the trunk gives her "licence and authority to wear an elegant hat on her head and an ostentatious coat on her back instead of a shawl. Without the trunk her lady-outfit would be an insult to God. If she let it out of her sight for as much as a second as like as not those tricksome and showy garments would wither into rags and ashes about her body." As the convoy departs, her mother looks on in mute sorrow and exasperation as Máirín rides aloft with the trunk on a cart.[17]

As Máirín's emigrant outfit suggests, cloth—especially when it touches or covers human bodies—is an especially powerful form of material culture. Cloth connects people across time to their families, ancestors, and offspring. In the process of manufacture and the mechanisms through which it is bestowed and exchanged, cloth carries information, triggers memories, and binds individuals and groups among themselves and across generations. Women often play the central role in the manufacture of cloth and its transmission at key moments in the life cycle, including birth and marriage. In many Italian regions, handwoven bedcovers (*copriletti*) were central to women's dowries, which typically included a *corredo*—a trousseau of bedcovers, pillowcases, a bedspread, and lingerie, much of it embroidered or trimmed by lace. For many brides, the *corredo* represented the most treasured part of their dowry, symbolizing a woman's upbringing and status, her skill and work ethic, her moral worth, and her devotion to her future family. *Copriletti*, like other parts of the *corredo*, carried powerful messages of commitment to reproduction and familial survival, both when transmitted to a bride's new family and in ritual moments when a mother—often a migrant far from home—bestowed parts of her dowry to her own daughters upon their betrothal or marriage.[18]

Migration, then, involves rituals and, in particular, rites of passage. But who creates these rituals and rites? Our contributors suggest three answers: emigrants and their communities, their descendants abroad, and the officials who regulated departure, travel, admission, exclusion, and removal. The chapters that follow reveal how migrants created meaning in moments of transition and disruption, forging new bonds of solidarity in transit and abroad, how officials imposed order and discipline on board ships, and how state agencies created new hierarchies of inclusion and exclusion by regulating the process of departure and arrival. Studying these everyday practices brings to life the world that migration created.[19]

* * *

Rituals of Migration contains three parts: "On the Eve," "In Transit," and "Return." The resemblance between the book's structure and the elements of a rite of passage is hardly a coincidence, given that the model for these rites is itself a physical journey. The three chapters in Part I—by Bernadette Whelan, Linda Reeder, and Donna Gabaccia and Joan Saverino—examine migrants as they prepare to leave, along with some of the connections they form abroad. Using folklore sources and firsthand accounts, Whelan looks at rituals of departure from Irish communities, with an emphasis on the emotive power of material objects and the American wake. Reeder, focusing on women and gender in southern Italy, exposes a dichotomy between external framing of emigration as funereal and the more celebratory preparations

Figure 1.8. Held at Ellis Island; *undesirable emigrants to be taken back by steamship company that brought them*, 1902. *Quarantine Sketches: A Pamphlet Published as Advertising in 1902 by the Maltine Company for Distribution to Physicians* (New York: The Maltine Company, 1902). Courtesy of the Library of Congress, www.loc.gov/item/93512789/.

by families during the week leading up to departure. Gabaccia and Saverino focus on *copriletti* from Toscana and Calabria, using oral history and genealogy to trace women's creativity and family connections across time and space. Family, community, and emotion emerge as the overarching themes of this opening section of the book.

Part II, "In Transit," examines migrants at sea and in the ports of arrival with an emphasis on regulation, discipline, and order. The emigrant ship functioned as a liminal space where people from different backgrounds came together in a confined setting, with some customary rules of behavior suspended and other rules newly fashioned. Cian McMahon's chapter demonstrates how Irish Protestant ministers used religious rituals during ocean voyages to control and discipline the emigrant poor, who were mainly Catholic, and how emigrants found meaning in rituals confronting death at sea. Jill Bender's chapter on Irish emigration to Australia in the mid-nineteenth century shows that shipboard routines extended patterns of social control from the domestic to the maritime arena, yet unruly passengers flouted these rules to forge new bonds of community. Lauren Braun-Strumfels and Clara Zaccagnini focus on Italian immigrant brokers in turn-of-the-century New Orleans, revealing how rituals of entry and exit—arrival, inspection, confinement, and exclusion—regulated migration as government bureaucracies expanded. All three of these chapters examine how institutions—workhouses, religious bodies, or state agencies—relied on repeated patterns of action and behavior to legitimate and display their power and to distinguish between insiders and outsiders, and how migrants responded to these efforts.[20]

Part III, "Return," offers a multidisciplinary approach to the history of Italian and Irish migrants who went back to their countries of origin. The three chapters in this section view return from three different perspectives: forced, ambivalent, and desired. Hidetaka Hirota, applying the tools of social and policy history, identifies admission to the poorhouse as the key ritual moment that made a small but significant

Figure 1.9. Final Discharge from Ellis Island, 1902. *Quarantine Sketches: A Pamphlet Published as Advertising in 1902 by the Maltine Company for Distribution to Physicians* (New York: The Maltine Company, 1902). Courtesy of the Library of Congress, www.loc.gov /item/93512805/.

number of Irish paupers eligible for expulsion from the United States in the nineteenth century. Sent back across the Atlantic Ocean against their will, these deportees were disowned by their original communities and found themselves without a place to live. Gráinne McEvoy, adopting a literary-historical approach, examines the return of young women to Ireland as represented in literary fiction. These women enjoy the once familiar landscapes, foods, friendships, and comforts of home yet find that they no longer fit in. Focusing on two sustained introspections about the initial moments and weeks of return, McEvoy's chapter shows how rituals of return—encounters with the landscapes and spaces of home, enjoyment of food and material comforts, and repositioning oneself within the home community—take on distinct meanings when examined from the point of view of the returnee. Joseph Sciorra's chapter, using visual-cultural analysis, explores Italian return migration via the medium of photography. Examining the production, use, and dissemination of images within and across generations, Sciorra identifies ritual expressions of personal and familial obligation. This sense of obligation and care—or the abdication of care—provides a unifying theme for the final section of the book.[21]

Written during a period of virulent anti-immigrant rhetoric and dehumanization of people on the move, the contributions in this book remind us how painful and terrifying, yet also how exciting and transformative, the process of migration can be. The authors reveal how everyone involved in the migrant experience—the migrants themselves, the families they left behind, and those in charge of regulating mobility—tried to make sense of a process filled, by its very nature, with peril and uncertainty. We hope that the chapters that follow, by reconsidering familiar moments in the cycle of migration through the lens of ritual, will encourage scholars to ask similar questions about other migrant groups.

PART ONE

On the Eve

1

Leaving for America

Rituals of Packing and Departure

BERNADETTE WHELAN

"Do-ell Érinn" (He Turned Away from Ireland), a poem by the sixth-century pilgrim Saint Columba, tells how "his sad heart ever bleeds" as he left Ireland for exile in Iona in Scotland. This correlation of passionate sadness, loss, and leaving characterized the experiences of political exiles. Yet not all of the approximately eight million people who left Ireland between 1801 and 1921 were exiled. By 1900, eighteen-year-old or even younger individuals wanted to fulfill personal ambitions, experience higher living standards, and reunite with kin. Leaving Ireland was ritualized from an early period. Acts and actions were repeated, conducted in a prescribed order, and carried meaning. If an object was involved in the performance of the ritual, although inanimate, it has a story to tell.

Except for the persistent exile trope preserved in songs and poems and the events surrounding the American wake, little is known about rituals associated with departure. Analyzing the minutiae of each of the different stages of emigration from the eighteenth century to the twentieth centuries, this chapter argues that each step involved in the processes from packing to leaving became ritualized, suggesting that emigration—particularly to America—became a self-sustaining activity. The chapter examines whether and how rituals of migration, defined here as multiple performances of acts in communities, eased the pain of leaving home, comforted family and friends, and prepared the emigrant emotionally and practically for a new life abroad.[1]

The Fare

Once the decision to leave was made, the emigrant sought a passage on a boat. During the eighteenth and early nineteenth centuries, when it could take six weeks or more to cross the Atlantic, most of those leaving the northern counties of Ireland were Presbyterians, generally family groups who could afford the fares and maintain themselves upon arrival. Many of the individual leavers at the bottom, or close to the bottom, of the economic scale often secured a passage by contracting themselves to the ship's captain or owner as an indentured servant or laborer; credit and bounty schemes whereby the settler paid the emigrant's passage and was repaid later were also used. Other schemes had developed by the mid-1840s in which the poor or destitute received full or part assistance from landlords or their agents, philanthropic societies, and Poor Law guardians (local officials who administered public relief).

From the 1830s onward, land consolidation and economic improvement prompted landlords to become increasingly interested in emigration. For the tenant, the choice was often between eviction and departure. When Patsy McDermott, a tenant on E. P. Shirley's estate in Farney, County Monaghan, was given the choice of "paying up or emigrating," he replied, "I have no money to pay for my passage, nor to buy a hap'worth of the journey." William Steuart Trench, Shirley's land agent, told McDermott he would have a free passage to any place in America, a respectable outfit, and a sovereign in his hand on landing. McDermott responded, "You may put me down for Boston." From the onset of the Great Famine in the 1840s, irrespective of how landlords justified emigration schemes from their estates, the choice remained between eviction or emigration, although departure could also be tenant-driven. Arthur Holland, another Shirley tenant, petitioned for a ticket. Usually, the agent for the landlord or the Crown chose the candidates and provided them with the passage, typically through a ship's agent or broker.[2] After the 1850s, many estate emigrants were no longer assisted. Instead, many were evicted and left to fend for themselves. Others left with a passage paid for by family and friends already in their intended destination, which became known as "chain migration."

During the famine years, Poor Law unions increasingly helped inmates to leave. Like landlords, guardians were driven by financial imperatives. The pauper's path to the local workhouse was known in some places as *cosán na marbh* (pathway of the dead), and thus the offer of a free passage by the guardians was a welcomed escape. Guardians selected suitable candidates. Sometimes only a single female or the head of a household was chosen and given the fare. Married women and children in workhouses in parts of County Clare whose husbands had emigrated to England or America and promised to return with money were known as "deserted women" or "the desertion." Between 250,000 and 300,000 Irish people received full or partial assistance to emigrate to North America in the nineteenth century.[3]

Others sold or pawned clothes or furniture and other belongings to buy their passage to America. Evidence of chain migration exists by 1845 when a scheme, started in Philadelphia, facilitated an American-based Irish immigrant to buy a passage from a local shipping agent, who informed a counterpart in Ireland, who in turn notified the recipients that their ticket was paid. After the 1850s, as a second generation of Irish became established in the United States, the regular arrival of the passage and remittance into a home meant inevitable departure for younger siblings. The philanthropist Vere Foster favored assisting young, single women to emigrate to the United States in the 1880s and 1890s because they were the least able to leave but also the "most liberal" in sending home help to bring out their brothers and sisters and parents if they wished to follow. By the turn of the century, 75 percent of young female emigrants had their passage paid by a sister, and most were joining a sister. Between 1848 and 1900, Irish Americans sent $250 million back to Ireland, of which $104 million (40 percent) took the form of prepaid tickets. Sometimes the promise of a fare did not mean departure: the hopeful emigrant Peig Sayers was disappointed when her friend Cháit Jim hurt her arm in America, was unable to work, and "*ná raibh fheidir lei an costas a chur chugan*" (she was unable to send the passage). Later in the twentieth century, Peig's children all departed the Blasket Islands for America. Within the kinship network, mutual obligation dictated the sending home of the fare and that the receiver would leave.[4] Receiving the fare not only symbolized dependency on the American connection; it made departure a ritualized and inevitable reaction.

Luggage: The Constant Memory Container

Before 1845, depending on personal resources, emigrants used a variety of containers for their belongings: wooden trunks or chests with a heavy metal frame; wooden boxes; bags made of leather, carpet, or coarse fabrics; sacks; duffel or sea bags; blankets and patchwork quilts used as a bundle; baskets; and barrels for food. In that period, there were few complaints about poor handling of or loss of luggage because so few transatlantic passengers brought goods valuable enough to tempt thieves. In other words, most traveled with bundles rather than bulky containers. Many were also aware of the poor conditions on board the vessels, which into the early nineteenth century were designed primarily to carry cargo and ballast. From the 1830s onward, a further factor dictating one's choice of receptacle involved the journey to the port or the local railway station. The wealthier emigrants traveled by horsedrawn carriage, which could carry all manner of luggage, while the poorer emigrants going steerage class may have walked. Paupers brought only what they could wear and carry on board in a small string bag or bundle. Starting in the 1840s, workhouses and prison-sponsored destitute emigrants were given "luggage," a generic term for the variety of containers. Many of the Shirley estate emigrants were given boxes, chests, or barrels with locks and keys for the journey. James Brenan's evocative 1876 painting *The Finishing Touch* shows the young female emigrant's modest traveling box.

A wooden box might be made for the journey by a local carpenter, or a tin box bought in a shop, suggesting the development of a commercial enterprise. Such boxes could also be used as a chair or a table during the transit. After 1892, when Ellis Island replaced Castle Garden as the main port of arrival in the United States, photographs of the baggage room show the ubiquitous trunk, bag, and bundle and reveal that the suitcase had become popular. Some containers traveled over and back across the Atlantic and survive today in households in Ireland, moving reminders of the transience of society and luggage's role in the emigration rituals. Each box had obvious practical purposes, but their contents were value-laden.

Examining packing as a ritual rather than a burden leads to consideration of premeditation, preparedness, anticipation, and hope.

Figure 1.1. James Brenan (1837–1907), *The Finishing Touch*, 1876. Oil on canvas. Painted by the artist while resident at Buckston Hill, Sundays Well, Cork. Irish Great Hunger Museum, Quinnipiac University, Hamden, CT.

Items were determined by personal wealth, emotional attachment, shipping-line regulations, emigrant guidebooks, letters from friends and family, expectations of needs upon arrival, and increasingly by returnees. Many of the prefamine Ulster-Scots traveled light. On April 17, 1728, James Wansbrough from Ballinlug, County Westmeath, and his family intended to bring £300 to join his sister, Ann Shepherd, in New Jersey. Writing from the American colonies, recent arrivals advised intending emigrants to bring gun oil, iron, saddles, teakettles, seed potatoes, quills, writing paper, feather beds, porter, spirits, ready-made clothes, and bolts of cloth. Such practical items were dictated by prior experience in the Americas. Emigrants were cautioned against bringing specific tools that were unsuitable for colonial conditions. Robert Parke of Chester County, Pennsylvania, advised his sister and brother-in-law, Mary and Thomas Valentine, to bring servants for their own use

Figure 1.2. Anonymous pupil of Nathaniel Grogan, circa 1740–1807, *Emigrants at Cork,* c.1840. Oil on canvas. National Folklore Collection, University College Dublin, Ireland.

and for sale after arrival. Emigrants were advised to clothe themselves "very well" in woolen and linen garments, shoes, stockings, and hats for the journey and arrival. After 1800, other practical items could include official passport-type documents. Quaker, Presbyterian, and Anglican authorities provided letters of introduction or testimonials and certificates of transfer to emigrants in good standing. The prepaid passage might include sea provisions, particularly after 1803 when British legislation sought to deal with reports of suffering and privation on board ships by requiring ship owners and captains to provide each passenger with water, vinegar, salted provisions, and wholesome ship bread. But passengers still brought their own stores packed in barrels and chests, including bread, butter, cheese, eggs, coffee, porter, spirits, and potatoes. Additional necessities for the journey, such as tin cans and kettles, could be purchased at the quay side as depicted in the painting *Emigrants at Cork* around 1840.[5]

The indentured servant, laborer, or, increasingly, the assisted emigrant traveled with few or no belongings. Many lived in the workhouse, in houses built of mud and other perishable material, in stone hovels, or in semi-underground dwellings. Such emigrants had few material possessions, domestic luxuries, mementos, toys, tools, or furniture to pack. Yet the mother of a poor but respectable Presbyterian, James Patton from Tamlaght Finlagan in County Londonderry, furnished him with two suits of clothes, two dozen shirts, and other necessary items packed in a chest so that he could save money when he arrived in Philadelphia in 1783 and bring out his siblings. For other prefamine emigrant families, packing was well planned and organized. Many carefully freed themselves of goods that realized cash and packed according to practicality more than emotion. They traveled in a group and intended to join family and communities in the Americas. From the 1780s and 1790s the "new Irish"—mainly Roman Catholic and increasingly young, unmarried female emigrants—had little to pack.[6]

During the Great Famine, Widow Tomalty, who had been evicted from the Shirley estate, had neither money nor bedclothes to give to her daughters emigrating to America. Shirley's assistance for the journey and arrival in America included the provision of frocks, shifts, flannel petticoats, aprons, gowns, slips, shirts, trousers, coats, and vests, as well as stools, chairs, pots, pans, water bottles, boiler, plates, mugs, coffee pot, panicans (pannikins, or small drinking cups), chamber pots, frying pans, dishes, plates, and food supplies, including stone biscuits, oatmeal, bacon, tea, coffee, sugar, salt, vinegar, and treacle. Even though some of Shirley's emigrants seemed to have been well kitted out for the journey, his agent complained about the ragged state of groups arriving into Liverpool for their ship to the United States. The sight of emigrants wearing homespun clothes and carrying a bundle tied to the end of a stick in hopes for a better life remained part of community memory in parts of Ireland into the mid-twentieth century.[7]

Advice on Packing

Pamphlets and posters advertising emigration, along with letters from America, offered advice on packing rituals. From the 1840s, guidebooks became popular. Each guide was different, but among the common topics were what to bring and what not to bring. Vere Foster's *Work and Wages; or, the Penny Emigrant's Guide*, first published as a broadsheet in

1851, went through several editions, and at least 280,000 copies were eventually published. Foster, who regularly crossed to America as a steerage passenger recording the often brutal and inhumane conditions on board ship, advised intending emigrants to pack a tin water can, a large tin hook-saucepan, a frying pan, a large tin basin for washing and for preparing bread, a tin teapot, a tin kettle, two deep tin plates, two pint mugs, two knives, forks and spoons, small calico gags, towels, and blankets. Along with having a sea outfit, the pamphlet recommended that extra articles of clothing such as woolen items, boots, and shoes should be taken because they were expensive and of lesser quality in the United States. Foster advised that the ship's provisions—water, bread or biscuit, wheaten flour, oatmeal, rice, sugar, tea or cocoa or coffee, salt and salt pork, molasses, and vinegar—be supplemented with extra supplies packed in a barrel with a padlock. He also recommended Epsom salt and pills to prevent seasickness. Light tools and sewing or embroidery material could be packed in separate boxes, clearly marked with the emigrant's name. Foster advised against overpacking because of the cheapness of most goods, except for woolens, and the different styles of clothing in the United States.

TABLE 1.1. Taxonomy of possessions and values.

	Practical	Spiritual	Comfort, physical emotional	Reminder of home
Ticket/money/documents	☘		☘	☘
Food/drink	☘		☘	☘
Clothes	☘			☘
Food preparation objects	☘			☘
Work implements	☘			☘
Prayer books, penal cross, rosary beads/talisman		☘	☘	☘
Hairbrush, ointment	☘			☘
Gifts packed/messages			☘	☘

Even on the new steam-powered ships introduced for Atlantic cross-ings in the 1850s, steerage passengers were required to bring their own bedding, often dumped into the sea prior to arrival or confiscated by the US authorities owing to concerns about infectious diseases such as cholera and typhus. The Reverend Alex Peyton's guide, published in 1853, was aimed at a wealthier class who traveled by the more expen-sive steamboat. He advised against emigrants encumbering themselves with clothes, furniture, and bedding, and, instead of money, he rec-ommended a certificate or draft drawn on an American bank or gold placed in an inside vest pocket or in a leather belt under a garment. The less well-off also sewed coins and paper money into the lining of a coat, money that, when replenished in America, could be sewn back into a garment, for example a coat or dress, and sent home. Concealed money crossed the Atlantic many times until the "last had gone."[8]

Margaret Ann Cusack, a member of the Poor Clares female religious order, described how by the 1870s young, single, Catholic female emi-grants adopted a ritual-like approach to gathering information about the clothes to take, the best place to go to, the cheapest tickets, and wage lev-els in America. Cusack wrote "it was your duty to get all the information you could." Some female emigrants kept addresses inside their pockets and purses so they knew where to go when they arrived in America.[9]

Among the 20,000 young women from County Mayo assisted to emigrate to America by Vere Foster in the 1880s was the orphan Anne Dyer. She was miserably clad when she left even though Mrs. Strick-land of Loughlyn House, wife of the local land agent, had given her the clothes. Her brother James was dressed only slightly better. Fortunately for them, Anne's friend Ellen Green wired money to Queenstown port, where they leased ocean outfits and found suitable lodgings. Many other emigrants funded by Poor Law guardians and prisons in the 1880s were given a ticket, clothing, and landing money but carried little else except food. Packing was not just a personal and family activity but also a community ritual. After the 1850s, neighbors presented the emigrant with gifts, including clothes such as stockings and underwear for the girls or money for the boys. Both received supplies of hard-boiled eggs, dried rye, or oatmeal biscuits for the journey. The emigrant might also be asked to carry presents for and to deliver messages of good wishes to relatives and friends in America.[10]

Figure 1.3. Woman's Purse (undated). Made of leather. Personal item obtained from a donor in Portaferry, Northern Ireland. Ulster-American Folk Park, Northern Ireland.

From the 1850s onward, the American letter was the main source of knowledge for most intending emigrants. Receiving, opening, and reading the letter was heavily ritualized in some places and almost ceremonial in nature. Family, friends, and neighbors would gather in the recipient's home to attend the reading. Letters exaggerated successes in America, concealed undoubted failures, and manipulated readers to leave or stay. Writing on January 20, 1859, from New York City, Mary Brown told her friend in County Wexford that "you will have to come to the country where there's love and liberty." Twenty year later, Denis Sullivan in St. Louis, Missouri, wrote that he would "cut my head off before I encourage a man to come to this country."[11]

Letters also detailed what to pack, wear, and carry; described conditions on board ship; and identified an address in America. Intending emigrants looked to them for advice and guidance on the journey. The physical presence of a returned migrant for long or short visits

Figure 1.4. James Brenan (1837–1907), *News from America*, 1875. Oil on canvas. Presented by the artist to the Crawford Art Gallery. Crawford Art Gallery, Cork, Ireland.

was similarly influential in the preparation process, even though the rate of permanent return by Irish emigrants to the United States was less than 10 percent between 1899 and 1924. Asenath Nicholson noted their presence in the 1840s. Forty years later, the American consul John J. Piatt commented that the returner's appearance and behavior had "a great influence upon the minds of those with whom they come in contact and lead many of them also to emigrate."[12]

Emigrants did not have to worry about visas and passports to enter America except during the American Civil War (1861–1865) and World War I (1914–1918, when mass departures from Ireland virtually ceased anyway). Until the 1870s, individual American states regulated immigration. Federal legislation thereafter required the American consular representative in Ireland to ensure that the passengers and their baggage were disease-free. Soon, passing medical and fitness examinations became a normal event for most Irish emigrating to America. Chain migration provided evidence for immigration officials that they could support themselves and were less "likely to become a public charge." After 1924, securing a quota visa required attendance at the local consulate office in Ireland for an interview and possession of a passport and birth certificate. Undoubtedly a stressful event, this ritual became a customary part of the departure process.[13]

Possessions packed had practical purposes, but they also held a variety of emotional attachments. Kate Moran, who emigrated to the United States during the 1880s from Waterville, County Kerry, packed the first book that she learned to read at primary school and planned to use it to help her write letters home. Emigrants from County Donegal, among others, were known to pack musical instruments. Those who could afford luxuries brought a hairbrush, soap, ointment pot, and mirror. Clay pipes and marbles were packed to reduce boredom while on board, and perhaps a spinning top, rag doll, or homemade broomhandle doll for children to play with.[14]

Packing rituals were always influenced by the culture of the sending-out society. Prayer books, penal crosses, prayer cards, religious pictures, rosary beads, or a St. Brigid's cross, sometimes given to them by the local Roman Catholic parish priest, reminded migrants of their faith and gave them a sense of attachment to home and a feeling of safety during the journey and in America. These religious items represented the increasing prevalence of Roman Catholicism as a belief system and institution and its growing presence in people's lives. Yet parallel to organized religion within rural Ireland was a strong tradition of superstition and belief in otherworld powers. In the mainly rural sending-out counties, for example, "frog bread" was packed as a charm. Prepared by a neighbor or the family of the emigrant, it was made by killing, roasting, and crushing a frog and then mixing the powder with oaten meal to prepare the bread, which it was believed kept the emigrant immune from fever. Another talisman carried was part of the caul, an inner membrane covering the fetus prior to birth, often borrowed from a neighbor. Believed to keep the wearer traveling by sea safe from drowning, it was posted back to the owners after safe arrival in the

United States for use by the next emigrants. Packing love charms was also popular. For example, pubic hair from a special girl or boy or siblings left behind might be secretly sewn into clothing. A small drop of menstrual fluid might be soaked into a piece of linen and then stitched into a male emigrant's clothes. It was believed that his love would subsequently remain constant.

In every period, even the poorest emigrants carried some kind of luggage from the home country. Integral to the packing ritual was that each possession held a personal meaning, whether practical or spiritual or comfort-giving, and each was a reminder of home. The item was value-laden, symbolizing attachment to family and place but also personal agency, control, hope, and expectation of a better life abroad.

Taking Leave

The origins of the American or living wake tradition are difficult to locate. They may derive from how missionaries, pilgrims, soldiers, fishermen, and emigrants embarking on lengthy and arduous journeys and unlikely to return home were memorialized in song and story as going into exile. Alternatively, their source may be found in funeral rites involving public participation, kinship, grief, and gaiety. Between 1675 and 1815, despite the range of the early emigrant experience, there are few references to an American wake. But it was still "no easie [easy] task" to say farewell and leave family, friends, and country. Some Presbyterian families visited their places of worship; for example, the Mellon family called to the Meetinghouse in Mountjoy, County Tyrone, before leaving on their transatlantic journey in 1816. In 1830, a "big bottle night" was held for an uncle of Mary Malin in County Donegal. Also prior to the Great Famine, the Quaker philanthropist Asenath Nicholson, touring Ireland, visited a house in Urlingford, County Kilkenny, where a daughter was emigrating to join four family members in New York. She was to leave with three others at ten o'clock in the evening, traveling by horse-cart to eventually embark at Dublin. During the previous hour there had been silence, but as departure grew closer there was crying, keening (wailing in grief), howling, kissing, and lamenting by friends and family from the whole parish—men and women, young and old. Nicholson did not describe the event as an "American wake," but the gathering of people, and the vocal and emotional intensity, presaged the rituals of migration of the postfamine period.[15]

Funerals and wakes largely disappeared during the famine years owing to apathy and fear of contagion. Similarly, beyond saying goodbye to family and friends, few ceremonies attended the departure of emigrants. By the mid-1850s, however, the custom had resumed. Depending on where one was leaving, the "American wake," "live wake," "*suipéar*" (supper), "spree," "parting spree," "old farewell supper," "American bottle night," "the bottle thing," or "the bottle drink" became a ritual for the departee, whether male or female, and where the wake was used to describe the departure was a further example of respect for otherworld spirits.[16]

In the week before leaving, the emigrant would call on friends and neighbors to say goodbye and invite them to his or her home for the wake. Preparing the house for the visitors was another ritual, usually performed by women who cleaned, baked cakes and biscuits, and cooked meats. If, as one source noted, there was "no food, no dance, no refreshments," women would bring fresh eggs or butter, jam, tea, and bread, while men brought porter, stout, and *poitín* (distilled beverage). A collection of money might also be taken for a poor family to pay for the food and drink. As commerce expanded during the nineteenth century, hosts provided minerals (nonalcoholic drinks) for young people, bought at a shop on credit until money from America paid for it later. Money for the wake could also be included in the letter from America.[17]

The event usually started on the evening before departure and continued through the night until the physical departure of the emigrant. Young and old arrived at the house, gathering in the kitchen, which was cleared of furniture for dancing. Twice or three times women served food and drink, while the father conducted the ceremonies. Stories handed down from generation to generation were told, embellished with accounts of previous emigrants and how America was the land of plenty. Singing and dancing, polka sets, jigs, reels, and music played on fiddles and melodeons added to the façade of merriment. Even though Catholic authorities frowned on drinking alcohol at wakes, liquor flowed, intensifying emotions. Usually, an older woman noted for her talents would start keening, delivering a long, mournful tribute in a shrill, high-pitched voice resembling a continuous cry, and eventually others joined in. As the time for departure arrived, the exhausted emigrant embraced grieving parents, kissed their mother, and promised to write and send back money. Knowing they would not see aged parents and neighbors again was heart-rending. Sarah Doherty from Malin in north Donegal recalled from her own "bottle night" that "it was as if you were going out to be buried." Harriet Martineau's description of a wake in 1852 near Castlebar, County Mayo, resonated with her:

> The last embraces were terrible to see; but worse were the kissings and the claspings of the hands during the long minutes that remained. When we saw the wringing of hands and heard the wailings, we became aware, for the first time perhaps, of the full dignity of that civilization which induces control over the expression of emotions . . . the pain and the passion: and the shrill united cry when the car moved on rings in our ears and long will ring when we hear of emigration.[18]

Prior to leaving, the emigrant might perform another ritual by taking a shovel out to some secluded spot on the land and mounting it in the ground, putting a stick standing beside it and a small heap of stones. Later, when the emigrant had left, the missing spade was found with "God be with the days! Mary or Tom" scribbled on it, bringing them to the mind of the finder. The words "Done by Mary" might be written on a piece of paper and put into the neck of the bottle with the end protruding and then concealed in rafters to be found afterward. Elsewhere, names were written on a stone followed by "*iad uilig imight go Meirceá*" (all have gone to America). Prior to leaving home in Scartaglen, County Kerry, to join their children in America, Tom Kerin and Nell Cournane left the door of their cottage wide open. Others brought fire embers to neighbors to keep alight for their return.[19]

The final stage in the American wake ritual was known as the "convoy" or the "American funeral." Remoteness and poverty might mean the emigrant left home on foot, on a cart drawn by a horse or mule, or in a sidecar. Neighbors, friends, and family set off on foot or in other carts after the leaver—a custom so associated with America in west Kerry that it was known as "convoying the Yankee." After arriving at the edge of the home place—perhaps the "Rock of the Weeping Tears" in west Clare, the "Bridge of Tears" in north Donegal, "Golden's Height" in west Kerry, the "ford (later bridge) at *Muing na Bó*" (the swamp of the cow) river in northwest Mayo, or a crossroads—older members of the procession said their last goodbye. They gave full vent to their sorrow in a loud and prolonged keen and stood on the road until a bend hid the emigrant. Younger members of the convoy continued to the nearest town, where dancing, singing, smoking, and drinking resumed until the arrival of the mail cart, sailing vessel, or the train that most could afford by the 1880s. At Patrickswell railway station in County Limerick, the station master called out "change here for America," again setting off "sorrowful partings and the bitter crying and leave-takings."[20]

The purpose of the convoy was to ensure that the emigrant's final hours at home were as cheerful as possible and would bring luck to the departee. Biddy Argue left her "spree" in Bailieboro, County Cavan, before the final departure and never saw her mother again. Others "stole away" to avoid the wake and convoy ordeals, and some admitted that they would not have attended if they had known it was going to be "so hard to go." Sarah Doherty recalled the singing going down to Moville port in Donegal, but when she got on the ship the crying started. The arrival of the era of air travel did not end the American wake. From 1945 onward, Shannon Airport, a transatlantic hub in Ireland, became the site of many such scenes.[21] Emigrants on board ships often took their "last look back"—*amharc déanach*, as it was known in the Blasket Islands, or "last view" elsewhere—between County Donegal and Tory Island off the northern coast; or at Fastnet Rock, "the teardrop of Ireland," off the southern coast; or in the later period at the departure gate at the airport.[22]

* * *

For over three hundred years, emigration—particularly to America—was a daily feature of life for most Irish families. From the eighteenth to the mid-twentieth century, the passage, the luggage, its contents, and the American wake and convoy became rituals for the departing emigrant. Each step was laden with meaning. The fare provided the means for departing, although the circumstances of receipt illustrated

Figure 1.5. Suitcases, 2024. Contemporary image. With kind permission of EPIC The Irish Emigration Museum, Dublin, Ireland.

not only the material status of the emigrants but also their chances of survival in America. Luggage and contents had practical and emotional importance and symbolized both the dislocation of life and the hope of opportunity abroad. The evolution and persistence of the American wake and convoy emphasizes the mixed emotions surrounding depar-ture. Practicality, sadness, regret, hope, and ambition characterized the process of leaving but did not guarantee a safe journey or success in America. Nonetheless, Irish rituals of migration, performed according to a certain order, reveal deep personal and communal values and beliefs. They were laden with cultural meanings, providing the emigrant and their community with a greater understanding of the momentous decision to leave and some degree of comfort to all.

2

La Partenza

The Gender and Political Implications of the Rituals of Leaving

LINDA REEDER

After reading an article describing the devastating effects of emigration in southern Italy in the early twentieth century, Senator Angelo Mosso, a doctor by trade, boarded a train to observe conditions firsthand. As his train pulled into the station on the outskirts of Castrofilippo, a small Sicilian hill town, he stood at the window watching a stream of men dressed in black, their bags slung over their backs, racing to scramble aboard the third-class wagons. Mosso's gaze shifted to those left on the platform, as friends carried away one woman, while others stood howling and weeping. "When the train began to move," he recalled, "there was [a] heartbreaking cry, like a thunder of tears erupting from a crowd in the midst of a tremendous calamity." Alongside the road that followed the train tracks, Mosso described how relatives and friends sat in their "festive carts characteristic of Sicily, with the horses decked out in embroidery, bows, and red harnesses, with plumes on their heads. . . . The women crowded on the carts pulled their black shawls from their head to reveal their large eyes overflowing with tears. And everyone, men, and children alike, had an expression of unbearable pain on their face . . . as if they were saying goodbye for the last time."[1]

Mosso's description of the lamentations, silent processions, and women dressed in black echoed the funeral rituals of South Italy, equating leaving for America with death. As South Italians left in ever growing numbers to seek work overseas, journalists, novelists, and government officials often depicted the moment of departure in terms of grief and the pain of a permanent rupture. Evoking the rituals of death to make sense of emigration seemed reasonable to most Italian and

Figure 2.1. Underwood & Underwood, Work and Gossip at a Fountain by the Cappuccini Gate in Taormina's Old City Wall, Sicily, 1906. Library of Congress Prints and Photographs Division, Washington, DC, https://lccn.loc.gov/2003670996.

foreign observers. Transnational migration in the early twentieth century was difficult, and often those who left never came back home. The moment of departure seemed to crystallize the unbearable pain emigration brought to many families. In their memoirs and letters, migrants often recalled the tremendous sadness and loss in leaving kin, community, and homeland.[2] The fusion of emigration with the emotions of death was more than a description of individual sorrow; it worked to manage the emotions that shaped the social and political significance of emigration at the beginning of the twentieth century in Italy.

Framing the act of departure as funeral ritual, however, erased the complexity of the emotional landscape surrounding emigration. The power of the funeral imagery in government reports, newspapers, and fiction diminished or concealed the wider range of emotions that defined departure, including the excitement and joy that ran through the sorrow. This chapter looks at how departure assumed a different meaning in rituals within the migrant communities themselves. In focusing on the preparations that marked the days and weeks prior to departure, I reveal how these intimate and public rituals appear more like a wedding than a funeral, with a sense of loss mixed with anticipation and optimism. This distinctive framing of the rites surrounding departure served to gender migration in ways that had wider political implications.

Scholarship on migration and identity is a rich and interdisciplinary field. Numerous volumes and articles have focused on the ways in which processes of migration constitute social relations, including gender relations, in both receiving and sending communities. Scholars have moved beyond focusing on the experiences of men and women to examine how migration reconfigured family relations, sexuality, work, and gendered notions of national belonging.[3] This shift accompanied a closer look at the role intimacy, affective ties, and emotions played in gendering migration and highlighted the ways migration blurred the lines between the familial, intimate spaces of migration and political and civic debates.[4] And while the scholarship has traced the ways individuals, states, and institutions wielded emotions in migration debates, there has been less attention to how the sentimental dimensions of migration are made, enacted, and performed. What is the role of rituals in the making of the emotional landscapes of migration? And what are the impacts of these emotional assemblages on identity and politics?

Historians and anthropologists have long recognized the significance of ritual in the creation of community, social hierarchies, and power dynamics. Their work has embraced the messiness of defining and recognizing rituals—repetitive actions that mark some kind of transformation. These transformations can be physical, temporal, social, or political, marking changes in the shape of an individual or a community in addition to shifts in relations between people and communities.

They can be ceremonial rites of passage, such as a coronation that happens once or twice in a lifetime, or quiet personal activities that mark the start of each day (a cup of coffee with the newspaper). They can be public and collective or intimate and solitary. Emile Durkheim insisted that ritual was the basis of society—"the 'collective effervescence,' produced through ritual created social cohesion and group identity, placing ritual at the heart of social life." Scholars have widened the definition to include many forms of repetitive events as "essential to the creation of self and society," recognizing how three different kinds of rituals—private, ceremonial, and public—serve distinctive functions in shaping social and political relations yet are very much entwined.[5]

Scholars interested in the centrality of ritual in the creation and maintenance of social identities, communities, and institutional and political power increasingly emphasize the emotions attached to these rituals. This work, as the historians Merridee Bailey and Katie Barclay note, has generated a wealth of new scholarship into how emotions "work in organizing, mediating[,] and constructing social, cultural, and institutional relationships." These "rituals are formed to manage emotions (such as grief) as much as rituals are designed to create emotion in the participants." Centering emotions as a driver of ritual practices, not just as a byproduct, highlights their role in constructing individual and collective identities.[6]

This chapter applies the insights of historians of gender and emotion to the rituals surrounding *la partenza* (departure from Italy). By choosing to frame these rituals as a kind of death, journalists, politicians, and critics strengthened the notion of emigration as a permanent rupture that posed a lethal threat to individuals and communities. The evocation of a funeral ritual reinforced the notion that emigration killed the men who left and condemned all who remained behind, especially women, to sink into despair or die. Yet community rituals around leaving—family dinners, visits, packing, and exchanges of letters—produced different gendered and political narratives of mass Italian emigration. From within the villages, predeparture practices echoed other rites of passage that reconfigured the contours of family and place, casting migration as separation but not as permanent loss. These rituals of leaving often centered the agency and participation of women, pointing to alternate political possibilities about the long-term impacts of migration on their home.

Figure 2.2. Underwood & Underwood, A Typical Courtyard, Home of a Local Policeman on San Michele Street, Trapani, Sicily, 1906. Library of Congress Prints and Photographs Division Washington, DC, https://lccn.loc.gov/2003670817.

Rituals of Grief and Mourning

Angelo Mosso was not the only observer struck by the emotional weight and grief in the moment of departure. Regardless of their opinions on mass migration, politicians, journalists, and experts from Italy and the United States who traveled through South Italy spoke of the pain of departure. Even the American journalist Broughton Brandenburg, who focused on the more positive rituals of migration at the community level, lingered on the pain of separation in describing the act of departure: "[W]hen night settled in, so did grief. . . . As the silence of the outer night crept into the house, there became audible the sobbing of the poor old mother as she lay thinking of the near separation of her own flesh and blood." In the morning, "the tumultuous grief of the night before had given place to a sort of hushed woe." In the streets, "hundreds came to see the party off," silently accompanying them to the donkeys waiting at the edge of town, and some of the townsfolk accompanied the emigrants to the train station. "Antonio's father," Brandenburg noted, "was as completely broken down as if he was giving his favorite son and the other to the grave instead of their departing for a happy land."[7]

The evocation of funeral rituals suggests that the communities the migrants left behind had to manage the emotional and material consequences of both individual and communal death. The departure of the emigrants left the living bereft, facing a future of precarity and pain. Evoking feelings of rage, anguish, and heartache around the moment of departure crystallized the image of those who remained as widows or orphans. Regardless of whether critics viewed emigration as a sign of national failure or as a necessary safety valve for a newly minted nation, nearly all agreed that emigration injured the communities they left behind.

Journalists, politicians, and scholars who depicted departure as a form of death focused on the silent procession following the emigrants to the train, evoking the processions accompanying the dead to the cemetery. They emphasized the grief of loss, reinforcing fears that transnational migration meant a permanent absence. The women and men who stood at the station bade farewell to those who might one day return and to those who never would. Rates of return migration to Italy were unusually high, yet over half of those who left did not go back, carving out new lives in new lands instead.[8] Channeling the emotions surrounding death gave voice to the fears underlying a family's decision regarding emigration. The emotional framing of emigration as akin to death included the emigrants and those who stayed behind. While emigration could improve a family's opportunities and material conditions, it could also destroy them. And even if emigrants returned, they might not be the same. In Maria Messina's short story "Le Scarpette," for example, Vanni, who leaves for America to make enough money to marry the woman he loves, returns eighteen months later only to find she has married someone else.[9]

The emotions produced through the funereal descriptions of rituals of leaving consolidated gender norms and shaped political debates over emigration. Framing the moment of departure in terms of grief and loss reinforced notions of rural femininity as defined by dependence on men and on reproduction. The emigration of husbands and sons would either kill the women left behind or leave them so bereft they would sink into insanity or prostitution. Emigration thereby marked the death of the family.[10] Fictional representations of migration channeled the emotions of grief and loss, describing the ways emigration destroyed the women who remained behind. The moment of departure signified the end of their lives as they had known, or envisioned, them to be. In Messina's "La Mèrica," when Catena's husband announces his intention to emigrate, she forbids him to go unless he takes her with him. They fight for weeks, and eventually he books passage for her and their small son. They arrive at the port of Palermo, where the port doctors diagnose her with trachoma, and she is sent back to her village. The local pharmacist there treats her condition with caustic poultices, and she goes blind. Mariano disappears into America, while Catena, lost in her own darkness, goes insane.[11]

Critics and supporters of unregulated migration amplified collective fears about the effects of departure, insisting that it destroyed families and left men unfit as husbands, fathers, or citizens. Distance weakened a man's ability to protect his women, turning husbands into cuckolds. Newspapers carried stories of emigrants who had returned, found out that their wives had taken lovers, and chose to either avenge their honor or close their eyes and pretend nothing was amiss, both being indications of the ways in which emigration compromised masculinity.[12] If men did not return home morally damaged, they were likely to be unfit to work. Politicians, medical officials, and journalists observed that emigration took a toll on emigrants, leaving them susceptible to disease. In his study on emigration, Dino Taruffi—a member of the parliamentary committee sent to investigate conditions in Calabria—described the returnees as wracked with tuberculosis or suffering from alcoholism. Giovanni Lorenzoni, an economist sent by the parliament to explore the agricultural conditions in Sicily, echoed Taruffi's observations in his study of rural Sicilian communities, where men returned "home to die."[13]

The evocation of the funeral also addressed the abandonment of the elderly. According to custom, family obligations dictated that sons care for their widowed mothers. Yet time and distance could undermine filial loyalty. If a woman's son left for America, there was a good chance that he would forget his responsibilities to his widowed mother. The bond between a mother and son was considered the strongest tie between any two family members, broken only by death or its near equivalent, emigration.[14] In "Nonna Lidda," Messina describes the devastation a grandmother feels when her son announces his plans to leave for America. Her only consolation is that he leaves her grandson in her care. A year after her son leaves, he writes to tell her he has married a woman from a neighboring town. She realizes that "now with the new family he would no longer have time to think of the old one. But patience, at least the little one, when he had grown would support her, he would stay with her." Within a few months, however, another letter arrives, instructing Nonna Lidda to use the money enclosed to buy a ticket for her grandson and put him on the next boat to America. A day after the little boy sails, she is found frozen to death in a nearby field. Messina's story reflects the importance placed on the mother–son relationship that represented a fundamental piece of Sicilian women's self-image. With the last physical tie to her son on a boat bound for America, Nonna Lidda dies. As for the emigrants, *la partenza* meant death for their wives and mothers.[15]

The sense of mourning extended to the homelands and villages that—like the women—would wither and die when the men left. Critics lamented the desolation left in the wake of mass migration, pointing to rising crime, increased poverty, and family dissolution. The anguished descriptions of the effects of emigration—"almost complete ruin," "disastrous"—often came from large landowners who watched as their profits fell.[16] In 1904, Anthony Mangano, a Baptist minister and missionary, described Amalfi as "row after row of empty, desolate houses." "In Potenza," he wrote, "the chief secretary of the city, while talking with me on this subject, opened the windows of his office and pointed out the barren mountain sides and said, 'There is the result of emigration for us.'"[17] Government officials filled their reports with laments from local officials describing how emigration "is the great scourge that hangs over our land."[18] Senator Angelo Mosso noted that the "departure of the emigrants, is like a great hemorrhage and blood-letting that is always damaging to weakened organisms."[19]

The equation of emigration with damage, disease, and death seeped into political debates around the "southern question" and emigration regulation. In the decades after Italian unification, the image of the South as economically, morally, and racially different from the North crystallized in both popular and political imaginations.[20] Framing emigration as the moral death of men and women across the South reinforced the idea that they were unable to prosper in a modern world. Framing through funeral rituals also supported the racialized arguments of those who argued that the people of the South were constitutionally ungovernable, justifying the extension of repressive laws and height-ened police presence.[21]

The image of emigration as a threat to individual and collective well-being also informed debates around regulating migration. In a country committed to freedom of movement, as enshrined in the civil code of 1865, legislative discussions sought to avoid outright restrictions on emigration and instead mobilized the language of protection. Legisla-tors referred to the need to protect emigrants from fraud and theft at the ports, and from the increasingly restrictive regulations imposed by the United States.[22] Italy's emigration law of 1901 sought to protect em-igrants from rapacious ticket brokers, fraudulent labor contracts, and deception at the ports of departure. The erasure of migration as a collec-tive project from legislative discussions reinforced a vision of departure as an act of individual liberty and of the South as a desolate land.

Rituals of Kin and Community

Leaving for the Americas was a collective experience across South Italy. Although husbands and wives usually made the decision to send individual family members to work overseas, villagers departed together. Sometimes villagers were recruited by labor brokers or representatives of the large shipping agencies, but even those who were following in the steps of their cousins, neighbors, or friends rarely traveled alone. Preparations for sending a relatively small group of emigrants often involved a range of overlapping kin and friendship networks. Focusing on the way that rituals of migration defined local, national, and transnational communities highlights the emotional dimensions that shaped the individual and collective experience. These rituals marking the moment of departure informed notions of gender, family, and the wider political landscape surrounding transnational migration in important ways.[23]

It is difficult to find descriptions of the collective familial and public preparations and rituals that marked the departure of emigrants from a village. Journalists, politicians, and academics interested in understanding the impact of emigration on South Italy commonly fixated on the train station. Those interested in the emigrant overseas understood departure as the moment the boat slipped away from the quay, when villagers left Italy behind.[24] Yet in memoirs and letters migrants evoked the moment of departure in final meals shared with family and friends or the hugs and tears as they left for the station. When we expand our view to consider the week or so prior to leaving, an alternate emotional landscape emerges.

In 1903, Broughton Brandenburg and his wife sailed to Italy to write an investigative series of articles on immigration the United States published in *Frank Leslie's Popular Monthly*. On board they met Antonio Squadrito and his father, Giovanni, who were returning to Campania from Brooklyn for a short visit. Brandenburg and his wife joined Antonio and Giovanni as they traveled home to see family and friends and accompany yet another emigrant group to America. Brandenburg's articles provide a detailed description of the rituals and practices that marked emigration. The rituals surrounding departure began days before the emigrants left. First came the packing. Families packed entire wardrobes for those leaving, as well as food and bedding. Brandenburg writes: "Carmela crammed into the huge boxes two sets of heavy mattresses with all the accompanying bedding, large cans of pomodoro [tomato], olive oil, sticks on which dried figs were impaled, flasks of wine, forms of cheese, old clothes, cooking utensils." Neighbors and friends pressed letters into the hands of those leaving to deliver to their kin in America, often containing urgent pleas for money or tickets and longer letters recounting recent news from the family and community.[25]

Four days before they left, emigrants and their family and friends joined together for a special evening service asking for protection on the voyage and prosperity in America. After the service they gathered at the house for feasting and dancing. "The large room on the ground floor of the Casa Squadrito was ringed around with a double row of guests," Brandenburg wrote, "while others crowded in the street outside." The next morning, a Sunday, the celebrations turned solemn, as the rituals that marked the end of the week—Mass and the *passeggiata* (leisurely walk or stroll)—took on a new weight. Emigrants laid flowers on the tombs of their loved ones buried in the cemetery. Monday evening brought more neighbors with messages, cheese, and olive oil for those in America. Only on the eve of departure did Brandenburg focus on the grief and pain of the impending separation.[26]

Taken together, the rituals of celebration and exchange—channeling a range of emotions of excitement, anticipation, fear, and grief—marked a new stage in the community's evolution. The packing of certain foods, the sending of notes and letters, and the insistence on Masses for health and wealth rather than in memory of the dead channeled emotions in ways that heightened the sense that emigration was like a marriage, a communal project that reconfigured the boundaries of kin and family. Like a marriage, emigration ran similar risks of joy, prosperity, and heartbreak. Descriptions of packing an emigrant's trunk full of olive oil, tomatoes, olives, herbs, clothing, bedding, and even particular pots and pans echoed preparations for a newlywed couple's home. As with newlyweds, these celebrations of food, bedding, and clothes reinforced a migrant's emotional connection to home and their place within a wider kin group, evoking memories of the colors, sights, and smells of the land they left.[27] As Charlotte Chapman Gower notes, "the homesick emigrant speaks of his native land largely in terms of its produce—the bounteous fruit and the excellent bread. For him the season to visit Milocca is the summer."[28]

One aspect of leaving that had a powerful ritualistic dimension was the exchange of letters. In nearly all accounts of the moment of leaving, there was a flurry of tucking letters into trunks or handing them to those departing. These letters—mixing information about family at home, recent deaths, births, marriage, expressions of longing and love with pleas to send money home or to ask why the emigrants had fallen silent—reinforced physical and emotional ties that underpinned the construction of transnational communities.[29] Across Sicily and South Italy, where illiteracy rates varied between 50 percent and 70 percent of residents over the age of six, reading letters was often a communal affair.[30] When letters arrived, by mail or via returning emigrants, they were often shared with neighbors, friends, or the local priest. The letters served not only to remind those overseas of their obligations back home but also to urge friends and relatives to come to the Americas. Antonio Mangano recalled one villager telling him that he had twenty-seven relatives in America, all writing to him to cross the ocean and try his fortune.[31] The ritual of tucking letters into the trunks of departing migrants transformed individual and collective emotions of love, hope, and fear into something tangible.

Focusing on the inclusive aspects of the rituals of departure carried gendered and political implications. Constructing emigration through rituals of family formation, far from emasculating men or destroying women, reconfigured the roles of men and women in positive ways. Relatives and friends eagerly awaited the return of an emigrant. "He is entirely transformed," as Mangano put it. "The rough, home-spun clothing and raw linen shirt are replaced by a 'store suit' and a stiffly starched shirt [that] shows through his open vest. . . . He has learned better how to carry himself and shows a new spirit of independence when he meets his former padrone without an obsequious bow: 'He is a man.'"[32]

Just as migration altered the meaning of manliness, it also changed the position of women within the family, the village, and the state. Rituals of departure reinforced the new position of women within the family and community as the keepers of transnational family ties and as household managers. The women who remained behind were not victims of emigration but rather active participants in the process. They took on new roles as financial managers, household representatives, and overseers of children's education.[33] Seen from the perspective of the community, rituals of departure mark transnational migration, like a wedding, as a generative force with social, cultural, and political implications. Each marriage may not be successful, but marriages ensure the continuation of the collective into the future. Yet few outsiders viewed departure through a lens of expansion, political agency, or growth.

Journalists and politicians fixated on the rituals of departure as a kind of collective death.

Recognizing the framing of rituals of migration is significant on multiple levels. What can appear to be the appropriation of funeral rites can, from another perspective, be understood as generative practices, with clear import for the ways migration defines community and family. But it may also have wider political significance. The insistence of Italian journalists, politicians, and experts portraying the moment of leaving as a permanent loss reinforced the notion of migration as an exodus, as an emptying of southern Italian villages, and diminished the agency of Southerners as cultural and economic actors on the national stage. This insight suggests that historians of Italy need to examine how the framing of rituals may play a significant role in reinforcing cultural tropes of the South as "backward," perhaps justifying central government decisions to focus industrial investments and infrastructure growth in the northern regions. The meanings attached rituals of migration are equally important to scholars as we seek to understand the construction of migrant identities at home and abroad.

Trousseau Textiles

Transnational Travels of Two Copriletti

DONNA GABACCIA AND JOAN L. SAVERINO

In almost all human societies, marriage is a central institution, a rite of passage, often marked by the wedding ritual.[1] In Italy, during the nineteenth and twentieth centuries, important ritualistic practices preceded the wedding. One was the presentation of the *corredo* (trousseau), an essential inclusion in the dowry given by the bride's family to fulfill part of a marriage agreement between two families. This chapter analyzes two handwoven bed coverlets (*copriletti*) that were part of two families' *corredo* in Toscana and Calabria, two provinces of Italy. They were fashioned by feminine hands during periods of economic change and global mass emigration that disordered and reordered local traditions. Both coverlets subsequently made transnational voyages—from Toscana to Chicago in 1921 and from Calabria to Winnipeg in 1960.

Migrating Italians carried material possessions with them, including household linens. Yet systematic examinations of migrants' choices about what to carry and why or how these material objects might be associated with ritualized practices scarcely exist. This chapter offers a gendered analysis of changes in the meaning, value, use, and preservation of handwoven bedcovers that traveled with migrants.

The production of textiles was once central to household labor in the Mediterranean. In Italy, the *corredo* consisted of clothing and household linens. The *corredo* was emotionally and symbolically valued because it was positively associated with a woman's artistic skill, her moral worth, and restrictions placed on her sexuality. Bedcovers literally adorned and legitimized the intimate space—the bed—where new kin were created, thereby emphasizing women's contributions to expanding a family's network of mutual support.

Recent scholarship has emphasized how the creation of household textiles provided women with an avenue to artistic expressivity. Working from childhood in groups, displaying their handwork in public at the time of marriage, and dressing the bed with embellished linens afforded ordinary peasant women opportunities to excel, take pride in their creative work, and judge others' prowess. Fabric was a rare and precious commodity before the prevalence of machine-made cloth. A loom in every home was a necessity. A particularly talented textile artisan became known and admired in the community, making her work sought after and more highly valued.[2]

Women's textile labor fit within a restrictive Mediterranean cultural code of honor and shame that required women to remain chaste before marriage and to comport themselves properly in public. Women, being the "repository of family and lineage honor," were subject to community scrutiny and sanctions.[3] Domestic textile production was an expectation associated with being a good woman and future wife. Thus the presentation of the *corredo*—a realization of a woman's domestic abilities—was a ritualistic affair carried out in the presence of both families, while neighbors examined, assessed, and appreciated the displayed trousseau items.

Both Toscana and Calabria experienced massive emigration and economic change in the nineteenth and twentieth centuries. A century ago, as the Italian statistician Anna Maria Ratti has noted, emigration rates were 298 per 100,000 from Toscana in 1876 but only 73 per 100,000 from Calabria. That soon changed: for the period 1911–1914, emigration rates from Calabria (2,778 per 100,000) far surpassed Toscana's.[4] The difference reflected changes in local economies. In Toscana, industrialization began earlier and proceeded rapidly, creating new jobs that absorbed considerable rural labor, while Calabria saw evolution mainly in its agricultural and pastoral economy. This chapter's comparison of two regions hints at ways that emigration, industrial life, and agricultural change transformed the already malleable gendered social practices, symbolism, and notions of femininity associated with the ritual of marriage and *corredo* in Italy and its diasporas.

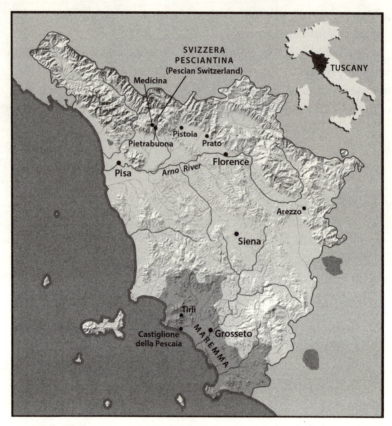

Figure 3.1. Toscana, with key sites mentioned in text. Matt Kania Map Illustrations.

Studying Migration and Material Culture

There are good reasons for scholars of migration to overcome the methodological challenges of studying the mobility of material culture.[5] The investigation of textiles, long an interest in cultural anthropology as indexical to identity, was largely ignored by historians until the twentieth century, perhaps because textiles' association with intimacy and femininity marked them as unworthy of serious attention. Historians focused instead on the industrialization of textile production, which was well documented in written sources. Yet for more than 10,000 years, textiles have been economically, politically, and socially central

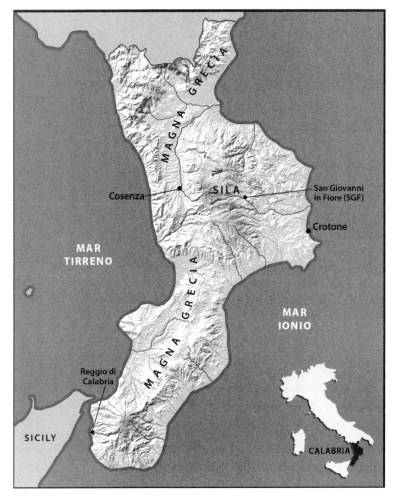

Figure 3.2. San Giovanni in Fiore, Provincia di Cosenza, Calabria. Matt Kania Map Illustrations.

to human societies that needed cloth to fulfill basic human needs for shelter and clothing. While the importance of fabric has changed over time, the domestic production of textiles remained significant in all the regions of Italy that sent migrants abroad.

A focus on *copriletti* as traveling material objects allows us to acknowledge the kinds of property that mattered to the iconic "huddled masses" and to generate insights into their changing cultural values and

Figure 3.3. Woman with Spindle in Roggiano Gravina, Calabria, 1950. Copyright UNESCO / David Seymour. By permission of Magnum Photos.

practices. These artifacts reveal how ordinary migrants valued beauty and creativity and allow us to understand what handmade items they especially wished to possess, use, and preserve.

Objects of material culture have their own histories. By adopting a historical, contextual, and comparative place-based analytic model, we illuminate the two bedcovers within temporal trajectories. The analysis connects their travels to human reproduction, kinship, social customs, and the gendering of everyday life—topics that can often be teased out only with great difficulty from written sources. Research on travel-ing *copriletti* required the use of mixed methods. Since 1991, Saverino's ethnographic and ethnohistorical research has focused on women's daily lives and expressivity, especially the production of textiles, in San Giovanni in Fiore (SGF) in Calabria, her maternal great-grandmother's hometown. In 2013, she began researching the *ozaturù*, a handwoven bedcover once included in every *corredo*. She conducted interviews and examined *ozaturi* in homes and in the local ethnographic museum. For this chapter, she also interviewed emigrants Anna and Stanislao Carbone, who owned the Calabrian *copriletto*, which was part of the *corredo* of Vittoria Carbone (Stan's mother). Because Saverino was unable to physically examine this *ozaturù*, she depended on photographs, correspondence, and secondary sources.

A coauthor of this chapter, Donna Gabaccia owns the Toscana *copriletto* and could physically examine it with the eye of an experienced hand weaver and crocheter. Gabaccia received the *copriletto* as a gift from Alex and Mary Batinich of Minnesota, together with a 3-by-5 index card explaining the cover's provenance in the Toscana-origin family of Cristiano and Vittoria Bastiani of Chicago, who gave it to Mary Ellen Mancina Batinich, the first wife of Alex Batinich. By the time Gabaccia obtained the *copriletto*, around 2009, Cristiano and Vittoria Bastiani, their daughter (Dorothy Kellberg), and Mary Ellen Batinich were all deceased, precluding oral history methods. The COVID-19 pandemic blocked ethnographic research in Toscana, so Gabaccia consulted the Mary Ellen Mancina Batinich family archive at the University of Minnesota's Immigration History Research Center Archives, traced the Bastiani family's genealogy on Ancestry.com, and reviewed the *Chicago Tribune* for notices about the Bastiani and Batinich families.

Domestic Textile Production in Toscana and Calabria

Both bedspreads studied were handwoven products of women's skilled domestic labor. Both reflected the differing regional economies of central and southern Italy after 1861. Figures 3.1 and 3.2 locate Toscana and Calabria within Italy and identifies sites mentioned in this chapter. Figures 3.3 and 3.4 give a general sense of the tools and labor of domestic spinning and weaving in the Italian South.

Vittoria Bastiani, who owned the Toscana bedspread until the 1970s, described its provenance in 1973 (see figure 3.5). The *copriletto* was woven around 1873 in Tirli in southwestern Toscana. The fiber used

Figure 3.4. Domenico Caruso standing next to his family's seventeenth-century horizontal loom in his shop. On the loom is a partially completed *ozaturù* that he was working on. SGF, June 28, 2013. Photograph by Joan L. Saverino.

was hand-spun linen, extremely uniform in coloration and thickness, suggesting the work of a highly skilled spinster. An equally skilled weaver prepared and mounted a warp of about nine meters on a domestic loom. Likely wooden, roughly constructed, and about a meter wide, Toscana looms were similar to the Calabrian one depicted in figure 3.4. Weavers attached harnesses of string loops ("heddles") to over-

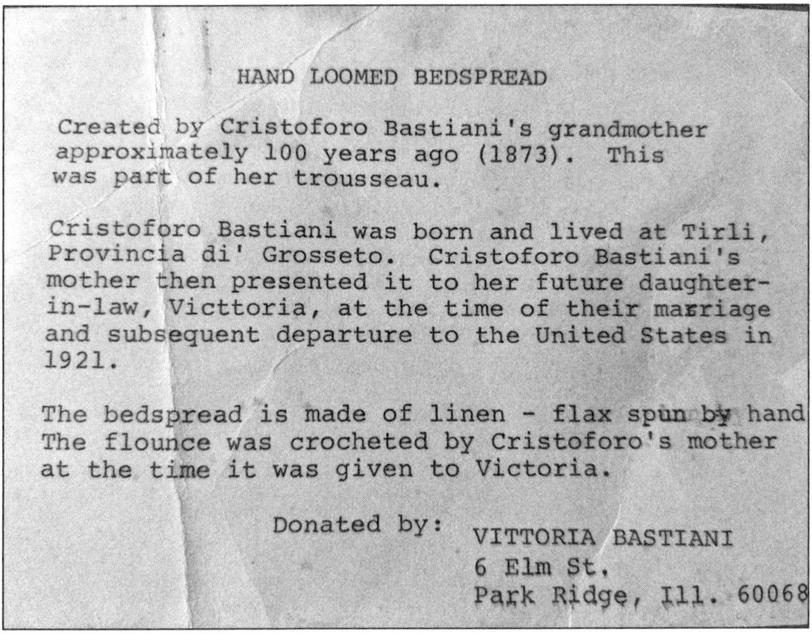

HAND LOOMED BEDSPREAD

Created by Cristoforo Bastiani's grandmother
approximately 100 years ago (1873). This
was part of her trousseau.

Cristoforo Bastiani was born and lived at Tirli,
Provincia di' Grosseto. Cristoforo Bastiani's
mother then presented it to her future daughter-
in-law, Victtoria, at the time of their marriage
and subsequent departure to the United States in
1921.

The bedspread is made of linen - flax spun by hand
The flounce was crocheted by Cristoforo's mother
at the time it was given to Victoria.

Donated by: VITTORIA BASTIANI
6 Elm St,
Park Ridge, Ill. 60068

Figure 3.5. Provenance card accompanying Tuscan bedspread. Photograph by Donna Gabaccia.

head wooden rods; after passing warp threads in a set order through the heddles, weavers could lift the harnesses in distinctive combinations to create woven patterns.

Figure 3.6 shows a basic block of the four variations on the honeycomb (*nidi di api*) pattern used in the Toscana bedspread. Once cut off the loom, whip stitch and linen thread were used to combine three woven segments into a bedspread measuring 1.95 x 2.325 meters. The provenance card established that a wide flounce was added later (see figure 3.5). The flounce fiber was manufactured cotton thread worked in double crochet and chain stitches to form a diamond filet crochet design with a scalloped edge. The flounce was attached to the bedspread's three sides with whip stitch to round its square bottom ("foot") corners. Of simple design, the regular and consistent crochet stitches were also the work of skilled and experienced hands.

The provenance card established that the Toscana *copriletto* was created for a woman's *corredo*. At the time the *copriletto* was woven in

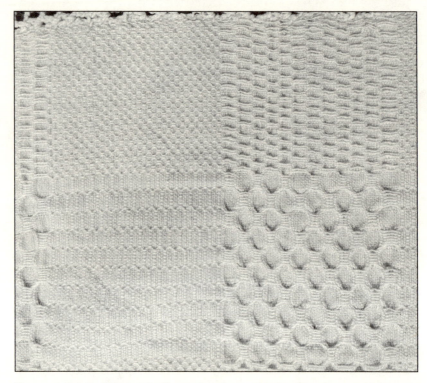

Figure 3.6. Detail of Bastiani family *copriletto* showing blocks of four honeycomb patterns. Photograph by Donna Gabaccia.

1873, domestic production of textiles for home use was still thoroughly integrated into the overwhelmingly agricultural yet diverse and changing economy of rural Toscana. The inclusion of household fabrics in a *corredo* had deep roots: studies of marriage and family in Toscana emphasize the importance of dowries and trousseaus among the region's urban elite already during the High Middle Ages; other studies describe how Catholic charities developed to provide cash for the purchase of a *corredo*, allowing the most impoverished Toscana girls to purchase linens and to marry. Especially within the complex households of Toscana's sharecropping peasants (*mezzadri*), women in 1870 were still expected to bring household linens to their marriage as a form of treasure.[6]

In the nineteenth century, Tirli, the site of the *copriletto*'s creation, was a tiny village of thirty or forty peasant families living in the hilly

Figure 3.7. Detail of Bastiani family *copriletto* showing crocheted flounce and corner construction. Photograph by Donna Gabaccia.

hinterlands of the much larger town of Grosseto. Local families owned or leased land to raise their food; seasonally, children or shepherds drove sheep, goats, or cattle into the Maremma coastland swamps and bush. Flax, the plant source for linen, was grown above the water line in such boggy coastal areas. With all members working, a peasant family in Tirli could still obtain a modest and hard but relatively secure subsistence.

After Italy's unification in 1861, rural change accelerated in Toscana. Privatized large estates pushed Maremma agricultural development, draining swamps and depriving hill peasants of access to the pasturage and flax bogs that facilitated subsistence. The Italian state also demanded new taxes, to be paid in cash, which peasants living far from urban markets obtained with difficulty. Finally, Italy chose to protect new textile manufacturers developing in Toscana in an arc stretching from Arezzo to Florence, Prato, and Pistoia. An exodus from mountainous Toscana began as growing numbers of peasant children survived to adulthood but were constrained to seek wages elsewhere. Many moved to areas of modernizing or intensifying agriculture or took employment in textile (or other) factories in Toscana's growing cities. Well before 1876, people from Toscana migrated long distances in search of work.

By contrast, the Calabrian coverlet was woven from local wool and was produced much later, in 1950. In SGF, it is called an *ozaturù*, a local-language term derived from the raised stitch technique most representative of the textile tradition there (see figures 3.8–3.10. The town, known as an artisanal center since the nineteenth century, was founded in 1188–1189 by the mystic Gioacchino of Fiore, a Cistercian monk. During the twentieth century, with a population of about 20,000, its economic base was agriculture and sheepherding, with goldsmithing and weaving arts also of great importance. In all of southern Italy, the economic system was based on the latifundium (large agricultural estate), which replaced the feudal system in 1806 after the passage of French conquerors' laws. The latifundium was a transitional stage from feudalism to capitalism and varied in form and function depending on the area. The largest Calabrian latifundium was the Barracco estate, which included SGF and spanned territory from the Tirreno Sea to the Ionio Sea. It was a uniquely successful model characterized by diversified production, administration, and labor relationships for most of the nineteenth century. The latifundium finally ended with the agrarian reform of 1950. Its goal, only partially

Figure 3.8. Stanislao and Anna Carbone's *ozaturù* woven in undyed natural local wool from the brown and white sheep in 1950, San Giovanni in Fiore, Calabria. The length is 2.265 meters; the width is 2.261 meters. The central design is *mattunella* (Calabrese), meaning "tile" (*mattonella* or *piastrella* in Italian). The edging design is a Greek geometric pattern. Photograph and measurements by Anna Carbone.

achieved, was twofold: to distribute land to the peasants, and to create positive conditions for agricultural development.

Isolated by its mountainous location, snowy winters, poor or nonexistent roads, and absence of a train line linking it with Cosenza before 1950, SGF experienced change more slowly than Toscana. Of course,

Figure 3.9. Maria Romano's multicolored *ozaturù*. Estimated age is 150–200 years old. It was passed down through her maternal line. Pattern, *ciampa e cavallu* (Calabrese, meaning "horse's hoofprint"). Photograph by Joan L. Saverino.

outside influences—such as manufactured goods, including textiles—were introduced to SGF much earlier, but these were limited to the wealthy. Local artisans, including textile- and woodworkers and other specialists, were integral to the economy until the end of World War II. Stan Carbone's mother was part of that World War II generation experiencing the shifts that so affected Italy and the global economy. Stan noted that she was the "last generation of artisans that were actually working with their hands."[7] While generally true, there are, of course, still some local artisans today.

In SGF, the *ozaturù* was the most expensive textile in the *corredo*, woven from local wool, a necessity in the frigid winters. Women wove on a Calabrian horizontal loom (as described for the Toscana loom) composed of four vertical axes (about 1.5 meters tall) and four horizontal harnesses with heddles, operated by pedals at the base of the loom. Local woods—chestnut, pine, beech, and birch—were used.

The loom permitted the width of the fabric to be 90–100 centimeters (and 60 centimeters wide in the oldest fabrics). Thus, as occurred with the Toscana coverlet, three separate lengths were woven in succession, with identical patterning, and then handsewn together to produce a coverlet wide enough for the marriage bed.[8] A handmade crocheted fringe was almost always added afterward, usually made by the woman herself.

Owing to their complexity, the *ozaturi* were fabricated by weaving specialists. Since the area was part of Magna Grecia, there were many intercultural and multicultural influences on patterns. The oldest multicolored *ozaturi* (figure 3.9) were naturally dyed, incorporating floral or geometric designs. Traditionally, weavers used vegetable dyes made from plants, roots, and fruits collected in the region or, as in the Carbone example (figure 3.8), employed undyed natural local wool from the brown and white sheep.

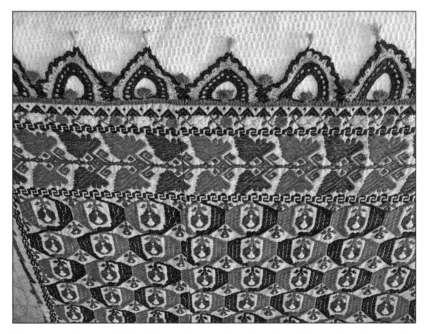

Figure 3.10. Close-up of Maria Romano's *ozaturù* with crocheted fringe. Note the underlying white *copriletto*, which closely matches one of the patterns of the Toscano one. Photograph by Joan L. Saverino.

The production technique was referred to as *pizzicotto* (pinch) or *pizzulune* (in regional language) because of the raised design it created. For this type of *ozaturù*, the warp (or base fiber) was cotton and the weft for the design was wool.[9] A cotton weft thread was also used to "beat" or secure the woolen weft threads that were pulled through the warp to create the design. The overall geometric or floral design was produced by pulling supplementary wool weft threads up through the warp with a metal or wooden hooked tool (much like a crochet hook).

Once completed, the *ozaturù* was placed in a large wooden trunk. For wealthier brides, a decorated cart and horse or donkey transported it and other belongings to the new patrilocal home. The exact customs associated with the transfer of textiles at the time of marriage differed from region to region in Italy, but every aspect of a *copriletto*'s preparation led up to the rite of passage, marriage.

Two Italian Families and Their Traveling Bedspreads
From Toscana to Chicago and Beyond

In 1973, Dorothy Kellberg, a Chicago schoolteacher who was forty-nine at the time, typed the provenance card (figure 3.5) describing the Toscana *copriletto* based on a conversation with her mother, Vittoria Bastiani, seventy-two, who owned the bedspread and who had carried it with her to Chicago. Vittoria provided a very short, somewhat confusing account, likely because the bedspread had originated in the family of her husband, Cristoforo, who had died in 1961.

We know little about the bedspread's creator. According to Vittoria, Cristoforo's grandmother wove the *copriletto* as part of her wedding trousseau. Vittoria noted the flax had been spun by hand but did not name the spinster. The grandmother, too, remained nameless: Was she the mother of Cristoforo's father or of his mother? Vittoria probably erred—Cristoforo's mother, not grandmother, married in the 1870s—but Italian and American records on Ancestry.com further confuse this simple narrative.

Cristoforo's parents were Emilia Paggiola (1850?–1925?, born in Tirli) and Giuliano Alsano Bastiani (1848–1925?, born in Medicina). After their first son, Alceo, was born in Tirli in 1878, the family settled in

Giuliano's hometown, Medicina, in northern Toscana. Presumably, the *copriletto* traveled with the family from Tirli to Medicina. Four sons and two daughters were subsequently born in Medicina to Emilia and Giuliano between 1880 and 1896. Cristoforo Bastiani was not listed among them. Medicina was in the mountains north of Pescia, 160 kilometers from Tirli. Oak and chestnut forests dominated the landscape. Local agriculture was increasingly dependent on waged workers, and Giuliano and Emilia's adult sons all described themselves as irregularly employed farm laborers when they emigrated.[10]

Born in 1898 or 1899, when Emilia Bastiani was around fifty years of age, Cristoforo sometimes listed Tirli and sometimes Medicina as his birthplace. When his well-documented oldest brother, Alceo, emigrated to Chicago in summer 1902, his parents' residence was listed as Medicina. Brother Alceo also seems to have been pursued to the United States in fall 1902 by a young woman traveling with her own brother from Pietrabuona (a village near Medicina); the woman told American immigration officials that Alceo was her husband and the father of a four-year-old son who bore his name and who accompanied her. Alceo must have refused to acknowledge the child since he soon married a much younger Tuscan woman in Chicago.

By the time brothers Alvise, Settimo, Domenico, and Paolino Bastiani followed Alceo to Chicago in 1907, Emilia and Giuliano had moved to Pietrabuona, the young woman's place of residence. Given this residential change, Gabaccia felt she had to consider the possibility that Cristoforo was in fact Alceo's natural child, born out of wedlock. If Emilia Bastiani was Cristoforo's grandmother, rather than mother, then she could indeed have woven the bedspread for her trousseau, as Vittoria claimed on the provenance card.

Once grown, Cristoforo Bastiani married in Medicina. In preparation for his marriage and departure for America, Emilia Bastiani crocheted and affixed the coverlet's flounce to the *copriletto*; she also roughly embroidered at its "head" edge her future daughter-in-law's name, using outline stitch (see figure 3.11). The act signaled a mother-in-law's affection and esteem for the bride for it departed from usual *corredo* practices, which ordinarily gifted a mother's bedspread to one of her daughters.

Figure 3.11. Emilia's embroidery of Vittoria's name on the Tuscan bedspread. Photograph by Donna Gabaccia.

Cristoforo and Vittoria left for Chicago in 1921, carrying the bedspread with them. Cristoforo described himself to immigration clerks as a literate agricultural worker, listed Giuliano Bastiani in Medicina as the couple's next of kin, and named Alceo (Cristoforo's oldest brother or natural father) as their Chicago host. After staying initially with Alceo in Evanston and working as a laborer, Cristoforo moved with Vittoria to Horner Park on Chicago's North Side. There he found employment as a carpenter, operated his own cement contracting business, and enjoyed modest success.[11]

Cristoforo and Vittoria had only one child, Dorothy Elizabeth, born in 1924. For fifteen years, the family rented apartments on the North

Side. Vittoria then took waged work as a dressmaker in the 1930s, facilitating the purchase of a simple frame house in the city. The fact that the *copriletto* became (and remains) slightly discolored from the oil and sweat of sleeping human bodies suggests that it continued to be used on the marital bed in the Bastiani home. After graduation in 1942 from Carl Schurz High School, Dorothy Bastiani trained as a teacher and worked in Chicago elementary schools until marrying Robert Kellberg—himself a teacher and the child of Swedish immigrants from a North Side neighborhood. Dorothy did not take possession of the *copriletto* from her mother upon marriage, as tradition might have predicted.

When the Kellbergs' three children began public school in Park Ridge, Dorothy returned to teaching and eventually became a principal in a school educating Mexican immigrant children, a fitting assignment given her documented interests in bilingual education—an interest that connected her to Mary Ellen Batinich, another Chicago schoolteacher and principal with Italian immigrant roots.[12] The two first met as members of the Illinois Reading Council, which Batinich led in 1970–1971. Intimacy and friendship based on their interest in bilingualism likely grew when both women lost their positions as principals during the racially charged era of school busing politics in the early 1970s.[13]

By 1973, after a second removal, Batinich was becoming a community activist and documentarian of Italian immigrant life. Apparently neither Vittoria Bastiani nor Dorothy Kellberg was still using the coverlet when Mary Ellen began collecting heritage items for an envisioned Italian American museum in Chicago. Unfortunately, no museum materialized before 1980, when Mary Ellen and Alex Batinich returned (with the *copriletto*) to Minnesota and Vittoria Bastiani died in Chicago.

Once in Minnesota, Alex and Mary Ellen wanted to donate the coverlet to the Immigration History Research Center but discovered that its collection policies excluded three-dimensional gifts. In 2009, Alex Batinich and his second wife, Mary, instead gifted the bedspread to Gabaccia as director of the research center. The coverlet then traveled with Gabaccia to Toronto and South Carolina. After completing research for this chapter, Gabaccia has decided to fulfill both families' original intentions by bequeathing it to Casa Italia/Italian Cultural Center near

Chicago.[14] A journey that began in Tirli with the production of a *copri-letto* fulfilling Italian expectations for a bride's *corredo* had transformed the material object into a museum artifact to be appreciated aesthetically by strangers.

From Calabria to Winnipeg

The *ozaturù* in figure 3.8 is owned by Anna Girimonte Carbone, gifted to her by her mother-in-law, Vittoria Lopez.[15] Vittoria met Rocco Carbone in 1945 in SGF shortly after World War II. Anna says that Vittoria "fell in love right away because his father [Stan's father, Rocco] was a beauty." After about five years they married in SGF in 1951. Vittoria, born in 1929, became an expert seamstress, learning from neighborhood women. Vittoria's mother, Maria Candelise, was widowed when her husband, Francesco Lopez, died, leaving her with five girls and two boys to raise. She bought a Singer sewing machine that Vittoria used to contribute to the family economy by creating and mending clothing.

In that early post–World War II era, a *corredo* was still essential for a prospective bride. Anna listed the minimum requirement: seven pillowcases, two sheets, and especially the *ozaturù*. The presentation of the trousseau was a transaction with the mother-in-law as the person designated to examine it. Anna said, "It was very stressful for the family." Since Vittoria did not have a mother-in-law, the job was left to her future sister-in-law. Anna and Stan agreed that Rocco was not one to view the *corredo* as a necessity. Stan explained how "it was a tradition as well but it was also a question of pride that you brought something into it. . . . She did it to save face"—that is, to avoid criticism and to fulfill expectations.[16]

Vittoria did not have the money to buy an *ozaturù*. Being resourceful, she decided to barter with the shepherds who came through town during the transhumance (seasonal migrations of herded animals). She offered to mend their clothing in exchange for the sheep's wool. They agreed, and she did the difficult and dirty work of cleaning and spinning the wool. Stan and Anna think that Vittoria hired Annamaria Cannizzaro, her neighbor, to weave the *ozaturù*. Vittoria brought it in her luggage when she left with her small children, Stan and Caterina, to join Rocco, who was working in a garment factory in Winnipeg,

Canada, in 1960. Anna commented on Vittoria's decision: "She left everything behind in Italy and she brought that *ozaturù*!" . . . When she came to Canada, she said, 'What can I bring? I can't bring plates, I can't bring glasses, just let me bring the *ozaturù*.'" Once settled, Anna stated: "She used it for many years because when they came here, she [had] nothing. So she put this on the bed." We cannot discount the symbolic nature of Vittoria's use of the *ozaturù* in Canada, a preservation of a local tradition of the dressed bed.

Anna first met Vittoria when she arrived in Winnipeg, in 1983, at age eighteen, to attend her sister's wedding. Anna says about Vittoria:

> She . . . said, Oh my god, you're so beautiful, maybe you're good for my son. . . . But that way she fell in love with me honestly and I fell [in love] with her too. She was a sweet mother-in-law. . . . We connected right away [be]cause we came from the same town, same idea, same tradition. . . . It's good to keep the tradition so at least we, we [left] Italy, but we have Italy in our heart.

Vittoria bequeathed her *ozaturù* to Anna, who brought it out of storage for the interview. She commented: "She gave me this BEAUTIFUL *ozaturù* . . . it is in great condition . . . it was beautiful to see honestly. I put it on my bed and it looked so wonderful. Very heavy, very heavy." Anna's sister-in-law did not want the *ozaturù* and told her mother to give it to Anna because she knew how to care for it:

> I said to my mother-in-law, I don't know why you give these things to me because I don't have children either. She said to me, you know what, I am giving [it] to you because I know you [will] take care [of it]. One day you choose who appreciates [it]. It doesn't have to be family . . . it can be one of your sisters, [it] can be in a museum, you make a choice. . . . I say, Ma, I appreciate it but why [do] you give it to me, you have two grandchildren? She said, no Anna, I give [it] to you because, I KNOW it's in good hands.

Since Anna and Stan have no offspring, Anna intends to donate her *ozaturù* to the Museo Demologico in SGF. The connections to the town are still vibrant given that Anna has immediate family living there and the couple returns yearly. Anna said: "See today I value this . . . [it] has a piece of memory and a sentiment because I know where it comes from. I don't know what it's worth." Stan, the director of programs and exhibitions at the Jewish Heritage Centre of Western Canada in Winnipeg, expressed a professional perspective. He noted that the *ozaturù* is part of the historical and social context of SGF. Its return to its birthplace would be a transnational, full-circle voyage. The *ozaturù* once symbolized and expressed through ritual behaviors the embodiment of the feminine ideal. Still valued and passed down intergenerationally, it has evolved into a contemporary symbol of local identity.[17]

Some Final Thoughts on *Corredo*, Rituals, and Migration

Although woven fabric was a key component of *corredo* in both Toscana and Calabria, the exact practices, production processes, and aesthetics of weaving differed in the two regions and changed over time. The case of the Calabrian *copriletto* might appear to reflect cultural conservatism and belated change when compared to the Toscana case, but we urge readers to reject simple evaluations about "more" or "less" conservatism in the two regions. As late as 1951, Vittoria Lopez was compelled to demonstrate to the neighborhood and her soon-to-be in-laws that she had a *corredo*. That was only thirty years after Vittoria in Toscana also brought a *copriletto* into her marriage to Cristoforo Bastiani. Scholars know little about how and when changes occurred in the symbolism, production, and use of *corredo* items, just as they know little about the changing associations of the *corredo* with female comportment and morality. It seems certain, however, that regional differences persisted, that changes intensified or accelerated during internal and international migrations, and that change never obliterated emotional and artistic appreciation for *copriletti*.

It also seems highly likely that economic changes in Toscana in the second half of the nineteenth century, mainly a decline in subsistence production, allowed the daughters of agricultural laborers (perhaps including the two daughters of Emilia and Giuliano Bastiani) to marry with little or no dowry or *corredo*. Folklorists' studies have confirmed that, by the mid-twentieth century, rural women in Toscana substituted eight to twelve purchased sets of sheets for homespun or handwoven *corredo* items. Still, the Toscana *copriletto* continued to hold emotional value as part of the marriage ritual evidenced by Emilia's embroidering of Vittoria's name in 1921.[18]

Subtle changes occurred in SGF, too, and "differed with terrain, crops raised, altitude and location, and micro-history" without eliminating the value—both financial and aesthetic—of *copriletti*.[19] Traditions of domestic textile production were deeply embedded in subsistence practices, which became less stable over time. In Calabria and Basilicata, especially along the new train lines, female textile production and other domestic and proto-industrial forms of production eventually collapsed, and the status of women declined with the importation of textiles from northern Italy and elsewhere in Europe. With male migration, women increasingly bore alone the weight of subsistence production of food in addition to domestic industry. Still, peasant subsistence production remained common for most families in SGF until after World War II— partly as a result of postwar impoverishment. These factors at least partially explain the town's apparent cultural conservatism.[20]

Similarly, scholars might best regard the changes in rituals and practices that accompanied migration as the further development of malleable traditions adapting to new contexts and circumstances. Traditionally, an *ozaturù* or Toscana *copriletto* passed from mother to daughter. Yet both Vittoria Lopez and Emilia Bastiani bequeathed *corredo* items to their daughters-in-law, Anna and Vittoria. Clearly, relations of mothers- and daughters-in-law were not always strained; they could be loving and warm. Because a woman's *corredo* was her own personal property, she could do with it as she pleased, needing no husband's permission. The interview with Stan and Vittoria Carbone indicates that the gifting of a *copriletto* sometimes reflected donors' esteem for a woman they believed would appreciate, value, and know how to care for it. Tellingly, both authors of this chapter (Saverino and Gabaccia) fell into that category when, during their research, they were given *corredo* items as special gifts.[21]

While immigrant mothers may have wanted to create a *corredo* for their daughters, American women like Dorothy Kellberg felt less tied to village mores. The impact of American-style "white weddings" on the practices and marriage rituals of Toscana and Calabria certainly deserves more scholarly attention. We suggest that shifts occurred during immigration from the brides' families' investments in *corredo* to investments in elaborate weddings with expensive, dedicated dresses, the hosting of large family-and-community celebrations with lavish displays of cookies, food, and drink, and the presentation of gifts to the newly married couple of cash and material gifts. (These arguably continued the intergenerational transfer of wealth but spread its costs throughout entire kin groups.)

As marriage practices changed, and the most important financial functions of the *corredo* diminished with life abroad, the artistic value and beauty of the handwoven objects—always important for the women who made such objects and used them in traditional ways—not only persisted but also became more evident and may even have increased in each owner's estimation. In both the Toscana and Calabria cases, familial memories and emotional attachments (e.g., of mother- and daughter-in-law) became associated with them. The individual artistry of the handwoven *copriletto* as part of the dressed bed shifted away from its status as a necessary treasure and highly symbolic object associated with female devotion and modesty to become an object of enhanced aesthetic worth honoring female skill and artistry.

Finally, in both destinations—1970s Chicago and twenty-first-century Winnipeg—families expressed desires to make *copriletti* available for wider appreciation by museum-going publics. For both families, the pride taken in a *corredo* was transformed into prestige and pride in possessing a *copriletto* deemed worthy of inclusion in a museum collection. The two bedcovers, rather than losing significance and meaning as they traveled, have, over time, become increasingly esteemed as products of female skill and artistry, deserving of an audience of persons outside the family who might view, learn from, and appreciate them as expressions of female creativity. Family members also became less certain their descendants could be trusted or would commit to materially preserving and valuing the bedspreads, so that roughly fifty years after emigration, both the Bastiani and Carbone families had come to see museum professionals and curators as guaranteeing a more secure future for their treasured *copriletti*.

The two families nevertheless envisioned *copriletti* finding homes of honor in very different settings. With their ongoing connections and recurring visits to their hometown, Stan and Anna Carbone imagined their *copriletto* making a return transnational voyage to Italy. They knew that the struggling museum in SGF (current population 17,000) had a small collection of *ozaturi* and that there was some professional interest in the town's weaving heritage. Because Vittoria Bastiani had last visited Italy just a decade before she gifted her *copriletto* to Mary Ellen Batinich, she surely understood that the populations of both Tirli and Medicina had stagnated after a century of rural exodus. (Today their populations are 200 and 100 respectively.) Already in 1970, it was far easier to imagine the creation of a museum honoring the heritage of Chicago's half-million Italian Americans than to envision their *copriletto*'s return to Toscana. As this volume goes to publication, we can anticipate these trousseau textiles will travel again in the future. Tracing the continuing movement of individual material culture objects reveals dimensions of migration experiences and changes in central rituals such as marriage that written records cannot always document.

PART TWO

In Transit

4

Sabbath on the Ocean

*Rules, Rituals, and Religion on Irish Emigrant Ships
in the Mid-Nineteenth Century*

CIAN T. MCMAHON

When Samuel Harvey emigrated from Belfast to New York City in the late summer of 1849, he found that his religious sensibilities as a devout Protestant overlapped with broader feelings of loss and isolation. "Sabbath on the ocean is peculiarly lonely," he mused in his journal after ten days at sea, "owing to the thoughts, which it awakens in the mind, of home." In particular, there was something disconcerting about the natural environment of a Sunday at sea. "I felt the want of solitude and rural scenes this evening to fit me for the coming Sabbath," he wrote. "Oh, how sweet have I sometimes felt the still hours of a summer Saturday evening when at home! Yes, I have felt as if the Sabbath on its approach flung its fragrance before it." Beyond these feelings of dislocation, there were many dangers to contend with, including the wind, rain, and "waves breaking like thunder" against his ship's "quivering and creaking sides." Other threats emanated from among the passengers themselves. The "weak state" of female passengers had to be protected, and the supposed ignorance of the lower-class Catholics in steerage threatened discipline aboard the ship.[1]

If millions of people like Samuel Harvey had formative experiences while completing sea journeys in the nineteenth century, why have relatively few historians written on the subject? Part of the answer probably lies in the fact that, for many years, historians considered it their job to explain the rise and fall of nation-states and empires. School children might be expected to memorize the names and dates of famous sea battles, but history was generally viewed as something that happened *on land*. In recent years, however, as part of a broader trend toward understanding world history, scholars have become more interested in maritime social history. Several books have been written on the experiences of pirates, slaves, and mutineers at sea. Others have looked at the emigrant voyage. David Cressy has argued that the journey "left an indelible mark" on seventeenth-century Puritans, while Stephen Berry has shown the "dissociative break" it furnished for emigrants a century later.[2]

For those leaving Ireland in the mid-nineteenth century, embarking aboard a sailing ship meant temporarily embedding oneself in a small, seaborne community. This "city afloat," as one eyewitness called it, was strictly organized along the same lines of social class and gender that structured Victorian society on land. As Samuel Harvey made clear, religious rituals were important in this respect. They were used by those in power to maintain control over their subordinates, and they could help make sense of the voyage experience, which could

Figure 4.1. A ship's officers conduct roll call on a mid-nineteenth-century emigrant vessel. Victorian rules on order and discipline were replicated at sea. *Illustrated London News*, July 6, 1850. Courtesy of the British Newspaper Archive (www.britishnewspaperarchive.co.uk) and British Library Board. Image © Illustrated London News Group.

sometimes be quite chaotic, by bringing communities together in times of loss and death. Moreover, for emigrants from nineteenth-century Ireland, where wealth and power were typically concentrated in the hands of a Protestant minority, the shipboard experience also highlighted tensions between poor Catholics and well-off Protestants. These anxieties were exacerbated by the fact that Catholics refused to attend Protestant worship services. As this chapter demonstrates, pious Irish Protestants such as Samuel Harvey used seaborne religious rituals to bring order and comfort to a difficult and dangerous voyage.

Rituals of Faith and Piety

On the morning of Wednesday, August 15, 1849, the emigrant ship *Rienze* sailed out of Belfast Lough before veering left, up and over the north of Ireland, en route to New York. As the vessel pushed through choppy waters, Samuel Harvey stood at the capstan, taking notes in his journal. The capstan was a horizontal mechanical device that the sailors used to drop and weigh the anchor, but Harvey preferred to employ it as his "writing table." There were, Harvey noted, around two hundred emigrants aboard, most of whom were Catholics housed in a long wooden dormitory in the belly of the ship known as "steerage." For his own part, Harvey (who was traveling with several others in the relative comfort of a second-class cabin) was part of the male Protestant elite that governed society in Britain and Ireland at the time and was explicitly entrusted by the government to help maintain discipline and propriety at sea. The *Rienze*'s officers also were Protestants. Captain Baugs, "an excellent man to the passengers," was assisted by a first mate named Pratt, whom Harvey described as "a fine, little, agreeable fellow and capital dancer." There were only two first-class passengers, a mother and her young daughter, on board the *Rienze*. Harvey did not seem to pay them much attention, but the first mate was annoyed by the daughter's affected pride. She was a "sensitive and accomplished young lady," Harvey wrote, but Pratt declared "he could find it in his heart to kick her out of the cabin" as she was "only a hotel-keeper's daughter." Many passengers struggled with seasickness as the *Rienze* made its way out onto the open ocean, but Harvey interpreted the wind and high waves in terms of God's power. "Here, the Almighty displays the strength of His omnipotent arm and performs a hymn to His praise on the strings of the storm," he reflected in his diary, "awakening the terror or sweetening the slumbers of the wandering Sailor Boys."[3]

It was not uncommon for pious people traveling in the mid-nineteenth century to describe what they experienced at sea in religious terms. "How immense is the ocean!" gushed an anonymous author in an 1847 issue of the London-based *Sailors' Magazine*. "But oh! how incomparable is it to the vast ocean of God's everlasting love! This has eternity for its bounds and an extent only known to the adorable Being from whose compassionate bosom it had its rise." The evangelical Protestant British and Foreign Sailors' Society, which was originally founded as the Port of London Society in 1818, drew clear connections between piety, power, and profit on the high seas. The goal of the organization was to bring sailors "under the power and into the practice of real piety," explained its secretary, Edward Muscutt, in 1846. Religious observance, he continued, "makes men more courageous [and] attentive to ship duties," and thus "not only do the men themselves gain an immense benefit, but merchants and shipowners reap an advantage [too]." The problem was that sailors were proverbially bad at following God's laws, at least as defined by religious ministers such as Muscutt. "A ship is a dreadful nursery for immorality and ungodliness," complained another anonymous author in the *Sailors' Magazine*. "The tide of corruption, which flows on board a ship, sweeps all before it, and it requires a powerful force to stop it; but, alas! there are very few who exert themselves for the cause of truth and righteousness." In an 1847 article in the New York *Sailor's Magazine*, a periodical published by the evangelical American Seamen's Friend Society, Reverend C. M. Butler explained that the pious sailor was a ready-made missionary. "Let our merchant vessels be made floating bethels where God is owned and worshipped," Butler suggested, "and then wherever they sail, they shall set up the banner of the cross on heathen shores, like the first discoverers of the Western world."[4]

Religion was a keystone of social order on emigrant ships in particular. The patriarchal hierarchies that framed society in Ireland, Britain, and the United States were explicitly replicated on ships at sea, in part because their physical distance from "civilization" seemingly exposed them to working-class anarchy. Admiralty laws on both sides of the ocean empowered the captain and his officers to employ violence to maintain discipline. This could include flogging or even execution, but women could also be subjected to medicalized punishments such as induced vomiting, bandaging into bed, or head shaving. Whenever possible, however, the soft power of religious persuasion, embodied in respectable rituals, was preferred. In their 1845 printed guide for emigrants, John Wiley and George Putnam strongly encouraged their readers to participate in religious practices at sea. "By all means, fail not in attending divine service," they urged. "It is not only proper in itself, but it is a mark of respect, which is due to the preacher and the captain." Worship services reminded emigrants of their place in the ship's hierarchy.[5]

Even before ships departed, clergy often encouraged their flocks to be well-behaved on board. In the early 1850s, Reverend James Buck of the Liverpool Seamen's Friend Society and Bethel Union regularly performed religious services on the decks of vessels preparing to embark for Australia. "Would to God that every emigrant ship carried, not only able seamen, and an able commander, and an experienced surgeon," he rued in the *Liverpool Mercury*, "but also an able and experienced minister of the gospel." When several passengers thanked Buck for ministering to them on the eve of their departure in April 1853, he urged them to demonstrate their appreciation by maintaining "a spirit of perfect subordination to the rules of the ship, and a habit of respectful and accommodating courtesy among themselves throughout their long voyage." Some believed that those who ignored their religious duties at sea would face God's wrath. In 1850, the New York *Sailor's Magazine* told the story of a ship captain who had been harangued by passengers for refusing to set sail on the Sabbath, even though the weather was good. Weeks later, when it emerged that those ships that had left on the Sunday had been subsequently held back by bad weather, "the complainers were ashamed and expressed regret," the magazine explained, but the captain interpreted the experience as "new evidence of the wisdom, as well as the duty, of not violating the command of God." Of course, the command of the captain was also implicitly confirmed by the story.[6]

On board the *Rienze*, Samuel Harvey recognized the connection between religious duty and social discipline. As a Protestant minister occupying a second-class cabin in a "floating cradle," he was one of the men responsible for organizing and officiating over religious worship services designed in part to impose restraint on the passengers aboard. "Had social worship in Second Cabin at 11 am, three of us officiated," Harvey wrote on Sunday August 19. "About sixty or seventy male and female were present, mostly half-dressed. They were very orderly and attentive." His patriarchal self-image, as gallant protector of weak females, was never far from the surface. On August 26, Harvey and his fellow celebrants conducted social worship at midday. They "asked me to close but I declined keeping the female passengers any longer below on account of their weak state and the great heat of the place," Harvey later noted. When he did deliver a sermon that night, the congregation was deeply moved, and "many a tear stole down the cheeks of several who were present."[7]

Roman Catholic passengers, who composed over half of the emigrants on board the *Rienze*, did not attend Protestant worship services and celebrated their Sunday Mass only on those rare occasions when a priest was on board. Still, Harvey used Catholics' behavior during Protestant worship services as a metric for their character. On August 24, he wrote in his journal that there was a prayer service every evening. "There are a few Roman Catholics in second cabin," he noted, "and though they do not join us, they keep a respectful silence during the exercise." Two days later, however, the behavior of some Catholics sparked a different kind of discipline from one of the Protestant passengers. "After our [religious] exercises, I was scarcely able to prevent [a Protestant] young man, Magill, from taking summary vengeance on a couple of young men (Roman Catholics) who trampled and made much noise on deck above our heads during worship," Harvey reminisced. Religious rituals designed to enforce respectability and decorum could also, ironically, spark righteous, sectarian violence.[8]

Although Harvey generally kept the *Rienze*'s Roman Catholic passengers at arm's length, many evangelical Protestants saw clear connections between the lack of religious leadership and indiscipline on emigrant ships. As Catholic priests rarely sailed on emigrant vessels, their allegedly superstitious coreligionists were considered prone to collapsing into anarchy. In January 1847, the London *Sailors' Magazine* published a story written by Edward Muscutt related to him by an officer who had recently sailed on an emigrant ship from Ireland to

Figure 4.2. Poor emigrants in steerage. Authorities employed religious rituals to counter the perceived anarchy of working-class life. *Illustrated London News*, May 10, 1850. Courtesy of the British Newspaper Archive (www.britishnewspaperarchive.co.uk) and British Library Board. Image © Illustrated London News Group.

Quebec. The vessel's passengers were all, bar one family, Roman Catholics and, "for the most part, lamentably ignorant and deeply prejudiced against all religions but what they called *their own*." They refused to attend prayer meetings and often interrupted them on purpose. When the officer tried to talk to them about the Bible, they told him that their priests had said "it was all lies." One passenger, named Pat Battle, was "more shrewd and intelligent than the rest." Before leaving Ireland, a priest had given Battle "a kind of spiritual commission . . . to watch over his companions," and he "exercised his authority to the utmost of his power." Over the course of their voyage, the ship encountered many violent storms. "During these trying times," Muscutt recounted, "the poor Irish were in dreadful alarm and were seen on their knees counting their beads and using the fancied holy water." When Battle asked the officer why he was not scared in the face of such of danger, the man showed him his pocket Bible and replied, "I trust in the God of the Bible, and this gives me comfort at all times." When they finally landed in Quebec, the passengers crowded around the officer to thank him for his skill and bravery. "'Oh, don't thank me, give God thanks,'" he replied, "'Let's have a prayer-meeting and all of you come to it.' To this, all consented."[9]

The story of Pat Battle and his fellow passengers was one of many designed to demonstrate that the voyage experience was a golden opportunity to convert Catholics to Protestantism. A pious common sailor could serve as an instrument of God's message. At an anniversary meeting of the Baptist Bethel Society in Boston in 1848, one of its officers, Reverend William Hague, celebrated "the influence of sailors on the multitude with whom they associated, both at home and abroad." The Bethel Society did its best to convert sailors who, "like a revolving orb in their intercourse with the emigrants, both on the sea and on the land, [are] effectual missionaries." Through the work of pious sailors, Hague said, "we might hope to see the midnight gloom resting upon them dissipated and the chains of Romanism forever broken." Although many emigrants were Irish speakers unable to read English, the distribution of free religious tracts and pocket Bibles was seen as a key to converting them to Protestantism. Missionaries envisioned the simple ritual of quiet reading as opening the door to understanding God's love.[10]

In March 1855, John S. Pierson of the New York Bible Society reported that Irish emigrants responded well to kind patience. "Catholics (more generally Irish) frequently refuse to receive, and occasionally receive, only to destroy [the Bible]," Pierson claimed, "but, in a very large majority of cases, the Word of Life finds a glad reception, and what one refuses, another takes." One ship captain, for example, told Pierson of "a party of six decent young Irish women, who refused entirely to take the Bible at the beginning of the voyage but who were all duly furnished with copies at its close. They could often be seen reading, with the book half-hidden in their aprons." Another ship's officer reported that "even the rowdy ones among the Irish passengers, the real surly fellows that make us the trouble on shipboard, when they saw the rest take [a Bible], would side along and take also, and could be seen reading afterwards."[11]

In sum, pious Protestant emigrants like Samuel Harvey, and their coreligionists on land, often interpreted sea voyages in religious terms. They saw the unfamiliar, dangerous natural environment as a reflection of divine power, where God "performs a hymn to His praise on the strings of the storm." Yet the built environment of wood, hemp, and iron on which emigrants found themselves was equally unfamiliar.

Here, men employed religious rituals to maintain the social order that they feared would collapse so far from home. Ships' officers and sailors used religious rituals such as prayer meetings, worship services, and the distribution of religious tracts to buttress the faith of Protestant passengers while converting Roman Catholics. As we have seen, however, male passengers such as Samuel Harvey also took it upon themselves to maintain the social order by ensuring that religion was observed at sea. When death and dying impacted these shipboard communities, religious rituals became doubly important.

Rituals of Death and Dying

It was critical for sailors and emigrants to effectively manage mortality precisely because it constituted an existential threat to the social fabric on board sailing ships. In mid-nineteenth-century Ireland, most people saw strong correlations between the treatment of dead bodies and the health of a society as a whole. "It is as essential to bury the dead as to feed the living," editorialized the *Galway Vindicator* in 1851 after six years of excess mortality caused by the Great Famine had decimated the population. For his part, Samuel Harvey was troubled by the indifference with which some of his fellow passengers treated the death of an emigrant child. "Most of those present when [the corpse] was cast overboard seemed to think no more of it, than if it had been a dead cat," he wrote in his journal. "Beginning to feel time hang heavy on our hands." For a population accustomed to the idea of burying a loved one in a particular spot in the landscape, which they could revisit from time to time, the reality that those who died at sea disappeared into the ocean was deeply galling. When another Irish Protestant, James Duncan, emigrated to New York in 1847, he mourned the loss of one of his friends and shipmates, a Miss McKee, toward the end of the voyage. In the days before she died, consumed by a dread of being left in the ocean, Miss McKee begged Duncan to "join her brother in speaking to the captain" to have her body buried ashore. "We knew it was a hopeless task but I promised to do so," Duncan noted in his journal. McKee then "seemed much relieved and lay easier for a while." She died later that night. After they sewed her body into a canvas shroud the following day, some "weights were attached, and the corpse [was] quietly lowered over the side." That evening, the other McKee sisters "were all in gloom, sitting in the dark," so Duncan and their brother "got a light and prepared some hot drinks and then got to our berths."[12]

Protestant missionaries recognized that life at sea presented unique dangers to the bodies and souls of emigrants and sailors. They therefore emphasized that there were clear connections between the rigors of maritime life and the need for piety and prayer. Seafarers lived on the edge of death with nothing "but a board partition between them and eternity," explained one author. They must, therefore, always be ready, "with scarce a moment's preparation, [to] appear before the Eternal Judge!" Religious periodicals were dotted with graphic descriptions of shipwrecks to show that people at sea needed God more than ever. "It is a fearful thing, in a dismal and dreary night," proclaimed the New York *Sailor's Magazine* in February 1846, "when the gale is howling above and the breakers are roaring below, to be lashed helpless to some cleat, or mast, or shroud, while the wild waves beat over the sufferers." Two months later, the same periodical reflected on the social gap left by death at sea. "A burial at sea leaves no memorial," lamented an editorial. "There is no grave to which grief and affection may go. The deceased seems blotted out at once and forever from all the realities of earth." While many were unnerved by maritime burials, at least one writer saw human equality and God's love in the practice. "The noblest of cemeteries is the ocean," the author declared. "All other graveyards, in all lands, show some symbol of distinction between the great and the small, the rich and the poor. But in that ocean cemetery, the king and the clown, the prince and the peasant, are alike undistinguished." While graveyards on land featured various manmade monuments, crosses, and signs, maritime cemeteries have "ornaments of which no other can boast [for] in no other are so many inimitable traces of the power and glory of Jehovah." With thoughts of death and salvation woven so tightly into how people thought about life at sea, it is no surprise that they used religious rituals to make sense of the experience and thereby maintain social cohesion.[13]

Samuel Harvey clearly attached great importance to burial rituals at sea because he went into great detail describing them. In total, it seems as if five out of the estimated 200 emigrants on board the *Rienze* died, a death rate within the normal range of expected mortality rates

Figure 4.3. The *Edmond* is wrecked off the west coast of Ireland in 1850. Mortality shaped the social fabric of seaborne emigrant communities. *Illustrated London News*, December 7, 1850. Courtesy of the British Newspaper Archive (www.britishnewspaperarchive.co.uk) and British Library Board. Image © Illustrated London News Group.

of 1–2.5 percent at the time. When two women died of dysentery on September 8, Harvey described the funerary practices that followed. "Those who can afford it generally dress the corpse as is done on land," he explained. By this, Harvey meant that the body was washed by other women and dressed in the finest clothing available, probably the same outfit they would have worn to Sunday services. "The sailors then sew a piece of new canvas around them, over [their heads] and all," before tying a hundredweight of pig iron to the shroud's feet to ensure it sank immediately upon hitting the water. At one o'clock in the afternoon, the captain ordered that the ship "heave to," bringing its progress to a near standstill by rearranging the sails. "The two bodies were drawn up in sheets from their respective hatchways," Harvey recalled, "and deposited on two planks placed for their reception." A sheet was placed over each body, the planks were picked up by Harvey and three other pallbearing men, "each with our cap in hand," and the corpses were carried "towards the mid-ships, in slow and solemn procession, while a deathlike silence reigned on deck." Coming to a halt by the edge of the ship, the men "rested the feet end of the planks about a foot over the side, the other end resting on our shoulders." A funeral sermon from the Anglican Book of Common Prayer was usually read over bodies of dead Protestants, but in this case the husband of one of the dead asked that a different reading be used. As the last of the amens died away, Harvey noted, "we slowly raise the ends of the planks [. . .] while the eyes of the females are turned away from the melancholy spectacle." The shrouds splashed into the sea below and disappeared. By treating fellow emigrants' corpses with such solemnity, Harvey and the others reiterated their respect for their seaborne micro-community.[14]

The funerary practices employed on emigrant ships had been worked out by sailors over centuries, as changes in deep-sea sailing technologies allowed them to spend greater durations of time away from land and thus compelled them to bury their dead at sea. The strict discipline on military vessels, for example, was cemented by careful attention to proper burials rooted in respectability and religion. When a seaman named Spiller died on the US frigate *Congress* in 1845, the New York *Sailor's Magazine* described his journey from illness to death as a series of religious rituals designed to secure the victim's soul for God and to succor his shipmates. As Spiller lay dying in his hammock, he begged for Christ's forgiveness before falling into a "tranquil state." "It is not [. . .] death that I now fear, or being buried in the sea," Spiller whispered. "If my soul can be saved, it matters not what becomes of this poor body." He died that night. The following day, his fellow tars prepared his body, and in the evening all gathered to commit his corpse to the deep. Spiller's body, wrapped in his own hammock, "was borne by his messmates, preceded by the chaplain of the ship, from the gun-deck, up the forward hatch and round the capstan to the lee side," the eyewitness explained, as the band played the dead march and the marine guard presented arms. With the officers standing on one side of the shroud and the crew "in a silent, dense mass" on the other, the ends of the planks were raised, and Spiller's body fell into the sea with "a hoarse, hollow sound." The author reflected on the sadness of the scene, but another correspondent, writing of a burial he witnessed on a whaling ship, emphasized that death deepened sailors' respect for God. "I have witnessed funeral ceremonies on shore[,] but this is the first time it has ever fallen to my lot to be a spectator of a scene so solemn and imposing as this burial at sea," the anonymous author recounted. "The time, the place, and the occasion, all conspired to throw around us a feeling of loneliness and dependence, which I hope will prove profitable to us all."[15]

In light of the importance attached to decorous funerals, pious Protestants often struggled to make sense of the fact that burial practices were not always observed on emigrant ships. Sometimes, of course, the inability to follow these practices was simply attributable to the overwhelming conditions at sea. When the *Cataraqui*, carrying emigrants including many Irish, was wrecked on the coast of Australia in 1845, the "scene of confusion and misery that ensued" made it impossible to adequately take care of the corpses. Nevertheless, the surviving crew and passengers that scrambled ashore "employed themselves in burying the dead bodies they picked up" as best they could, "the mangled condition of many of which it is too painfully horrible to describe." At other times, however, alleged Catholic superstitions and ignorance were to blame for a lack of adequate funerary practices. While sailing on board the *Washington* to New York in 1850, to see for himself what conditions were like for emigrants, the Irish landlord and philanthropist Vere Foster was bothered by the fact that "no funeral service has yet been performed . . . over anyone who has died on board, the Catholics objecting . . . to the performance of any such service by a layman."[16]

Foster's demure reflection contrasts with a far more graphic description of Irish Catholic emigrants' superstitions, which appeared in the London *Sailors' Magazine* in January 1848. When typhus broke out aboard a ship bound for Canada in 1847, the "infatuated" Irish Catholics, "moved by some inconceivable and demonical spirit, would not separate themselves from the dead." Eventually, "the infection rose to such a pitch on board, that, frantic with despair," the captain and his Protestant passengers "succeeded in overcoming them, when, to their horror and dismay, they discovered above sixty dead bodies stowed away in chests or sewed up in beds!" Although this account was surely exaggerated and may have reflected a misunderstanding over Irish Catholic "wake" practices, its point was clear: it was up to Protestants to maintain discipline at sea by insisting on proper burial practices.[17]

Even Samuel Harvey had to admit that, while it was important to treat rituals relating to death and dying with great decorum, the challenges of life at sea sometimes rendered the task impossible. Approximately halfway through the *Rienze*'s voyage, one of Harvey's fellow cabin passengers fell ill and was soon close to death. "At the request of her husband," Harvey recalled, "a few of us from the second cabin read, sang, and prayed" with her. The physical environment of the ship itself made it hard to concentrate. "Oh, how distressing is such a place for a death-bed from the heat of the place, the noise of the passengers, and the pitching of the vessel!" Harvey complained. "Yet, she seems happy for God is with her. Thanks be to His name for such a religion whose holy influence can console the departing Spirit even under such untoward circumstances!"[18]

Harvey and his fellow passengers did their best to prosecute dignified funerals, but sometimes fear and danger required them to speed up the process. When a man died in steerage, allegedly of cholera, on the "dark and stormy" evening of September 15, his fellow passengers were afraid that leaving his body on the ship for too long would endanger themselves. "The funeral tonight was a very frightful and solemn scene," Harvey wrote in his journal. "After a hurried prayer was read over the body below, it was with some difficulty hauled up on deck, the ship at the time pitching very much. And as we committed it to the deep, the foam-crested billows boomed by, flashing like illumined winding sheets." In a gruesome afterthought, Harvey added "there is no doubt that the body was devoured by sharks, as immediately afterwards they appeared around us and continued to follow us all night." In Harvey's mind, however, even this hasty, dismal scene had a favorable effect on the religious inclinations of his fellow passengers. "More of the passengers resorting to prayer," he noted later that night, "and may these alarming lessons leave a salutary impression on our hearts!" Death and dying brought emigrants closer to God.[19]

* * *

As the *Rienze* finally approached New York City on September 20, 1849, after five long weeks at sea, a sailor, high above in the rigging, spied land. "I must leave the reader to his imagination for a description of the thoughts and feelings, which thronged in quick succession upon our hearts," Harvey scribbled in this journal, "as the glad announcement rung in our ears from the lips of the keen-sighted tar on his lofty perch." The passengers hurried to the sides of the ship for a glimpse of land, and as America slowly came into view, they responded with an almost religious awe. "And Lo! the world of many a bygone dream, and of all our future expectations, rises as if by magic from its azure bosom," Harvey wrote. "All again is silent, no one seems inclined to speak—every heart is engaged in its own thoughts—thoughts too deep or too sacred for utterance." The following morning, the passengers were up early, "getting breakfast cooked, dressing, and hauling up luggage on deck." Recognizing the solemnity and importance of the occasion, Harvey noted, all the passengers were "dressed in their best Sunday clothes."[20]

The experiences of Samuel Harvey and his fellow emigrants during their voyage across the Atlantic Ocean in 1849 offers a fresh perspective on the history of European immigration in the mid-nineteenth century. Many books and articles have been written on how and why people emigrated in search of farmland, jobs, or political and religious freedoms. Others have detailed the ways in which immigrants carved new lives for themselves in the teeming cities, forested mountains, and vast plains of North America. And yet we still know relatively little about the voyage itself, which served as the bridge between these two worlds. Harvey's journal is special because it sheds valuable light on the social dynamics of life aboard the floating city that was the sailing ship. In particular, it demonstrates that emigrants used religious rituals to handle the discomforts and dangers of life at sea. In some ways, rituals also helped to maintain order and discipline. In the patriarchal world of a deep-sea sailing vessel, Protestant men like Samuel Harvey replicated the social hierarchies established on land by ensuring that their fellow passengers followed prescribed rituals at sea. Sunday worship services were used as a weekly opportunity to reiterate the rules governing life below deck while simultaneously amplifying the sectarian differences between Catholics and Protestants.

At the same time, however, emigrants who might never have met one another had they not embarked on the same ship clearly used religious rituals to build a sense of community. By congregating to worship, passengers recommitted themselves to social norms, but they also fostered feelings of solidarity. Shipboard deaths threatened the seaborne social fabric, but funerals were highly ritualized in ways that respected the dead while offering comfort to, and unity with, the survivors. In these ways, although many old friendships were lost when emigrants took to sea, new ones could also spring to life.[21]

5

"Wild Girls" at Sea

The Assisted Emigration of Ireland's Workhouse Women

JILL C. BENDER

Australia! Australia! how proud may'st thou be
When the Ocean's encompass'd these wild girls with thee
Thy plains will rejoice and more beauties disclose
When these Shamrocks are join'd to the Thistle & Rose
—William B. Neville journal, 1848–1849[1]

Early in the morning of March 8, 1849, a riot broke out on board the *Digby*, an emigrant ship bound for New South Wales with 258 Irish orphans on board. Faced with an angry group of female orphans from County Cavan, and in a panic, the ship's schoolmaster called for assistance from the surgeon-superintendent and any married, male passengers on board. When the surgeon-superintendent, Dr. William Neville, reached the between decks, he found the disturbance suppressed, but he also found the schoolmaster "much cut and injured about the head," the young women having struck him numerous times with tin pots. While certainly the most dramatic event, this riot was only one of several disturbances to take place on board the *Digby* during its 110 days and four hours at sea. Shortly after arrival at Sydney, Neville submitted his private log along with the schoolmaster's diary and select comments from the ship's matron to Sydney's Immigration Board for review; these documents depict a voyage marked by significant chaos, violence, and abuse.[2]

Scholars have highlighted similar riots among the female inmates of Ireland's nineteenth-century workhouses and have noted how the oppressive nature of the Irish Poor Law shaped the behavior of these "wild workhouse girls." The workhouse was one of numerous institutions that advocated adherence to strict schedules, uniforms, segregation, and other disciplinary measures to instill order among the lower classes of Victorian society. Riots, violence, and vulgar language, in turn, provided a means for impoverished women to resist these practices and the social assumptions on which they rested. While many historians recognize the role that assisted emigration played in these larger social structures—providing women a potential means to escape poverty and offering workhouse custodians a means to control growing inmate populations—few have examined how these expected behaviors played out on board the emigrant ship.[3]

From the point of departure to the moment of arrival, emigration commissioners and shipboard authorities relied on rigid schedules, classification, oversight, and confinement to establish discipline and "protect" female emigrants from "ruin" during the voyage. As such, rituals permeated the entire migration experience, providing officials the structured and repeated practices necessary to construct and reinforce a particular social order. In this chapter, I focus on reports of violence, socializing, and punishment as they surfaced on two ships carrying Irish orphans: the *Earl Grey* and the *Digby*. While not written by the female orphans themselves, these reports of shipboard activities provide insight into the ways that impoverished Irish women navigated and sometimes challenged the prevailing social and gender expectations of the mid-nineteenth century. Furthermore, the ways colonial officials and shipboard authorities responded to allegations of misbehavior among the female emigrants reveal the difficulties of transferring Victorian rituals of social control from land to sea.[4]

Assisted Female Emigration

The *Earl Grey* and the *Digby* were part of a broader, government-sponsored migration scheme designed to transport impoverished individuals from Ireland's workhouses to the Australian colonies at the height of Ireland's Great Famine. Conceived by Colonial Secretary Earl Grey and members of the Colonial Land and Emigration Commission in London, the Earl Grey Orphan Migration scheme originally included both male and female emigrants. Noting the Australian colonists' wish to address the existing gender imbalance and their specific demand for female domestic servants, however, emigration commissioners quickly focused their attention on Irish girls between the ages of fourteen and eighteen who had lost either one or both parents. The resulting scheme was a highly organized endeavor, with multiple steps designed to ensure both the quality and safety of the young women selected to participate.[5]

First, as soon as the Colonial Land and Emigration Commission notified the Irish Poor Law unions of the developing migration plan, workhouse masters began to recruit local candidates and invite any eligible inmates to nominate themselves for consideration. Next, a committee of local Poor Law guardians screened the list of applicants and, following medical examinations, removed those deemed "troublesome or physically unfit" from the pool of potential emigrants. Additionally, the master and matron of the union workhouse, the young women's former employers, and local religious leaders all testified that each orphan was "a girl of unblemished moral character." Once satisfied with those selected, the Poor Law guardians submitted the names to the Irish Poor Law Commissioners, who had the opportunity to make further changes to the list. Inspectors from the Colonial Land and Emigration Commission then visited the workhouses to make the final selections. Before the emigrants' departure, the Poor Law guardians provided the young women with a change of clothes, boots, bedsheets, combs, and soap. Emigration commissioners arranged medical examinations for them, provided food and accommodation at sea, and ensured that the emigrant vessel was properly outfitted for a safe voyage. As a result of these efforts, more than 4,000 Irish female orphans participated in the Earl Grey scheme between 1848 and 1850, boarding twenty emigrant vessels bound for the ports of Sydney, Melbourne, and Adelaide.[6]

Once on board the ship, the women found themselves subjected to a highly regimented system, much like what they had experienced in the workhouse. As the product of the Irish Poor Law Act of 1838, "the workhouses were supposed to run on a system of Benthamite order, with schedules, bells, and silence." Inmates were separated according to classification: men kept apart from women, children from adults, the sick from the able-bodied. Emigration commissioners introduced similar measures of segregation, strict schedules, and detailed oversight on the

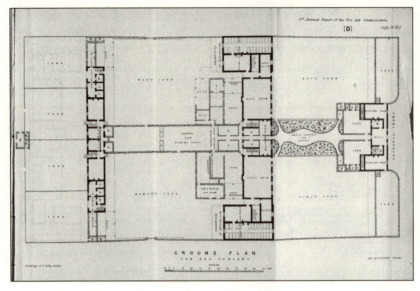

Figure 5.1. Ground Plan, *Fifth Annual Report of the Poor Law Commissioners*, 1839. Workhouse Drawings Collection, Irish Architectural Archive (85/138).

mid-nineteenth-century emigrant vessel to keep the emigrants in line. Indeed, legislators and authorities ensured that the orphan emigration vessels adhered to the patriarchal organizations and rigid hierarchies of Victorian society. In keeping with established military tradition, for example, the captain exercised "near autocratic power" as sole commander of the ship. Furthermore, all government-chartered emigrant ships bound for Australasia employed a surgeon-superintendent, who oversaw the health and behavior of the emigrants. In the eyes of officialdom, the predictable, ritualized nature of these practices both revealed and legitimized social hierarchies and power relations. Everyone had their appropriate place, and everyone performed their appropriate role.[7]

Additional regulations, of course, were needed for any vessels carrying large parties of single women, especially single Irish women. In the case of the Irish orphans, while emigration commissioners hoped that the women's young age and workhouse origins might "render them manageable during the voyage," they also acknowledged that their youth, sex, and class would necessitate close "moral and religious superintendence." With this in mind, the emigration commissioners insisted

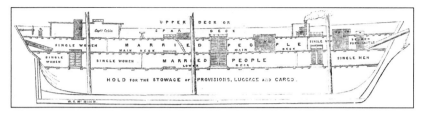

Figure 5.2. Cross-section of the emigrant ship *Bourneuf. Illustrated London News*, June 26, 1852. © Illustrated London News Ltd/Mary Evans.

that a "trustworthy Matron" and a religious teacher be appointed to all vessels carrying Irish female emigrants. While the matrons were expected to oversee the emigrants' daily activities on board ship, the teachers assumed responsibility for their religious instruction—and, together, both could supervise and protect the morality of their precious cargo. From the start, then, workhouse custodians and emigration commissioners sought to identify the most morally sound and healthy orphans from the workhouse population, with the hopes that the young women might become strong laborers, childbearing wives, and contributing members of Australia's colonial society. These hopes and expectations then shaped the methods of selection, protection, and control implemented across the emigrant experience.[8]

Despite, or perhaps because of, these regulations, chaos frequently plagued the Irish orphans' experience at sea. Reports of misconduct surfaced on board the very first orphan emigrant ship, the *Earl Grey*. Shortly after the ship docked at Sydney Harbor, the surgeon-superintendent, Dr. Henry Douglass, notified Australian officials that fifty-six of the Irish orphans from the Belfast Union had proven to be of particularly "bad character." Labeling this group the "Belfast girls," Douglass accused the orphans of violence, improper language, petty theft, and prostitution. Authorities in London and Sydney took the accounts of misconduct seriously, immediately launched twin investigations, and produced competing reports. Sydney officials sided with the surgeon-superintendent, agreeing that the Belfast girls were guilty of "indecent and disorderly" conduct and blaming workhouse officials for selecting unworthy emigrants. In response, the Home Office directed the Irish government to conduct its own inquiry into the matter.

Figure 5.3. Deck of an Australian Emigration Ship. *Illustrated London News*, January 20, 1849. © Illustrated London News Ltd/Mary Evans.

Over the course of June 1849, the Poor Law Commissioners interviewed those involved in the selection of the emigrants and came to a different conclusion, determining that "great care" had been exercised in the selection of the orphans and that any immoral behavior had clearly been learned at sea.[9]

Although the Poor Law Commissioners ultimately dismissed many of Douglass's allegations as "disproved" and "inaccurate," the damage had been done, and rumors of impropriety shaped subsequent Australian reports and colonial expectations of the orphan immigration scheme. In fact, of the eleven orphan ships that sailed to Sydney between 1848 and 1850, at least seven were accompanied, and sometimes preceded, by reports of misbehavior on board. The *Digby*, for example, was the fifth ship in the migration scheme to arrive in Sydney, and the surgeon-superintendent immediately filed a report highlighting the misconduct of young women from the Cavan workhouse. Like their Belfast counterparts on the *Earl Grey*, the Cavan orphans from the

Figure 5.4. Pencil drawing on pale blue paper of shipboard life on the *Thomas Arbuthnot*, 1849. National Museum of Australia.

Digby were accused of violent conduct, vulgar language, and theft. By the fifth ship, in other words, the Irish orphans had been typecast—all expectations of disorderly conduct were laid out before a ship disembarked and then came to fruition over the four-month voyage. Furthermore, these reports of indecent behavior continued to haunt the Irish orphan emigrants after their arrival in New South Wales.[10]

(Mis)behavior at Sea

The orphans' behavior, or misbehavior, at sea adhered to the gendered and class expectations of the mid-Victorian period. Owing to different socioeconomic realities, working-class communities frequently adopted notions of femininity and respectability that diverged dramatically from those espoused by their middle-class employers. Middle-class girls were supposed to be submissive, dependent, chaste, virtuous, and pious. Workhouse girls, by contrast, were supposedly independent, forceful, and more aggressive, as many sought to fend for themselves from the age of thirteen. As the matron of the *Digby* concluded when complaining of the orphans' "rebellious" attitudes and "thoughtless" behavior, it was "only natural to expect" a degree of unruliness among "such a class of persons."[11]

These class and gender expectations similarly shaped the attitudes of emigration commissioners and shipboard agents, many of whom anticipated aggressive and indecent behavior on board the vessel and planned accordingly. Authorities were particularly concerned that inappropriate socializing might compromise the orphans' virtue. Potential female immorality was a significant source of concern in Victorian society, and such worries only escalated on board emigrant ships where vulnerable young women came into daily contact with male crewmembers for months on end. The matron of the *Earl Grey* recalled concerns of inappropriate interactions being at the forefront of her mind, noting that from the start she had "wished to stop all intercourse between the immigrants and crew, and to prohibit the girls speaking to them." The potentially more experienced surgeon-superintendent, however, thought any complete prevention "impossible" and instead kept close watch over the Irish orphans and enforced strict regulations on their movements.[12]

Assuming no one could be trusted to behave appropriately in an unregulated environment, authorities organized orphan emigrant vessels to discourage any impropriety. The *Earl Grey* orphans, for example, were not permitted into the sailors' quarters; nor were the sailors permitted between decks where the young women slept. While the crewmembers and female emigrants could speak to each other (and even sit together) on deck, they were to do so only under the watchful eye of the matron or surgeon-superintendent and only during the day. Additionally, the matron would walk the deck every evening until eight o'clock, when the last orphan girl had made her way below, at which point all the young women were locked up until morning. When the occasional romance did blossom on board the *Earl Grey*, the surgeon-superintendent was quick to intervene. Following reports of a relationship between the ship's chief officer and a Belfast orphan, for example, Douglass "talked to them very nicely day after day about their conduct" until, eventually, "the Chief Officer promised to break off the intercourse." Overall, both the matron and the captain applauded Douglass's oversight of the orphans' contact with the sailors and insisted that nothing "criminal" or "improper" had passed among the young women and the crewmembers of the *Earl Grey*.[13]

Not so on board the *Digby*. On arrival at Sydney in April 1849, the surgeon-superintendent immediately filed charges accusing the ship's captain of allowing "the Sailors to be too familiar with the female Emigrants." Although the Board of Immigration hesitated to place sole blame on the captain, no one could ignore the numerous indecencies recorded in the surgeon's log and the schoolmaster's diary. The surgeon, Dr. William Neville, and the schoolmaster, George Binsted, frequently complained of the *Digby* orphans "lounging" in the men's laps and reported crewmembers being "between decks at improper hours." The ship's carpenter was of especially dubious character, surfacing multiple times in Neville's journal as a repeat offender yet rarely punished for his misdeeds. In early February, for example, the carpenter developed an inappropriate relationship with a submatron and later "boasted of taking unmentionable liberties" with her. In fact, he claimed that it was this indecent conduct that had kept him from making an honest woman of the submatron and admitted that, had they not conducted themselves in this manner, he likely would have "married her."[14]

Neville investigated the reports of the illicit liaison by questioning the other matrons, one of whom admitted to having heard similar accounts from the orphans. Those under her charge, she claimed, were "highly scandalized" by the submatron's behavior. In response, the surgeon-superintendent punished not the carpenter but the submatron. He removed her from her position and, in her place, reinstated a former matron who had resigned earlier because of illness but had since recovered. Just six weeks later, additional complaints regarding the carpenter surfaced. This time, two orphans reported that he had pulled the clothes of another orphan "completely over her head to the exposure of her person." Again, Neville complained that he was powerless to "punish or reprimand the man." The carpenter, he explained, was a favorite of the captain and disciplining him would simply "create another serious disturbance without attaining satisfactory results." The patriarchal structures of the mid-Victorian era were as evident on the emigrant vessel as they were on land, and they shaped shipboard efforts to protect and reform notions of female respectability. Furthermore, many recognized these rituals of control as legitimate methods to instill order. When exercised from the top down in an established social hierarchy, these disciplinary measures provided a means to enforce or maintain accepted boundaries, and any resistance to these efforts was deemed disorderly and disruptive.[15]

In reality, the orphans rarely relied on the assistance of the surgeon, or any shipboard authority, and instead chose to take matters into their own hands and resolve disputes in their own manner. Indeed, scholars have identified "a distinctly female pattern" of conflict in late Victorian working-class communities. Conflicts between women, they note, were often triggered by concerns surrounding property, male partners, children, and space. Furthermore, grievances tended to be aired publicly, "before an audience of other women." A remarkably similar pattern of conflict surfaced on board the orphan emigrant vessels. This was particularly true in the early weeks of the voyage, when the young women were staking out their personal territory and sought to solve any disputes among themselves. According to Douglass, for example, the *Earl Grey* orphans' behavior was the most "extreme" during the first month—"they used the most abominable language," he complained, "and actually fought with each other." The early weeks of the *Digby*'s voyage appeared similarly chaotic. Within days of departing Plymouth, for example, Ann Kekney of Athlone Union was "placed in confinement for violent conduct and bad language," and Mary Caserly of Longford Union was severely reprimanded for cutting another orphan on the head "with a Tin Mug."[16]

These individual disputes appear to have calmed down with the monotony of weeks spent at sea, or at least the reports became less frequent. Group dissent continued, however, and sometimes gained intensity as the women banded together to protest the perceived unfairness of their situation. On June 16, 1848, for example, Douglass reported being called to the between decks of the *Earl Grey* to quell a disturbance. When he reached the lower deck, he found two young women fighting, "one armed with a fork, with which she threatened to take the life of the other." Douglass ordered the perpetrator to be sequestered to the poop deck; his mode of punishment, however, resulted in an immediate backlash and "led to an absolute revolt among the Belfast Girls." It is unclear whether the women were frustrated with the surgeon-superintendent for prematurely ending what was likely a spectacle of entertainment or for intervening in what they considered to be a local, or private, conflict. Either way, the orphans rallied to support their compatriot and, in doing so, demonstrated their ability to challenge and potentially alter the existing power dynamics on board.[17]

Even if a surgeon-superintendent managed to rein in the most egregious acts of violence and establish a system of control, petty acts of theft continued throughout the duration of the voyage. At times, the young women stole food supplies from the ship's store, often flour or sugar. In fact, at one point, the captain of the *Earl Grey* complained that a young woman had taken a considerable amount of moldy bread that had been left out for the pigs. After looking into the matter, Douglass confirmed the charges, and the act of theft raised questions and confusion among government authorities as well as those on board the ship. Members of the Orphan Immigration Committee worried that the theft of moldy bread indicated the women were not being provided adequate provisions—a concern that both the surgeon and matron were quick to dismiss, lest they be held responsible for failing to see the ship appropriately stocked. As the matron explained: "The girls would eat all one meal sometimes and other times would leave it." She thought it more likely that the woman had taken the bread by mistake, because the man who usually fed the pigs would often give the orphans some biscuits at the same time. Douglass, for his part, dismissed the theft as the result of cultural upbringing: "Strange beings; they have complained of their bread being mouldy and yet so strong is there propensity for, or so little do they think of, about stealing, that on the first opportunity they steal the very quality of bread they complain of." Indeed, both the surgeon and matron insisted that the young woman took the bread out of habit rather than hunger.[18]

More often, the young women stole articles of clothing from each other, such as handkerchiefs, stockings, shoes, and petticoats. Douglass, for example, later recalled an occasion in which his attention was directed to a young woman who appeared pregnant. When he confronted her, however, she admitted that "she had four petticoats on, that being the only means she had of securing them." Just as they had dismissed the theft of food as common practice, the shipboard officials explained the theft of clothing as cultural and class-based. According to the captain of the *Earl Grey*: "They had curious ideas upon the subject of stealing, when they were brought up for it, they would say that somebody had stolen their clothes, and therefore they had the right to take the clothes of others." Similarly, both the matron and the surgeon dismissed any stealing as a "confirmed habit" of the orphans and "part of their nature." In committing repeated acts of petty theft, the young women were simply performing the mundane rituals expected of their class; indeed, in doing so they confirmed their place in a broader social order or cultural hierarchy.[19]

Discipline at Sea

The alleged crimes of the young women did not go unnoticed, and emigration agents and shipboard authorities debated the correct response to any misbehavior. Although flogging was still permitted, corporal punishment was generally not thought an appropriate means to instill order among refractory women. Instead, surgeon-superintendents adopted gendered rituals of punishment widely sanctioned across other Victorian institutions. Punishments such as the regular removal of an emigrants' privileges, isolation, or a restricted diet, for example, allowed surgeon-superintendents to promote good behavior, cleanliness, order, and discipline on board emigrant ships. Furthermore, the consistent use of such regulations likely lent the surgeon an air of legitimacy and reinforced the existing social hierarchy by suggesting a rational, reformative response to irrational, disruptive behavior.[20]

Certainly, the shipboard logs kept by Douglass and Neville reveal that both surgeons turned to similar social practices to reestablish or maintain control while at sea. Shipboard agents relied particularly heavily on the orphans themselves to regulate each other's behavior. The young women bonded quickly, forming kinship groups based on place of origin or religious affiliation, and they did not hesitate to report anyone who stepped outside of accepted social norms. As the matron of the *Earl Grey* explained: "The girls from various parts have invariably kept together. For instance, the Banbridge girls would not think of associating with the Belfast girls, . . . and if one of them did become acquainted with the Belfast girls the others would say 'you are no longer a Banbridge girl.'" One evening in February 1849, the impact of this potential social alienation became heartbreakingly apparent when Rose Riley, "of the 'Cavan Union,'" attempted to throw herself overboard the *Digby*. According to the ship's schoolmaster, Riley had suffered a severe scolding from the other girls of the Cavan Union for carrying on "an improper intimacy" with a member of the ship's crew, and this upbraiding from her peers had led to her "rash" attempt at "self destruction." Fortunately, Riley's foot caught in the main brace, saving her from death, but not perhaps from further ostracism. As the historian Cian McMahon notes: "Shame and fear were particularly powerful at sea, especially for those whose social identity was strongly rooted in the group they were traveling with."[21]

The mid-nineteenth-century emigrant ship was designed to facilitate various levels of oversight, and frequently surgeon-superintendents turned to social organization and spatial design to enforce existing hierarchies and establish (or reestablish) order. Traditionally, prior to embarkation, all steerage passengers, including single women, were organized into groups of eight to ten people called "messes." On board a female emigrant ship, the young women would sleep, dine, and complete their chores with other members of their mess, under the supervision of the matron. Douglass, however, turned to the mess not only to organize the orphans but also as a punitive measure. As the ship's captain later explained, the surgeon-superintendent put "the bad ones all in one mess." In fact, he put all the "very bad" orphans—or those deemed "past redemption"—in the No. 1 mess. He then positioned the No. 1 mess near the matron's quarters, so that she could keep a particularly close eye on the most disruptive orphans and ensure that they did not corrupt the others.[22]

When that did not work, as it frequently did not, the surgeon removed the alleged troublemaker from her cohort, sequestering her to the poop deck or placing her in confinement. During the first two weeks the *Digby* was at sea, at least four orphans were held in confinement for various lengths of time as punishment for anything from "violent conduct" to "filthy habits." In late December 1848, for example, the schoolmaster recorded that Jane Armstrong, from the Cavan Union, had been placed "in confinement for 8 Hours for refusing to produce her Bonnet" when asked; she was eventually "liberated on her promise of future obedience." Physically removing a resistant individual could prove challenging, of course, and sometimes resulted in additional conflict. The captain of the *Earl Grey* later recalled the crew's difficulties isolating a woman to the poop deck, as she struck them when they tried to get her up the ladder; the officers, he noted, nicknamed the orphan in question "thumb screw" after she injured the second mate in the process.[23]

Often, a surgeon-superintendent opted to increase the severity of a punishment to provide an example to others and dissuade future acts of misconduct. In the early weeks of the *Digby*'s voyage, for example, Neville ordered one Catharine Mourne to be confined for four days and restricted to a diet of bread and water. Mourne had been singled out for her "filthy habits and general bad conduct," but the punishment clearly did not have the desired impact, as the following week she was found guilty of stealing from the government stores. Although Mourne was assisted by three other orphans, the ship's officers immediately identified her as the ringleader and "a very badly disposed person." Such continued misbehavior, the officers argued, necessitated a punishment of "unusual severity for the sake of example," and they condemned her to a full week of confinement, with a diet of bread and water on alternate days. Even after Mourne was freed, they insisted that she remain separated from the other orphans until she showed "signs of reformation." Similarly, when the Cavan Union orphans rioted and attacked the *Digby*'s schoolmaster with tin pots, Neville immediately determined "it necessary to inflict on the most outrageous girl such a degree of mild punish[men]t as would act on the fears of her cooperators." In response, he ordered that the alleged leader, sixteen-year-old Rose Maguire, have her hair cropped as both a punishment and a warning to the other young women. Public humiliation, it seems, spoke volumes at sea.[24]

The numerous negative reports about the Earl Grey Orphan Migration scheme posed particular problems for the government-appointed surgeon-superintendents, many of whom found themselves attempting damage control on arrival. Once a ship docked at Sydney Harbor, members of the Board of Immigration immediately boarded the vessel to inspect its cleanliness, examine the immigrants, and record any complaints. If the board was not convinced that the surgeon-superintendent had performed his duties satisfactorily, it launched an investigation and reserved the right to withhold remuneration or dismiss the surgeon-superintendent from service. Surgeons arriving amid a flurry of negative reports immediately began to deflect blame away

Figure 5.5. Item 05: Sydney Cove, N.S.W. Emigrants Leaving the Ship, by O. W. Brierly, 1853. Mitchell Library, State Library of New South Wales.

from themselves and often cast their explanations according to existing gender and class norms.

Most frequently, of course, the orphans were held responsible for their own behavior. This, too, required a delicate balancing act. After all, surgeon-superintendents could not blame the young women to such a degree that the entire scheme might come to an end—and with it the surgeon-superintendent's employment. As a result, while the young women certainly suffered criticism and blame, most surgeon-superintendents sought to uncover the orphans' motivations and point to external explanations for their violent behavior. Douglass, for example, complained that the Irish emigrants of the *Earl Grey* were single women of abandoned character and no education, but he was also quick to argue that they deserved "pity" rather than "condemnation." The true fault, he argued, lay with Ireland's Poor Law guardians, who had failed to select respectable women for the voyage.[25]

The *Digby*'s Neville hesitated to show the Irish orphans any pity and instead described their behavior as intentional displays of resistance to

British authority. Early in the voyage, the surgeon-superintendent admitted that he found "them to be a very desperate set of vicious and perverse Girls holding everything in the shape of Governm[en]t at defiance." Regardless, he still cast the true blame elsewhere, accusing the *Digby*'s captain and his wife of exacerbating an already tense situation. According to the surgeon, Captain Tabor and his wife had withheld rations from the emigrants, encouraged inappropriate intimacies between the crew and the single women, and instigated much of the misconduct on the part of the orphans. The ship's matron agreed with Neville, observing that the captain and his wife "help'd to incite disobedience" and routinely worked "in opposition to the Surgeon's wishes." In fact, she worried that the resulting chaos would place both the surgeon and schoolmaster "in great danger" as the lone government representatives on board the vessel.[26]

Of course, it was easier to blame the captain and his wife than anyone tied directly to the migration scheme, such as the government-appointed surgeon-superintendent or the orphans. In fact, it was even easier to blame just one person, especially if punishing or removing that individual did not necessitate any modifications to the broader system. As a result, as blame trickled down the *Digby*'s hierarchy, it settled on the captain's wife, who suffered the harshest criticisms, embedded within existing gender and social expectations. According to the matron, the captain's wife was a "Ball headed Horse of a woman," illiterate and "uneducated," and "very much addicted to Brandy and profane oaths." She was no better, in other words, than many of the Irish orphans. Furthermore, her behavior at sea appeared intentionally manipulative. At one moment, she was a "crafty She-devil," subjecting the orphans to verbal abuse. The next moment, she sympathized with the Irish emigrants and encouraged them to "create disturbances." Her very presence was disruptive. She frequently distracted the captain with "her fears, whims & caprices." And while claiming a nervous disposition and tendency to illness, she denied the orphans regular access to the poop deck and prohibited the "trifling amusements"—such as singing and dancing—so crucial to high spirits and good health during a "very monotonous" sea voyage. In the end, the matron concluded, it was this marginalized woman—connected to the voyage only through the captain—who was the "acting cause of discontent." No other motive could be found to explain the Irish orphans' conduct at sea.[27]

* * *

When the *Earl Grey* and *Digby* docked at Sydney Harbor in October 1848 and April 1849, respectively, the orphans were immediately relocated to the immigration depot at Hyde Park Barracks. The recently renovated building provided the young women a place to wash, rest, and receive religious guidance as they waited to secure employment. Their time at the immigration depot followed a structure similar to what they had experienced first at the workhouse and then on board the emigrant vessel: at Hyde Park Barracks, they were placed under the watchful care of a matron and subject to a daily schedule, designed to enforce respectful habits of industry and cleanliness. On arrival at New South Wales, the Irish orphans likely found themselves in somewhat familiar territory, even in this strange new land.

Figure 5.6. Hyde Park Barracks, Drawings in Sydney, circa 1840–1850, Mitchell Library, PX*D 123, 5b, State Library of New South Wales.

As young, impoverished, single women, the Irish orphans were consistently subjected to the reformative impulses and gendered expectations embraced by middle-class society and upheld by mid-Victorian rituals of social control. From start to finish, colonial officials, shipboard authorities, and immigration agents turned to repeated practices and proceduralism to orchestrate the young women's status within accepted hierarchies. As the Irish orphans moved from workhouse to emigrant vessel to immigration depot, however, they were not passive participants in Britain's assisted emigration schemes. Instead, as this chapter has demonstrated, emigration officials and shipboard agents consistently struggled to explain and respond to the female emigrants' conduct. Ireland's "wild girls," in other words, established their own modes of accepted behavior and conflict resolution on board the emigrant ship. As they did so, they disrupted the rituals of social control central to Victorian power dynamics.

6

On the Border in New Orleans

LAUREN BRAUN-STRUMFELS AND CLARA ZACCAGNINI

In July 1901, Luigi Dell'Orto wrote to Antonio Polidori in the town of Senigallia, near Ancona in east-central Italy. He enclosed his "personal ticket No. 880," good for the journey from Palermo to New Orleans aboard the state shipper Navigazione Generale Italiana (NGI), for which his brother Arturo Dell'Orto was the sole agent in the American city. The ticket was financed by Sunnyside Plantation, a large employer of Italian cotton growers 300 miles north of the city in the Arkansas Delta. Following a standard format, Dell'Orto's letter informed Polidori of a series of steps he had to take to secure departure paperwork in Palermo, Sicily, including determining who to communicate with, what to say, and how much money to carry with him to pass inspection. The letter also included a list: "Questions to which the emigrant departing from Italy and arriving in the United States must answer." At no point should the emigrant say that anyone but he or his "relatives" had paid his fare. He should testify "so far as work is concerned you are not engaged or bound to anybody." All of this was false, as agents like the Dell'Orto brothers and subagents in their employ provided what they called "prepaid" passage only in exchange for signed labor contracts, which were illegal under US immigration law. Migrants who financed their journey in this way were then left to pay off the cost and interest at inflated prices, which generated a kickback for the agent of as much as $25 per family recruited.[1]

A 1907 Department of Justice investigation detailed how labor agents conspired to fabricate "calling affidavits," documents required for legal emigration supposedly issued by relatives already in the United States. Mary Grace Quackenbos, a special prosecutor appointed by the United States Attorney General at the urging of Italy's ambassador to the United States, Edmondo Mayor Des Planches, uncovered how Arturo Dell'Orto worked with his brother Luigi to operate their Agenzia Italiana on Decatur Street in New Orleans. Adjusting to the new rituals of inspection that the federal Bureau of Immigration and Congress had devised, Arturo Dell'Orto told migrants how to secure the required consular stamp. He coached them through border agents' questions with preprinted directions that, he warned, must be destroyed to prevent immediate rejection at the border. Because labor brokers like Arturo Dell'Orto also acted as steamship agents selling tickets for travel, they earned "double commissions" by recruiting migrants. They had a strong incentive, Quackenbos concluded, "to satisfy their greed [and] resort to methods which deserve contempt." Forged calling affidavits from supposed relatives were just the first step in a facilitated migration process laced with hope yet marked by fraud and deceit.[2]

Arturo Dell'Orto operated during a period of transition in the administration of border controls in the United States and Italy. The expansion of border controls at the turn of the twentieth century involved rituals of passage, inspection, confinement, and exclusion that "gave meaning and power to the enforcement of exclusion" while simultaneously generating fraudulent border-crossing strategies that US and Italian government officials sought to combat. In the case of Chinese immigrants, the historian Adam McKeown has explained how efforts to enforce exclusion laws led migrants and brokers to create devices for subverting the law, including the preparation of false documents and extensive coaching to pass the lengthy investigation and interview requirements of Chinese applicants claiming exemption. Although Italian immigrants did not face wholesale exclusion, their rituals of entry and exclusion featured similar practices of control and evasion.[3]

Brokers and Agents

Emigration from Italy grew exponentially during the first decade of the twentieth century, with more than 2.3 million people leaving. Most of the US-bound traffic from Italy, as from other European countries, led to New York. In 1903, when 74 percent of all shipbound arrivals to the United States entered through Ellis Island, only 0.5 percent landed in New Orleans. The disproportionate percentage of arrivals to New York has led historians to neglect European landings at other US ports, yet

Figure 6.1. Advertisement for *Navigazione Generale Italiana*. Palermo is depicted in the inset on the right with an image of the old port. Courtesy of Lauren Braun-Strumfels.

by the 1890s the passenger traffic connecting Palermo to New Orleans was robust, with the Navigazione Generale Italiana offering four departures a year. Although New Orleans was the busiest port of entry in the Deep South and the ninth-busiest immigration port in the United States, it lacked an adequate landing facility until 1907.[4]

The city of New Orleans, where the complicated dynamics of immigration control empowered both public and private actors in ways that blurred the lines of authority, offers a distinctive view into a critical era of migration between the Italy and the United States. In the late nineteenth and early twentieth centuries, tens of thousands of semi-illiterate peasants migrated from the rural countryside of western Sicily to the American South, most passing through the port of New Orleans. By 1900, Italians made up one-third of Louisiana's foreign-born white population. The same year, 90 percent of Italian immigrants in New Orleans were Sicilian. Italians spread from the city into the Deep South. By 1910, they made up 10 percent of the foreign-born population in the neighboring state of Arkansas and formed the largest foreign-born population group in both Louisiana (nearly 40 percent) and Mississippi (nearly 23 percent). Labor brokers working for employers based in the South, along with agents of shipping companies, were part of a vast recruiting process that delivered a flow of cheap labor between Palermo and New Orleans despite an 1885 US immigration law prohibiting the importation of contract workers.[5]

Focusing on Italian migration through the port of New Orleans offers an important perspective on how migrants responded to the rituals of inspection the US government was creating at this time. Arturo Dell'Orto amassed significant power through the cutthroat world of labor recruiting and ticket selling by combining the roles of shipping agent and labor broker. In his dual capacity, Dell'Orto belonged to a particular type of immigrant that historians have studied in other contexts. Joseph Tape, for example, a Chinese immigrant businessman in the historian Mae Ngai's *The Lucky Ones*, negotiated a position of wealth and influence that straddled Anglo-Chinese lines in Gilded Age San Francisco. Tape "gained prestige among whites," Ngai writes, "for his knowledge of both Chinese and English enabled him to communicate with a range of parties—the steamship company, customs officers, immigrants, district associations, merchants." The Chinese consul in San Francisco sometimes called on Tape to serve as an interpreter, augmenting his status in the city. For Tape, Ngai explains, "being a broker meant that he knew important white people in the transportation industry and the immigration bureau. Among the Chinese, his position was highly prestigious." This prestige came in part from his monopoly over Southern Pacific Railroad and steamship ticket sales as the railway's commission-earning "Chinese passenger agent." In the distinctive setting of New Orleans, Dell'Orto developed many of the same powerful connections as Tape did in San Francisco, but his relationship with the Italian government was more contentious.[6]

Dell'Orto's main goal was to advance his own business interests. After arriving in New Orleans in 1892 from Turin at age twenty-three with his older brother and sister, he worked his way into the city's business class, gaining direct access to government leaders on both sides of the Atlantic. He even boasted in one of New Orleans's leading newspapers of taking NGI's concerns directly to the Commissariat of Emigration in Rome, his way of telling English-speaking readers how influential he

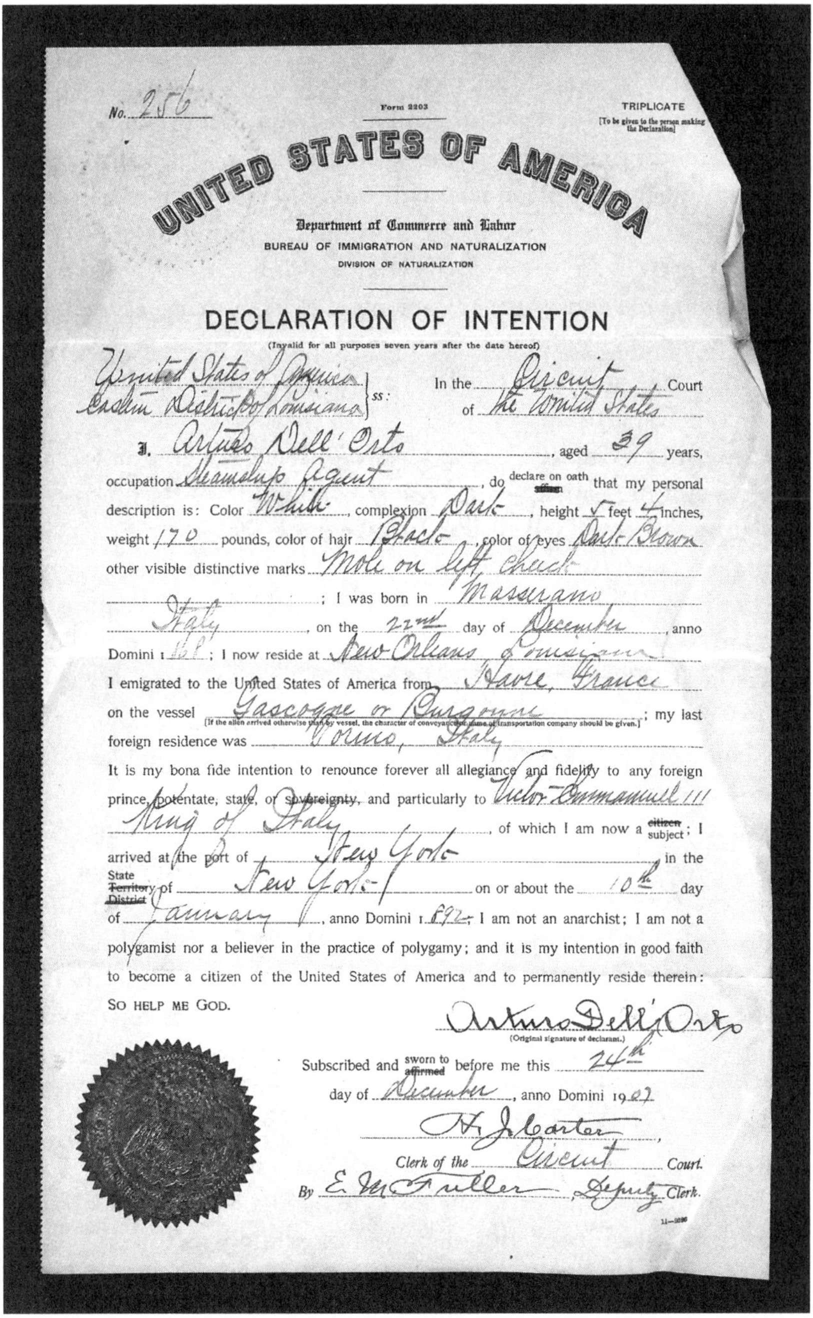

No. 256

Form 2203

TRIPLICATE
[To be given to the person making the Declaration]

UNITED STATES OF AMERICA

Department of Commerce and Labor
BUREAU OF IMMIGRATION AND NATURALIZATION
DIVISION OF NATURALIZATION

DECLARATION OF INTENTION

(Invalid for all purposes seven years after the date hereof)

United States of America, Eastern District of Louisiana } ss: In the Circuit Court of the United States

I, Arturo Dell'Orto, aged 39 years, occupation Steamship Agent, do declare on oath ~~affirm~~ that my personal description is: Color White, complexion Dark, height 5 feet 4 inches, weight 170 pounds, color of hair Black, color of eyes Dark Brown other visible distinctive marks Mole on left cheek ; I was born in Masserano Italy, on the 22nd day of December, anno Domini 1868; I now reside at New Orleans Louisiana I emigrated to the United States of America from Havre, France on the vessel Gascogne or Burgonne [If the alien arrived otherwise than by vessel, the character of conveyance or name of transportation company should be given.]; my last foreign residence was Torino, Italy

It is my bona fide intention to renounce forever all allegiance and fidelity to any foreign prince, potentate, state, or sovereignty, and particularly to Victor Emmanuel III King of Italy, of which I am now a ~~citizen~~ subject; I arrived at the port of New York in the State ~~Territory~~ ~~District~~ of New York on or about the 10th day of January, anno Domini 1892; I am not an anarchist; I am not a polygamist nor a believer in the practice of polygamy; and it is my intention in good faith to become a citizen of the United States of America and to permanently reside therein: So help me God.

Arturo Dell'Orto
(Original signature of declarant.)

Subscribed and sworn to ~~affirmed~~ before me this 24th day of December, anno Domini 1907.

H. J. Carter,
Clerk of the Circuit Court.
By E. McFuller, Deputy Clerk.

Figure 6.2. Arturo Dell'Orto's Declaration of Intent to Naturalize, 1907. In conformity with US immigration law, Dell'Orto testified that he was neither an anarchist nor a polygamist and that he intended to reside permanently in the United States. *Declarations of Intention, Compiled 03/1892–05/1903, Records of the District Courts of the United States*, Record Group 21, National Archives and Records Administration—Southeast Region, Atlanta, GA.

was in the Italian capital. Dell'Orto was signaling his intimate familiarity with the rituals of departure and arrival at a time when both Italy and the United States were trying to control Italians' mobility. As the volume of Italian migration increased and NGI consolidated its market power, Dell'Orto was the only agent working consistently in New Orleans. He exerted an extraordinary degree of influence—sometimes to the benefit of the consulate and sometimes to its dismay—as the Italian government struggled to manage mass emigration through regulations enacted in 1888 and 1901 to protect and control migrants during their journey and on arrival.[7]

Passed after a decade of rapid growth of Italian migration to South America and the United States, the emigration law of 1901 focused its regulatory power on independent emigrant agents. For the first time, the Italian government intervened in setting ticket prices, regulated conditions on board ships, standardized the documents required for exit, and created an oversight commission. Emigration agents, allowed under the 1888 law to operate independently, were limited by the 1901 law to a government licensing system that required working for a shipping company. Yet this crackdown did not achieve the desired impact of lessening corruption and abuses. Following a tour observing Italian communities and labor conditions in the American South in the spring of 1905, Ambassador Des Planches concluded that "immigration agents can be very good or very bad for our emigrants. It is a profession that should be subjected to strict standards and surveillance. The agent tries to profit both at the expense of the owner who asks for labor and at the expense of the foreign workers he procures for him." As border regulations on both sides of the Atlantic increased the demand for paperwork—permits, inspections, and, later, passports required for transit—the insider knowledge of a broker/agent like Dell'Orto became only more valuable.[8]

Historians have neglected the powerful actors in the transportation network that facilitated the migration of millions of Italians, especially shipping agents. By the 1850s, the major transatlantic shipping companies (then headquartered in Great Britain and Germany) had established bureaus in Italy and assembled a strong network of emigration agents, who wove wide-ranging brokerage and client relationships into the process of migration. With the creation of the NGI through mergers in 1881, the power of these intermediaries intensified, as they procured emigrant labor on behalf of employers and managed prepaid tickets for the transatlantic route. On the other side of the ocean, plantation owners and other employers in the American South used brokers to attract cheap labor. At the turn of the twentieth century, the Italian government set out to manage these agents and brokers, who were simultaneously necessary for, and detrimental to, the movement of its citizens. Limited administrative capacity, however, allowed men like Dell'Orto to take advantage of the experimental nature of the emerging rituals of control.[9]

Accused by their critics of enticing and then trapping migrant laborers, agents and brokers also fulfilled a critical role facilitating complex journeys with multiple checkpoints. "All manner of middlemen and brokers traded in the movement of strangers," Ngai notes, and migrants depended on them to deliver them to, and provide access to, distant labor markets. Their practices, like the calling affidavits from supposed relatives, raised concerns among American and Italian officials, though much of the criticism of labor brokers also reflected class and religious stereotypes about the immigrants themselves.[10] For Italians arriving in New Orleans aboard NGI ships, the barriers to entry included harsh and unpredictable immigration inspections and duplicitous behavior by the labor brokers and agents who arranged tickets for their passage. As the processes governing Italian migration became more standardized, these migrants navigated particular rituals of passage, inspection, and confinement.[11] In giving clear instructions on how to negotiate these rituals, Arturo Dell'Orto both exploited and assisted Italian migrants landing in New Orleans.

Rituals of Passage, Inspection, and Confinement

By the year 1900, government officials in both the United States and Italy wanted to distribute migration away from crowded industrial cities to alleviate poverty, labor competition, and the strain on public resources. At the same time, the growing demand for foreign labor in southern states, along with the supposed ease of access through the port of New Orleans, prompted an increasing number of Italians to prefer the route to Louisiana. Arturo Dell'Orto wanted to increase the number of NGI crossings from Palermo to New Orleans from four a year to one every month, but the enforcement actions of the federal Bureau of Immigration disrupted his plan. In September 1904, Commissioner Frank P. Sargent, wishing to set an example for the other major ports, visited New Orleans and delivered a message in person to the city's immigration inspectors, instructing them to enforce the law more rigorously.[12]

On October 17, 1904, one month after Commissioner Sargent's visit, the steamer *Liguria* arrived in New Orleans from Palermo. Since the port of New Orleans lacked a facility large enough to process all the passengers on board at once, immigration inspectors, led by Vincenzo Piaggio, boarded the *Liguria*. All 1,483 passengers were held for several days, during which the officers examined the passengers to determine whether they were, under US immigration law, "clearly and without a doubt entitled to land." Reports issued by Dell'Orto and the ship's captain, Francesco Ansaldo, indicated that the examinations were harshly conducted, causing the passengers considerable stress, exacerbated by miscommunication, as Piaggio did not understand the Sicilian dialect. Dell'Orto suspected that the federal immigration officers, following Sargent's rebuke of their work, were "determined to make an example of the next immigrant vessel to arrive" and eager to exhibit what Dell'Orto described as the "iron rigor" now required of them. But there was more to the story than that. Formerly an agent for the rival Fabre Line and Anchor Line companies, Piaggio had been driven out of business by Dell'Orto in New Orleans before moving to New York to become a federal immigration inspector.[13]

Immediately after the examination, Dell'Orto wrote to Senator Murphy J. Foster (D–LA), who had recently served as the governor of Louisiana, cataloguing the injustices experienced by passengers on the *Liguria*. Such injustices, he emphasized, were not witnessed in other ports of entry. P. H. Stratton, chief officer of New Orleans's immigration station, ordered a second examination, which determined that 400 people had been, in Dell'Orto's words, "erroneously detained" under suspicion that they were "likely to become a public charge." Without being notified of the reason for their detention, and without access to the appeals process in place on Ellis Island, 118 of these passengers were "ordered deported." Piaggio's team excluded almost 10 percent of the

Figure 6.3. The *Liguria*. Courtesy of Lauren Braun-Strumfels.

1,483 passengers, whereas the average in New York was "one half of one percent." Overall, Italians experienced a 2 percent rejection rate in the mid-1890s, compared to 1 percent for European arrivals as a whole at the turn of the twentieth century. Dell'Orto, whom the New Orleans *Daily Picayune* quoted anonymously as "one of the interested parties," challenged the basis for the exclusions. "Why," he asked, "should the examination of the immigrants of the *Liguria* have been so strict on the score of 'liable to become a public charge,' when no Italian pauper has ever been known here?"[14]

Immigration inspectors at every US landing station had considerable autonomy in deciding whether to accept or reject migrants, and the absence of a landing facility in New Orleans made the processing of immigrants even more arbitrary, as the *Liguria* incident showed. Dell'Orto accused lead inspector Piaggio of carrying out a "long-considered *vendetta*" against him to "to damage Italian immigration and discredit the port of New Orleans." Dell'Orto found much to criticize in Piaggio's execution of his duties. The immigrants in question, he complained to Ambassador Des Planches, "had made their arrival without being treated with equality, justice, impartiality and disinterest, like they are treated in all the other ports of the United States." Dell'Orto blamed his former commercial rival Piaggio for harming "not only the well-being of this State but also Italian immigration and our Company [NGI]." Dell'Orto himself would soon face the same accusations from the Italian consulate in New Orleans.[15]

After two years without incident, an NGI ship again encountered strict scrutiny on October 4, 1906, when the *Lazio* arrived in New Orleans from Palermo with 1,161 passengers, 96 percent of them traveling in third class. Eighty passengers were detained, but in the end only ten were excluded. Facing a fine of $1,000 if any of these ten were to escape, the "captain didn't think he could guarantee to keep them on board." Dell'Orto "suggested having them locked up in the Parish Prison until the departure of the steamer, on the 15 or 16 of October." For Dell'Orto, the jail was an unpleasant but tolerable location to house passengers at no cost to his shipping company, as he would otherwise have been required, under Italian law, to pay for room and board until those rejected could be returned to Italy on the next departing NGI ship.[16]

By contrast, for the Italian consul in New Orleans, Lionello Scelsi, and his fellow officers in the diplomatic corps, jailing Italian migrants alongside common criminals was an embarrassment. Vice Consul Luigi Villari did not "understand under what right can people not guilty of any crime be put in prison." When he visited the parish prison to inspect the conditions, he found that the male migrants were held in a "special space," separated from the other white inmates in the segregated prison because of "special treatment" paid for by NGI. The sole rejected woman was held with her baby among the other female prisoners, who Villari objected were prostitutes. If the passengers were indeed held in the prison on Dell'Orto's recommendation, this was an extraordinary exercise of power by one private individual over the federally regulated processing of migrants.[17]

Scelsi was determined to exert some control. Arriving in New Orleans to lead the consulate two months after the *Lazio* landing in 1906, he immediately became convinced that Dell'Orto was exploiting rather than helping Italian immigrants. Prior to Scelsi's appointment, a revolving door at the consulate had brought several consuls and vice consuls in and out of the office during the chaotic years of the *Liguria* and *Lazio* landings. This administrative churn undermined consular authority, allowing Dell'Orto to increase his influence. On January 10, 1907, Scelsi wrote to Dell'Orto instructing him to provide accommodation for migrants rejected by the US immigration authorities, as the city prison was not an acceptable holding place prior to repatriation. Much of this would have been impossible in many of the other ports receiving Italian migrants, where the presence of Italian and American authorities was more extensive but also more scrutinized by immigrant advocates and the press. By March 1907, Scelsi and Dell'Orto were engaged in an open feud in the pages of the New Orleans *Times-Democrat*, with the NGI's agent accusing the consul of obstructing the free emigration of Sicilian laborers to the city.[18]

From Rome, the Italian Ministry of Foreign Affairs (MAE) demanded an approach to detention for Italians that "would be more humane and more becoming for a self-respecting State." To detain passengers in prison, the MAE wrote to Ambassador Des Planches in Washington, "seems excessive to this office, nor is there news of similar measures in similar circumstances" in other ports. In New York and Boston, the MAE observed, rejected passengers remained under the supervision of the ship captain, who "prevents them from disembarking and provides for their repatriation." Acting on this guidance, Scelsi warned Dell'Orto's agency that the consulate "will not allow those new arrivals whom the federal immigration authorities will not admit to disembark . . . to be placed in prison." Dell'Orto and NGI, he insisted, were solely responsible to "provide another room to serve as shelter for the rejected emigrants." A new, larger landing facility—capable of processing ships the size of the *Liguria* and the *Lazio*—finally opened in New Orleans in 1907, donated by the Southern Pacific Railroad and to be maintained by NGI. As Italian and American officials refined their rituals of inspection, especially in peripheral areas, private interests continued to control immigration in vital ways, opening a space for intermediaries like Arturo Dell'Orto.[19]

"Middlemen without Morals"

In March 1907, after only a few months in his post as consul, Lionello Scelsi targeted the operations of emigration agents like Dell'Orto, men he called "middlemen without morals," in a scathing letter to Carlo Leone Reynaudi, the commissioner of emigration in Rome.

Scelsi labeled Dell'Orto "a chief of these immoral middlemen without conscience," whose power in the city was undermining "much of the protective action of this consulate." The conflict that erupted between Scelsi and Dell'Orto also implicated the *Times-Democrat*, which had reported the details of Scelsi's private diplomatic correspondence regarding the detention of the *Lazio* passengers. Scelsi accused Dell'Orto of colluding with the newspaper to undermine and discredit him. A series of three articles published over three days exhibited what Scelsi characterized as the "bad faith that distinguishes the local press." Dell'Orto used the sympathetic *Times-Democrat* to publicly accuse Scelsi of holding back Sicilian emigration by refusing to sign affidavits required to issue passports under Italy's 1901 emigration law. Scelsi countered that Dell'Orto was seeking to increase "emigration artificially provoked by the now all too notorious middlemen of planters."[20]

When Scelsi received four calling affidavit applications less than two weeks after his public spat with Dell'Orto, he suspected forgery. The consul doubted that the signatories were aware that their names had been affixed to these legal documents, which confirmed their financial support for their relatives once they arrived from Italy. Scelsi informed labor broker Augusto Catalani, who was recruiting "relatives" to work on the Sunnyside Plantation with tickets issued by Dell'Orto for transit aboard NGI, that he would no longer certify calling affidavits sent to him in the mail but would instead require in-person hearings at the consulate, where he could hear the signatories testify to their desire to bring their relatives to Arkansas. This evidence would be required before he forwarded his consular stamp for a legal document necessary to leave Italy called the "*nulla osta*" as part of the consul's efforts to make New Orleans–bound migration conform with US anti–contract labor law and the 1901 emigration law.[21]

Even as Scelsi was taking these measures, the *Times-Democrat* took Dell'Orto's side, making it seem like the consul was blocking emigrants from Sicily with overzealous enforcement. In response, using language that painted Dell'Orto in the harshest terms, Scelsi explained his concerns to Commissioner Reynaudi in Rome:

> It is clear that this office finds an obstacle to its protective work in the action
> deployed by the shipping agent General Arturo Dell'Orto, who is so inti-

mately associated with the interests of the inhumane cotton and especially sugar planters. He sets up all the deceptions, all the subterfuges in order to be able to sell the greatest number of prepaid tickets, without at all caring about the disastrous consequences to be met by the thousands of emigrants made to come here not against their will, but certainly deluded by promises of prosperity that then finds no basis in reality.[22]

Scelsi objected to what he saw as the unregulated power of an agent who benefited directly from commissions earned on each paying passenger, profits that increased in tandem with his efforts to expand the traffic between Palermo and New Orleans and to shut down his competitors. Scelsi took very seriously his mandate to enforce the Italian emigration law of 1901. But in Arturo Dell'Orto, he was confronting a power broker whose familiarity with New Orleans and its business and political leaders positioned him, in effect, above the law.

As government officials in Italy and the United States worked together to confront the worst abuses in the passenger trade and to enforce laws passed in both countries to regulate immigration, agents like Dell'Orto walked a fine line. Did his methods exploit or help migrants? In February 1905, Egisto Rossi, then the commissioner of emigration in Rome, wrote to Ambassador Des Planches in Washington, DC, informing him how Frank Sargent, his counterpart as the US commissioner of immigration, characterized the problem: "Mr. Sargent attributes the increase [of Italian immigration] in the last year to agents, sub-agents and correspondents of the navigation companies that plant spores in the most remote villages, who hunt relentlessly for the emigrant for commission they earn on every ticket sold; and says that the new restrictive measures will be necessary to curb the incessant work of these sub-agents." By 1907, Sargent would lead a bureau-wide push for consistent and stringent enforcement with the intention of combating the transnational agent network, amplifying strategies to question, investigate, and surveil.[23]

Mary Grace Quackenbos's Department of Justice investigation in 1907 revealed critical information about Dell'Orto and the operation of agents in his network bringing Sicilians through New Orleans. Government officials now knew how Dell'Orto operated: recruiting paying passengers and coaching them through a gauntlet of exit and entry examinations. They identified a letter written by Dell'Orto giving emigrants answers to inspectors' questions and instructing them to conceal information that employers in the United States had prepaid their fares in exchange for labor, a direct violation of the 1885 Alien Contract Labor Law and an excludable offense. Yet at the same time, the poorest immigrants faced exclusion under the "likely to become a public charge" provision of US immigration law. Forged testimony from Italians already in the American South who promised to maintain their "relatives" was designed to meet both objections by satisfying Italian bureaucrats and American immigration inspectors that the migrants had resources but had not violated American law by signing labor contracts abroad.[24]

In their investigations of fraud and other abuses in the emigrant trade during the Progressive Era, journalists' exposés and legislative efforts focused on the figure of the labor recruiter who used his familiarity with his countrymen's language and customs to entice them into exploitative contracts abroad. Arturo Dell'Orto was only one such figure, for the problem existed on a large scale. One investigation on behalf of the US Bureau of Immigration, for example, identified Frank Missler of the North German Lloyd and Austro-American steamship lines, whose "extensive and systematic" efforts in cooperation with immigrant bankers facilitated the migration in 1907 alone of as many as 300,000 men from Hungary, Austria, Bulgaria, Serbia, Turkey, and Greece to the United States. Operators in smaller markets copied the strategies of the most successful agents. Quackenbos noted that Dell'Orto "perfected a system in New Orleans, doing for the surrounding southern states what Peter McDonnell & Company," representing the Old Dominion Steamship Line, with offices at Ellis Island and Battery Place in New York City, "is doing on a larger scale for the whole country."[25]

In March 1907, Consul Scelsi wrote to Commissioner Reynaudi, implicating Arturo Dell'Orto in a raft of duplicitous activities and accusing him of undermining the consulate's mission. In Scelsi's words, Dell'Orto's conduct was causing "continuous damage to our emigration." Dell'Orto's double role as labor broker and emigration agent, the consul objected, stymied the attempts of Italy and the United States to regulate migratory flows between Palermo and New Orleans. Scelsi exhorted Reynaudi to "oblige the NGI to change its agent in this harbor." The consul objected to Dell'Orto's actions on two grounds. First, he found it "unacceptable that the agent of a company largely subsidized by the state should make himself in this port the main violator of emigration laws." Second, he believed that Dell'Orto was undermining the "protective action" of the consulate by "continually creat[ing] obstacles with maneuvers and subterfuges of all kinds" and profiting from misleading and misinforming NGI passengers. Yet as the proliferation of coaching documents and fake calling affidavits suggests, tighter entry requirements led to new strategies to subvert those rules. With an administrative apparatus for regulating immigration only just emerging at this time, Arturo Dell'Orto played a critical role in facilitating the arrival and admission of Italian immigrants in New Orleans, because he knew better than anyone else how to navigate the rituals of migration control.[26]

* * *

The incidents surrounding the arrivals of the *Liguria* and the *Lazio* illustrate the significant challenges emigrants from Italy encountered trying to enter the United States at its largest southern port during a time of transition in the regulation of migrant mobility around the world. After securing the paperwork needed to exit Italy and enduring a two- or three-week-long Atlantic passage, the final step of their journey consisted of rituals of inspection leading to admission or exclusion, encounters in which "middlemen without morals" played a decisive part. Multiple layers of authority shaped the border-crossing rituals of Italian migration in New Orleans. Even as the Italian government passed laws to regulate emigration, the Italian ambassador and his consuls recognized, as Commissioner Reynaudi put it to Ambassador Des Planches, that "there are limits to what our government can do." In the United States, the administrative apparatus for regulating immigration was still in formation, and the exercise of border controls in New Orleans shows how public and private actors contributed to making this system. Arturo Dell'Orto stepped into the gaps between laws as written and as executed—the space where new systems of ritualized bureaucratic border controls were being made. In so doing, he shaped the lives of countless immigrants.[27]

PART THREE

Return

7

Strangers in the Homeland

The Aftermath of Deportation from the United States

HIDETAKA HIROTA

Born in County Galway, Ireland, around 1821, Ann Gray emigrated to the United States in 1860. A few days after landing in Boston, Gray went to Portland, Maine, where she spent four or five months before moving to Island Pond, Vermont. Five years later, she returned to Portland, where her sisters had settled. Sometime during her stay in Portland, she became destitute and entered an almshouse. At the almshouse, Gray developed symptoms of insanity, and in June 1867 the institution sent her to a state almshouse in Tewksbury, Massachusetts. Portland officials likely thought that a state that had originally admitted her into the country should take care of this foreign "lunatic," a logic widely shared by charity officials in nineteenth-century America. Gray's two-year residence at the Tewksbury almshouse did not cure her insanity, and Massachusetts officials decided to deport her to Ireland in the spring of 1869, along with three other Irish women with mental illness, under the state's immigration law, which allowed for the overseas removal of foreign inmates at public charitable institutions. In late April, the officials sent them to New York, where they took the *City of Antwerp* to Cork.

When they arrived in the port of Queenstown in Cork on May 5, Gray and the three women were dropped on the street without money, food, or shelter. A local officer accidentally found them and took them to the workhouse in Cork. Yet the atmosphere of the workhouse was far from welcoming, and the Cork officials thought that they "ought not to come at all." Deported from the United States as undesirable burdens who did not belong to the American community, these Irish women were regarded as outsiders who did not belong to Ireland either. Thus,

Gray and the three other women became social outcasts in their land of birth.[1]

The immigration of the impoverished Irish during the Great Famine provoked a surge of anti-Irish nativism in the United States. This hostile sentiment resulted in the development of restrictive immigration policies in northeastern states. The most popular form of immigration control in these states was to discourage the entry of destitute foreigners into the United States by requiring shipmasters to provide special bonds for their landing, which fell due if they subsequently required public assistance. Massachusetts, however, developed a unique policy permitting the expulsion of foreign paupers already in the United States to "any place beyond [the] sea, where he belongs." This policy allowed for the deportation of foreign inmates at public charitable institutions in Massachusetts to other US states, to Canada, and to Europe. Between the 1830s and the 1880s, when the US federal government began administering immigration, at least 50,000 persons were removed from Massachusetts. The deportation policy largely functioned as an anti-Irish measure. Calling Irish paupers "leeches upon our tax payers," nativists in the state promoted the removal of "an ignorant and vicious Irish Catholic population." Viewed as a drain on the American community, indigent Irish migrants were expelled from Massachusetts to Britain and Ireland under the state's deportation policy.[2]

This chapter examines the lives of destitute Irish migrants after they were sent back to Ireland from the United States for being public charges in the mid-nineteenth century. While Massachusetts officials deported some Irish paupers directly to Ireland, Liverpool became the major destination in England. Regarding Irish paupers sent from the United States as burdens on their community, Liverpool officials forwarded them to Ireland under the British Poor Law, which provided for the removal of the transient poor. Many of these Irish paupers were thus doubly deported from Liverpool to Ireland after being expelled from the United States to Liverpool.[3]

Ritual shaped the history of Irish pauper removal in two ways. First, for the Irish poor, the act of entering charitable institutions functioned as a ritual—a familiar, repeated, and dreaded set of actions— that marked them as outsiders and made them legally deportable. The concepts of settlement and belonging were the central principles both in the British Poor Law and in Massachusetts deportation policy. Under the British law, people in need who had legal settlement in a parish were considered as belonging to the community and entitled to relief from the parish, including accommodation at a workhouse. But the parish could deny requests for relief from the transient poor, who did not possess legal settlement there, and forcibly return them to the places where they were judged to belong. The British system of poor relief was introduced to America during the colonial period, and the state of Massachusetts based its deportation policy on this model. Indigent people seeking relief at public almshouses and lunatic asylums but lacking legal settlement in any Massachusetts town could be expelled from the state. No unnaturalized foreigner, moreover, was eligible for legal settlement in the state.

In both Britain and Massachusetts, many destitute Irish men and women became removable outsiders upon their admission into charitable institutions as paupers. John Barry, an Irish immigrant from Cork who had lived in the United States for three decades, for example, was deported to Ireland on June 12, 1868, shortly after his admission into the Tewksbury State Almshouse in Massachusetts on April 16. John Francis Maguire, an Irish critic of the British Poor Law, had pointed to a similar feature of pauper removal from England during the Great Famine: "A poor man who had lived some ten or fifteen years in England, and did not secure what is called a settlement in any parish, might, on receipt of relief be transmitted with his whole family to Ireland." The historian Adam McKeown saw the enforcement of US Chinese exclusion laws at the turn of the twentieth century as a ritualized process consisting of standardized and repetitive procedures, including detention at landing stations and interrogation by officials. Those exempted from exclusion and entitled to land, such as Chinese merchants, still had to go through this rite of passage. If admission into landing stations for admissible Chinese was a ritual for entry, admission into almshouses for the Irish poor served as a ritual for forced exit.[4]

Yet the deportation experiences of the Irish poor were also significant in a second sense, because they *lacked* elements of ritual found in other kinds of migration. Lack of care was the defining theme of deportation from the United States and Britain. In both cases, deportees received little medical and material aid in the process of removal and were simply abandoned when they reached their destinations without provisions to support themselves such as cash, clothes, or food. As a result, they often sought relief at the local workhouse. When deported Irish paupers finally returned to Ireland, local charity officials considered them strangers undeserving of relief and protested the American and British removal policies. Whether the deportees ended up in Liverpool, Dublin, or Cork, local charity officials insisted, as their American counterparts had, that these migrants did not belong to their communities. Together, the rituals of admission into charitable institutions that led to deportation and the absence of care and social acceptance during and after the removal process reduced indigent Irish migrants to an early example of stateless people—men, women, and children without a country who were "made vulnerable by movement"—in the nineteenth-century North Atlantic world.[5]

Irish Deportees in Liverpool

Nineteenth-century Liverpool drew so large a number of Irish migrants that it came to be seen as the capital of Ireland in England. As one of the major European gateways to North America, Liverpool had a sizable population of poor migrants, but the Irish were noticeably poorer than other migrant groups. At the height of the Great Famine, with the Irish accounting for 88 percent of the sick people who received care from Liverpool's health authorities, British officials dubbed Liverpool the "hospital and cemetery of Ireland." Pauper deportations from the United States added another layer to Irish poverty, already recognized as a social, economic, and public health problem in the city.[6]

Once in Liverpool, many deportees entered the local workhouse to secure immediate or long-term shelter. Immigration officials in Massachusetts claimed that removals were conducted humanely, but in practice the deportees, including those with mental illness, were abandoned upon arrival in Liverpool. Speaking about mentally ill paupers being sent to Liverpool, a superintendent of a sanitarium in Massachusetts critical of the deportation policy asserted that "it not unfrequently happens that all trace of them is lost." A typical deportee was "unable to provide for himself" and "let loose on the public streets, to take his chance of what Providence may do for him." Those who witnessed

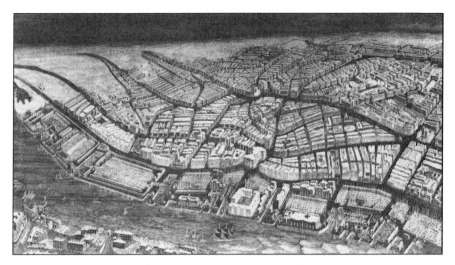

Figure 7.1. "Panoramic View of Liverpool, 1847." *Bygone Liverpool* (Liverpool: Henry Young and Sons, 1913). Courtesy of the Yale University Library New Haven, CT.

deportees' arrival described the scene as a "woeful sight," identifying the "hunger stamped upon them" as a result of neglect during the voyage. Once disembarkation was completed, the deportees were left helpless without basic necessities to support themselves. Under these circumstances, deported migrants sought admission to the Liverpool workhouse "in a condition of extreme wretchedness."[7]

The problem for the Liverpool authorities in receiving Irish paupers from the United States was that the city had already suffered a considerable influx of paupers coming directly from Ireland during the famine period. In 1847, the worst year of the Great Famine, nearly 40 percent of the passengers arriving in Liverpool from Ireland were categorized as paupers. The workhouses quickly became homes to famine refugees. The Irish accounted for approximately half the persons admitted to the institution in 1848. Many residents of Liverpool complained that they were suffering an Irish "pauperism invasion," a perception shared by residents of the major immigrant-receiving cities of the United States such as Boston and New York.[8]

Given the antagonism to Irish poverty, it is not surprising that Liverpool officials frowned on the admission to the workhouse of additional Irish paupers sent from the United States. In October 1855, after being informed of the arrival of fifty-four non-British paupers "in a state of great destitution," the Workhouse Committee within the Select Vestry, the governing body of poor-law administration in Liverpool, resolved that the Vestry Clerk write to the British Foreign Office "in the hope that some remedy may be provided against the recurrence of so great an evil." In a meeting in June 1858, reporting on the recent admission to the workhouse of two women and one man "who had been sent over from America as of unsound mind," the chairman of the Workhouse Committee remarked that "it was questionable what right the parties had to send them there." Three months later, one committee member called for the attention of the Select Vestry to "the importation of paupers from America." In the year up to November 1858, the Liverpool workhouse admitted 108 paupers sent from the United States, ninety of whom were Irish. One Liverpool official asked "why should not the Irish be sent at once to their own country instead of Liverpool"? Many of the deportees had lived in the United States for years, and they included women who had naturalized as US citizens through marriage to Americans and arrived in Britain with their American-born children. For the officials, such Irish belonged to the United States rather than to the United Kingdom, which should not be burdened with their support.[9]

Realizing that it could do little to stop deportation from the United States, the Liverpool Workhouse Committee attempted to reduce imported Irish pauperism by deporting the migrant poor to Ireland instead of paying for their maintenance. A Dublin newspaper in March 1855 reported that the authorities in Liverpool had sent to Dublin a group of mentally ill Irish women deported from Boston to Liverpool. In 1858, when the thirty-five paupers on the *Resolute* from Boston entered the Liverpool workhouse, one official proposed to "send home the Irish portion." In September 1859, when sixteen Irish paupers sent from Boston entered the workhouse "in a state of extreme destitution," the chairman of the committee remarked: "I was here when they came, and I never saw a more miserable lot of people." The paupers' testimony shocked workhouse officials. It turned out that the average age of five particularly old-looking paupers among the sixteen was seventy-one (considered very old in a time when the life expectancy of white Americans was slightly above forty). To the officials' inquiry, the five elderly persons answered that it was wrong that "after being 40 years there they should be sent back here." Within a week of these paupers' arrival, the workhouse officials forwarded eleven of the sixteen to Ireland and expressed their intention of sending the rest shortly. As in Massachusetts, admission into the workhouse in Liverpool functioned as a ritual that made the Irish poor removable from the community. Accommodation into the charitable institution was the first step in the uncharitable policy of expulsion.[10]

Irish Deportees in Ireland

Although Liverpool remained the most popular destination for deportation from Massachusetts, some deportees were also transferred from Liverpool to Ireland by British officials. American officials also shipped the Irish poor directly to Ireland. What sorts of lives awaited Irish paupers who were expelled from the United States, and in many cases from Britain, and finally returned to their land of origin?

In general, the paupers sent to Ireland followed paths similar to those in Liverpool. The Irish Poor Law Act of 1838 had divided Ireland into 130 regional administrative units, or Poor Law unions, and poor relief in each district was overseen by a Board of Guardians, consisting of local magistrates, often local landlords, and the elected representatives of the taxpayers in the union. The workhouses administered by these unions became the most immediate option for the deportees. In late January 1855, for example, Massachusetts officials deported eight Irish women inmates at the Worcester Lunatic Hospital to Liverpool. On March 4, six of them arrived in the port of Dublin, which implies the death of two women during the deportation voyage. According to the Dublin *Freeman's Journal*, one of the lunatic women "had in a great degree recovered her sanity upon the voyage across the Atlantic." She told the newspaper correspondent that, when they arrived in Liverpool, the port's authorities put them on board the *Trafalgar* to Dublin. Five of the arriving six—Anne Arbuthnot, Mary Shiel, Hannah Irvine, Anne Taggart, and Mary Sheeby [*sic*]— were found by a local constable "wandering about the quay, not knowing what to do or where to go," and were taken to the North Union Dublin Workhouse. Of the five, Irvine and Shiel left the workhouse within six months. Taggart, originally from County Antrim, spent nearly twenty years at the workhouse and in 1874 was transferred to a sanitarium, where she presumably spent the rest of her life. Arbuthnot from Antrim and Sheeby from County Kerry stayed at the workhouse until their deaths in 1858 and 1877, respectively.[11]

Liverpool officials forwarded many deportees to Dublin, but it was not the only Irish port that received Irish deportees from the United States. In the second half of the nineteenth century, Queenstown in County Cork acquired a stronger position in the transatlantic passenger trade compared to earlier periods. When two British steamship companies launched services at Queenstown in 1859, Liverpool still enjoyed its prominent status in the passenger trade. After 1870, however, Queenstown (and Moville, near Derry) surpassed Liverpool as the main ports of North America–bound embarkation for Irish migrants. With its growing presence in the passenger business, Cork emerged as a major destination for deportees from the United States during the 1860s, and the arrival of those suffering from mental illness became a recurring issue that caught local officials' particular attention. In April 1864, for instance, the Board of Guardians of the Midleton Union in Cork discussed the treatment of an Irish woman who "was sent over from America as a lunatic." In October 1867, officials found among the arriving passengers from the United States seventy persons who had been "sent back to this country by the American Government." Fifteen of them, including one "violent lunatic," were "in a sick and imbecile state."[12]

Like the Liverpool authorities, Cork officials regarded the deportees from the United States as an uninvited drain on their treasury. When five deportees entered the workhouse in December 1868, the Cork Board of Guardians called them "Irish-American lunatics" who "ought not to come at all." They used the adjective to underscore the outsider status of the returning paupers. The poor-relief fund collected from taxpayers in the Cork Poor Law Union should be spent only on the local poor, the officials believed, not those coming from outside their union in Ireland, let alone the United States. This sentiment was widely shared in Ireland. As the historian Catherine Cox has shown, relief for the mentally ill had become "a very significant drain on local and national financial resources." "Lunatics are a heavy charge on Irish taxpayers,"

CORK HARBOUR—'Statio bene fida carinis.'

Figure 7.2. "Cork Harbour." *Francis Guy's Illustrated Descriptive and Gossiping Guide to the South of Ireland* (Cork: Francis Guy, 1883). Courtesy of the University of Illinois Library at Urbana-Champaign.

declared the *Freeman's Journal*. According to the Dublin newspaper, this "evil" arose in part from the fact that "many insane, epileptic, and debilitated are often sent back from America as being unfitted for employment or military duties." The newspapers expressed frustration with "State Governments" in the United States for shipping the economic burden to Ireland.[13]

In an attempt to prevent the further entry of "Irish-American" paupers, the Cork Board of Guardians inquired into the American practice of deporting Irish migrants. In a meeting in December 1867, one board member revealed that nineteen paupers suffering from insanity had arrived in Cork from the United States during the year; this board member complained that it was a "very great hardship that this country should be made a place for the reception of lunatics from America." Upon hearing of the landing of returned "lunatics" at Queenstown in May 1869, one official stated that "it was a pity the people were not dropped at Liverpool instead." "When landed here," another board member lamented, "there was nothing for them but the workhouse."

From the perspective of the Cork guardians, the entry into the work-house of the so-called Irish-American paupers was nothing but a financial imposition on their union—a problem exacerbated by British authorities' refusal to receive or support them.[14]

Parallels Between American and British Deportation Policies

For Irish poor-law officials, the problem of American pauper deportation was not simply financial. Americans deported the Irish poor to Liverpool and Ireland at a time when the forcible removal of Irish paupers from Britain to Ireland provoked intense conversations among Irish officials over Irish sovereignty in the context of British colonialism. In this political setting, Irish officials perceived deportation from the United States as another case of a foreign government's imposing on Ireland debilitated persons who no longer seemed to belong to Ireland. The administrative and ideological parallels between American and British deportation policies, and Irish officials' criticism of returned paupers, demonstrate that the absence of care and social acceptance was a shared phenomenon among the United States, Britain, and Ireland.

On the eve of the Great Famine, poor relief in Britain was guided by the Settlement Act of 1662 and the Poor Law Amendment Act of 1834. These laws bound each Poor Law union to provide relief and medical treatment to poor people in the parish who had the status of "being settled" within the union, which could usually be obtained either on the basis of the father's settlement in the parish or by birth there. A person who claimed relief outside their settlement could be forced to return to the parish, where they legally belonged. Thus, if Irish migrants without settlement in Britain claimed relief in British unions, the unions had no legal obligation to support them and could forcibly remove the migrants back to Ireland. It was under this system that Irish paupers who entered the Liverpool workhouse after being returned from the United States were deported to Ireland.[15]

In Liverpool, with its large Irish pauper population, the impulse for removal was strong. In May 1847, Liverpudlians in a public meeting proclaimed with loud cheers "the Irish poor ought to be maintained by Irish landlords and Irish property." The high demand for the banishment of Irish paupers from Liverpool resulted in the passage of the

Poor Removal Act in June 1847. This act facilitated the expulsion of Irish paupers by simplifying legal proceedings for removal and enabling union officers to deport them to Ireland on the exact day when they claimed relief, upon confirming that they were born in Ireland and had no settlement in the British parish where they resided. Between 1846 and 1853, Liverpool shipped 62,781 Irish paupers to various parts of Ireland, chiefly Dublin but also the cities of Belfast, Cork, Drogheda, Dundalk, Newry, and Waterford. During these years, notes like "Sent over from Liverpool by the Authorities" frequently appear on the admission register of the Cork workhouse, indicating the entry of deportees from Britain.[16]

The British deportation of Irish paupers was extremely unpopular in Ireland. Above all, the practice appeared cruel and inhumane. The *Cork Examiner* objected that "in many cases, in most cases, these parochial authorities [in England and Scotland] might as well send those Irish outcasts to the deserts of Siberia, or the back-woods of Canada, as land them in the streets of Dublin, Waterford, or Cork." Criticizing the expediency in the implementation of removals, the *Belfast News-Letter* argued that "the inquiry is not where it is just or humane to transit the pauper, but where it is the least burthensome that he should be sent." For those who had lived for a long time in Britain, deportation to Ireland amounted to banishment to a foreign land where they had no family or acquaintances. The deportees included many British-born Irish paupers. Sixteen-year-old John Driscoll, for example, was born and grew up in England and spoke "with a thorough English accent." When he entered a workhouse in London, the officials put him on board a ship to Cork "against his will" just because his parents were natives of Cork, though Ireland was virtually a foreign place to him. For destitute Irish migrants in Britain, just as those in Massachusetts, accommodation at charitable institutions in search of relief constituted a ritual through which they were made deportable.[17]

If the Irish paupers had spent most of their lives in England, Irish officials believed, they belonged to England rather than Ireland and should be legally allowed to receive charity there. Certain Irish groups—such as persons who resided in a parish for five years without interruption, widows within twelve months of their husband's death, and persons applying for relief on account of temporary sickness and accident—were technically exempted from deportation under the Five Years Residence Act of 1846. The administration of pauper removal, however, proved so sloppy that British officials often illegally deported these so-called irremovable Irish to Ireland.[18]

Many Irish observers also found the manner of removal enraging. Like the deportees from the United States, those from Britain received only minimal provisions and were abandoned upon discharge at Irish ports. The historian Frank Neal explains the process of removal: "The relieving officer gave the master the pauper's fare while the unfortunate person was given some bread and a small sum of money, usually a shilling. On the master taking on board the pauper and signing the receipt, the parish had fulfilled its legal responsibility. . . . On putting the person ashore in Ireland, the master had discharged his responsibility and the pauper was left to his own devices." A letter to the editor of the *Belfast Morning News* in January 1858 pointed to the inhumanity of deportations to Belfast. Many cases of removal were "of a most pitiable and heart-rending nature, arising from nakedness, want, and night exposure, during the long sea voyage." "No attention seems to have been paid by our neighbours across the channel to extreme old age or ill-health," the writer bemoaned; "all were hurried over indiscriminately, as soon as they were found to be in want, and of Irish origin." Some commentators even compared deportation with the slave trade. In criticizing the removal of Irish paupers from England, an Irish member of Parliament argued that "sickness and misery of every kind was endured by those unfortunate persons on board the steamers into which they were huddled. The way in which they were transported across channel was such as had, that evening, called for their lordships' sympathy in the case of the African slaves." Absence of care was the essential feature of pauper removal.[19]

Most exasperating for Irish Poor Law guardians was the asymmetrical nature of pauper law within the United Kingdom. British Poor Law unions were legally authorized to deport Irish paupers to Ireland based on the law of settlement. Yet the Irish Poor Law did not include provisions on settlement. This meant that a pauper could obtain relief in any Irish Poor Law union and enter any workhouse as long as it had space, and Irish workhouses had no legal device to send their own British inmates back to Britain. Since the British population in mid-nineteenth-century Ireland was tiny (less than 5 percent of the population of the city of Dublin in 1851, where most of them lived), supporting British paupers cost the Irish Poor Law unions little. But Irish guardians expressed considerable irritation at the inequality in eligibility for relief between the British and Irish poor, which was rooted in the colonial relationship.[20]

From the standpoint of Irish Poor Law boards, if "the English born poor are entitled to and receive relief in Ireland, without being subject to removal," the Irish poor should be allowed to claim relief in England. Otherwise, the law of settlement, as North Dublin workhouse officials demanded, should apply to Ireland so that they had the means of "sending English and Scotch Paupers of whom there are a few sizable numbers in this House back to their own country." Irish officials thus claimed their right to deport British paupers in Ireland to Britain, where they belonged, just as American and British officials adopted the legal concept of belonging in their own deportation policies. In rare cases, Irish officials sent deportees back to England at their discretion. In October 1856, for example, when a poor woman named Moore and her three children were deported to Cork from London, where her unemployed English husband resided, the Cork guardians returned them to London. The protests of the Irish Boards of Guardians, however, went nowhere. In 1869, they were still denouncing the Poor Law within the British Empire as "manifestly and outrageously unfair." Irish people deported from England during the 1860s included a woman who had lived in Hartlepool for seventy years and, in another case, five children of a man who had spent a quarter-century in England.[21]

Given Irish workhouse officials' attitudes toward British deportation policy, it is not difficult to imagine how they interpreted deportation from the United States. The Irish officials found a clear parallel between American and British deportations. Precisely when officials in Ireland were struggling with the pauperism imposed by Britain, American officials were returning paupers to Ireland in a markedly similar manner. In examining the "vast increase of paupers" in the workhouse as a result of the British removal law, Dublin officials found that those sent "from America" also contributed to the expanded inmate population. In a report on the "Deportation of Paupers" between December 1857 and January 1858, the *Belfast*

News-Letter listed the admission of a young woman "who was sent here by the parochial authorities of Boston, in America," along with cases of paupers deported from Scotland. American policies for returning Irish paupers to Ireland aggravated the sense of injustice felt by Irish officials. The *Freeman's Journal* bitterly criticized American state governments for "outraging Irish feeling by playing the part of the English Board of Guardians in sending back used-up Irish labour." From an Irish perspective, American officials had joined the British government's scheme to compel Ireland to support paupers who had lost tangible connections to Ireland other than their birth there. Irish politicians and poor-law officials saw the British removal law as "selfish in its spirit" and "harsh and cruel in its operation," and they applied the same criticism to the American deportation policy as well.[22]

Officials in Cork in the winter of 1868–1869 saw clear parallels between pauper removal from the United States and British deportation policy. One official complained: "This city is the receptacle for every poor person who comes from America or England." The paupers returned from the United States through Liverpool posed an especially frustrating problem to the Cork Board of Guardians. Legally, these deportees, upon landing in Liverpool, entered the same category as Irish paupers who were removable from Britain under the British Poor Law. Another board member asked: "Are those people Irish-born subjects, or are they Americans?" "If they are Americans, you might remonstrate," he suspected, "but if they are not, I fear there would be some difficulty." The problem, he continued, was that, "supposing those persons (being Irish-born) are landed in England, they will, under the present law, become removable to Ireland, and there will be no redress." Cork officials could not raise any effective argument against deportees coming through Liverpool. In discussing paupers with mental illness brought from the United States, a representative of an Irish steamship company advocated a change in British passenger laws to compel shipowners arriving in ports within the British Empire to "take back the lunatic to the port from whence he came," for "similar law prevails in the United States." He suggested that with such an exclusion policy "it will probably become possible to prevent such persons from being shipped [from the United States] in future."[23]

Irish Poor Law guardians believed that they were enduring the worst part of the entire system of pauper removal. Large towns and cities in Ireland already received a growing number of the poor from rural areas in the country during the Great Famine. The North Dublin Union of the Board of Guardians was annoyed by the arrival of paupers, "all flocking to the metropolis in vain hope of relief." Alongside these domestic migrants, Irish workhouses received Irish deportees from Britain, over which they had no control under the colonial legal structure, as well as from the United States. By contrast, while they grumbled about the paupers from America, Liverpool officials could ultimately transfer them to Ireland. Despite the high expense of removals that the workhouse had to pay, one Liverpool official was still "thankful for the power to send the Irish back." When the Liverpool Workhouse Committee criticized American deportation policy in 1859, the chairman of the committee accurately pointed out that "we do the same thing to Ireland."[24]

Irish officials had no choice but to accept all the paupers returning to Ireland, whatever trajectory they might have taken in arriving there. In discussing the admission of mentally ill deportees to the Cork workhouse in 1869, one official asked "[c]ould we send any of our paupers to America," only to be told by other officials: "If you send the lame, the blind, or the mad there, they will be returned to you." British and American officials referred to their countries as a "dumping ground" in protesting the growing immigration of the Irish poor, but Irish officials thought that the term most accurately applied to the return of paupers to Ireland. Reflecting the officials' sentiment, the *Freeman's Journal* argued that Britain was expelling a class of Irish "whose sinews were worked off in England" from "localities where they had spent the better portion of their lives," while "their infirm bones were packed off to Ireland." Irish workhouses thus had to assume a disproportionate share of responsibility for the Irish poor, but all parties involved in the deportation of the Irish poor—American nativists, Liverpool officials, and Irish guardians—treated indigent Irish migrants as unwanted burdens on their communities. In their recent study of the removal of Irish paupers from Britain to Ireland under the British Poor Law during the Great Famine, Lewis Darwen and coauthors note that "responses to the arrival of these destitute masses on both sides of the Irish Sea were remarkably similar and undoubtedly punitive." These responses to indigent Irish migrants were shared not only across the Irish Sea but also across the Atlantic Ocean.[25]

* * *

A transnational system of social marginalization and physical expulsion shaped the experience of destitute Irish migrants in the nineteenth century. Irish paupers shipped to Liverpool under American state deportation policies entered a society where a very similar removal policy was operating, and some of these paupers were further deported to Ireland under this policy. Even though Irish workhouse officials had no legal authority to execute deportation, they took part in forming the world in which Irish migrant paupers were thrown out. American nativists, Liverpool workhouse officials, and Irish Poor Law guardians shared a resistance to the "importation of Irish paupers" founded on the concepts of settlement and belonging. The idea that the poor in need should be cared for in places where they belonged drove American and British removal laws, but it also influenced the way Irish officials responded to deportees from the United States, who hardly seemed to belong to Ireland. The deportation of Irish paupers in the United States stemmed from American nativism, but their long return trip— from embarkation at US ports to unfriendly reception at workhouses in Ireland—was shaped by a wider conception of belonging and exclusion shared by American, British, and Irish officials alike. The rituals of making the migrant poor deportable from charitable institutions and neglecting them in the process of removal unfolded across national borders, making indigent Irish migrants into people without a home in the North Atlantic world.[26]

8

Feeling Strange on the Shore

The Ambivalence of Return Migration in Irish Literature

GRÁINNE MCEVOY

> She had put no thought into what it would be like to come
> home because she had expected that it would be easy; she had
> longed so much for the familiarity of these rooms that she had
> presumed she would be happy and relieved to step back into
> them, but, instead, on this first morning, all she could do was
> count the days before she went back.
> —Colm Tóibín, *Brooklyn: A Novel*[1]

Admired and envied, scorned and begrudged, the figure of the returned Irish emigrant occupies a place in Ireland's cultural imagination that belies the tiny proportion of emigrants who returned to the homeland. Although numbers are difficult to determine, only an estimated 9 percent of Irish immigrants to the United States in the first quarter of the twentieth century returned to Ireland, compared to roughly 50 percent of Italians. And yet the experience and the idea of return have left an imprint on Ireland's plays, novels, short stories, films, and popular songs for well over a century. Fictional returned children of Erin have most commonly taken the form of the stereotypical "Returned Yank": either an abrasive presence characterized by, to quote Philip O'Leary, "flashy clothes, conspicuous wealth, ignorance, bombast, and a distressing accent," or a naïve sentimentalist returning in search of land, landscapes, and a sense of belonging.[2] Such figures include the wealthy, cigar-smoking St. John Hogan Hannafey, who coasts around the backroads of County Cork in his cream Lincoln in Seán O'Faoláin's *Come Back to Erin* (1940); the impulsive, tactile, and "heavily made-up" Lizzy Sweeney in Brian Friel's *Philadelphia, Here I Come!* (1964);

and the eponymous Sean Thornton of John Ford's 1952 film version of *The Quiet Man* (based on Maurice Walsh's 1933 short story of the same name), a retired boxer jaded by urban life in Pittsburgh who returns to his birthplace of Inisfree (the movie's rendition of Inishfree) in hopes of settling in his old family home.

Perhaps the quintessential response of the fictional returned migrants is their arresting reencounter with the landscapes of home, whether natural or built. Numerous late nineteenth-century popular ballads romanticize cottages, streams, and mountains that "sweep down to the sea." In his short story "Houses on the Mountain" (1959), Benedict Kiely recalls how his aunt and uncle, returned from Philadelphia, nostalgically but ill-advisedly built a new home on the side of Dooish Mountain in County Tyrone. Indulging in the foods and material comforts of home also takes on a ritualistic quality in depictions of return. In George Moore's "Homesickness" (1903), the ailing protagonist James Bryden feels fortified by the milk, bacon, and cabbage and the warming hearth that he enjoys during his first night at home in Duncannon after thirteen years in New York City's Bowery district. In Anne Enright's *The Green Road* (2015), Dan Madigan, driving home to Limerick after a red-eye flight from New York, acts on an impulse to buy a packet of Irish crisps while stopped at a petrol station, a ritual he offers to share with Constance, the sister he has not seen in several years. Perhaps the most complex, introspective ritual that characterizes the fictional returned Yank's reencounter with home is that of reencounter with community—whether family or friends, neighbors, or acquaintances—in which the returnee is repositioned as simultaneously or alternately a member, outsider, and observer. Michael Ridge in Tom Murphy's play *Conversations on a Homecoming* 1985 is just one example of a returned migrant navigating these dynamics.

Literary representations of the figure of Irish returnee offer a potentially fruitful way to access a somewhat murky historical and cultural experience. Historical evidence of return in this period is somewhat limited, but many of Ireland's leading writers spent time abroad, made a return to the land of their birth, and witnessed or wrote about returnees and their impact. Several scholars have turned to literature and other cultural forms to understand the perception and influence of return, both real and imagined—particularly Irish attitudes to nationhood, identity, tradition, and modernity. This chapter undertakes a close reading of two fictional migrants—Mairéad from Máirtín Ó Cadhain's short story "Floodtide" (1948) and Eilis Lacey from Colm Tóibín's novel *Brooklyn* (2009)—to illuminate the collective experience of how returnees encountered the homeland and how they were perceived by those who had stayed behind. In particular, the chapter explores elements of homecoming that are comparable across both texts. Published six decades apart and set in two quite different periods, both texts struck many similar chords, revealing the enduring power of rituals of return—both real and imagined—in Irish culture.[3]

In choosing Mairéad and Eilis, I give priority to fictional representations that are shaped by a historical moment, by gender, and by the returnees' perspectives. The two women's experiences depict migrations and returns undertaken from the late nineteenth into the mid-twentieth centuries. Written in the 1940s and set in the 1910s, Ó Cadhain's "Floodtide" evokes Gaeltacht (Irish-speaking) communities whose survival was threatened by emigration and language erosion. Writing in the early twenty-first century, Tóibín re-creates dynamics of migration in an east coast Irish town in the 1950s, where a returnee's embrace of modern American fashions and behaviors might be both scorned and admired. As the literary scholar Sinéad Moynihan has noted, the male returnee was disproportionately represented in Irish culture until the 1990s, limiting the array of fictional females both written and set before that period. Mairéad's and Eilis's experiences are connected by the ways in which their gendered roles as daughters, wives, and young women shape their own perspectives on return and that of their neighbors.[4]

Perhaps most important, as representations of female return, "Floodtide" and *Brooklyn* offer sustained reflections on the dynamics of homecoming from the perspectives of the returned migrants rather than that of the family, community, or society that received them. While Maura Laverty's *Never No More* (1942) and Edna O'Brien's *The Light of the Evening* (2006) feature female returns in the first half of the twentieth century, neither novel offers sustained reflections, from the perspective of the returnee, on the rituals and first moments of return. Through their introspections, Mairéad and Eilis reflect a shared experience of return that is both disappointing and discomfiting. Return brings into relief how much they have changed and the degree to which they now stand apart from those who never left. Compelled to reflect on their own senses of identity and belonging, Mairéad and Eilis emerge from their experiences of return with a deeply ambivalent sense of both the meaning and location of home.

Mairéad: A Disappointing Harvest

The opening scene of "Floodtide" (An Taoille Tuile), a short story from Máirtín Ó Cadhain's 1948 collection *The Cloudy Drop* (An Braon Broghach), sets the stage for a self-revelatory and emotionally ambivalent return to the homeland. After ten years in New York City, Mairéad has returned to her native Connemara for good. Having paid for the passages of three sisters to America, she has saved a small dowry to enable her to return and marry Pádraig, the constant and patient love of her girlhood. As her story opens, Mairéad lingers in bed and, with pleasure, contrasts the moment with her decade in New York toiling in a hot kitchen from before dawn, "for the sake of . . . for the sake of this day—a day when she could lie in or get up as she pleased." Her reverie signals a shift in mood. The ambiguous ellipses cast some doubt on whether the sacrifice of years of her young life to wage labor in America was worth it, and her thoughts are then interrupted by an irate reprimand from her mother-in-law in the back room, which reminds Mairéad that she is still answerable to people other than herself. Within minutes, her mood swings up again when she finds that her sweetheart "had put on a roaring fire and the kettle was humming to the boil." In response to Pádraig's welcoming hearth, cheerful voice, and affectionate smile, "Mairéad's irritation melted on the spot."[5]

Written from the returnee's perspective, "Floodtide" depicts Mairéad's readjustment to the impoverished, hardscrabble community on the shores of Galway Bay in which she had been born and raised. Mairéad's reencounter with home is driven by the rituals of return—she surveys the landscapes of home, indulges in familiar foods and material comforts, and engages with her native community conscious of a change in her status and identity—but it is unexpectedly difficult. Roused from her bed to participate in a communal harvest of seaweed, variously referred to as "dulse" and "caragean," Mairéad has a visceral encounter with her home, laboring on the Cora (the farthest point along the strand, constantly exposed to erosion by the open sea), that profoundly challenges her initial enthusiasm for return. In a single morning, her emotions swing from feeling revitalized by the sea air and saltwater to feeling broken by the "slavery" of foreshore scavenging, from being sure that she belongs and is deeply rooted in the place where she was reared to feeling scorned, unappreciated, and rejected by her neighbors. Mairéad comes to realize, with a heartbreaking sense of loneliness, that she has much to relearn about the unrelenting survival economy of the Connemara coast, and that her ineptitude and indulgence in nostalgia will try the patience of all, even of her beloved Pádraig.

The stakes of Mairéad's life choices—her decision to emigrate and then return to Pádraig and her native community—can be fully understood only when "Floodtide" is read alongside the other stories in *The Cloudy Drop*. Ó Cadhain is widely celebrated as, in the words of Louis De Paor, "the outstanding prose writer in modern Irish and a significant figure in twentieth-century world literature." *The Cloudy Drop* reflects the lives of real women in Ireland's impoverished west, the women whose lives Ó Cadhain, born in An Cnocán Glas, Spiddal, County Galway, in 1906, witnessed firsthand. Devoted to social as well as political revolution, Ó Cadhain wrote in response to the privations he witnessed in early twentieth-century Connemara. During World War II, he was detained in Tintown, the military prison in the Curragh, County Kildare, which he referred to as *Sibéir na hÉireann* (Ireland's Siberia). During his incarceration, he read widely and was inspired to represent in written form the economic inequalities that shaped the choices and fates of the people of the Cois Fharraige region of Connemara, using their own words and language. The stories in *The Cloudy Drop* explore, through the eyes of their female protagonists, women trapped in lives marked by loveless but pragmatic marriages, unrelenting childbearing, and the harsh physical labor of a subsistence economy. More often than not, these emotionally and physically bruising existences end in privation, starvation, and premature death.[6]

For generations of women and girls, the culture of Connemara dictated that emigration, when the opportunity arose, was their best chance for survival and security. Only one other protagonist in *The Cloudy Drop* takes up such an opportunity: Máirín, the emigrating daughter in "The Year 1912" ("An Bhliain 1912"). Written from the perspective of her preemptively grieving mother—with a brief segue into Máirín's inner world—this story depicts the hours leading up to a young girl's departure for America as she packs her trunk, changes into her comparatively gaudy traveling clothes, and bids farewell to a community that has gathered to send off another child of the village.

This ritual of departure foreshadows an experience of return. As they bid farewell to Máirín, the villagers laugh about how she might change, warning her against "getting the accent" or forgetting what a pig looks like, and they mock the behaviors of previous returnees to the village, reflecting that this is a community in which emigration is frequent and return is not uncommon. Her bereft mother—whose namelessness indicates her universality—also reflects on Máirín's potential return, with an external stoicism that belies a bleak inner world. While she protests aloud that Máirín will return in five years, the mother reflects with heartbreak:

> But she knew that if she did see her again, she would be nothing like the innocent, young country girl she was now at nineteen, her beauty like morning sunshine on a hillside in paradise. Her lips would have touched the bitter fruit of the Tree of Knowledge. . . . Her expression would be steely and cold. She would talk with a strange accent, as if a wicked step-mother had wreaked havoc on her speech. That was what all returned Yanks were like.

Máirín's story, like that of Mairéad in "Floodtide," reflects the dilemma facing those who left and then returned to villages such as this one. Although "tales of America were mother's milk," the returnee was assumed to be forever changed, an outsider to her community, and subject to scrutiny and begrudgery. The stories of Máirín and Mairéad are therefore connected by an emotional thread, casting the two women as versions of the same figure.[7]

In "Floodtide," Mairéad's morning on the Cora feels to her like a test of the degree to which she is still a daughter of the foreshore. Her appraisal of her experience with this type of agriculture, captured through the narrator's indirect discourse, reflects her awareness of how intrinsic that acumen is to the identity of those who belong to her native community:

> Mairéad was born and bred on the edge of the great bay. She had already gathered periwinkles and sand eels, laver, dulse, and carrageen. The spring before she went "over" she had helped her father cut seaweed on the upper part of the beach. But she had left before she was fully inured to the slavery of the seashore. Her hands had quickly become wrinkled from washing, scrubbing, and cooking, instead of acquiring the leathery skin of a foreshore forager. In the ten years during which the sea would have put salt in her blood and mettle in her bones, Mairéad saw salt water little over ten times.

Immediately following this critical self-reflection, "the salt wind in from the deep sea breathed new life into her veins," and the sight, sounds, and feel of the foreshore reinstate in Mairéad a confidence in her identity and her own heritage and history on the Connemara coast. Much of this shift in mood is stimulated by memories of and nostalgia for her childhood exploration of the beaches and its bounty. "The crisp and solid sand lifted Mairéad's heart," and the various fruits of the exposed strand—whelks, periwinkles, crabs, rockfish, and limpets—trigger comforting memories from her childhood as she recalls her father bringing shellfish home and roasting them on embers for supper.[8]

Mairéad's nostalgia for the animal and plant life of the Cora has been fostered by the culture around emigration and longing for home. Emigrants from the area typically brought these remnants of home with them: Máirín leaves with a handful of dulse in her trunk, and Mairéad remembers the bunches of carrageen a neighbor had brought to America that had "often jolted her mind back to the edge of the great bay, to the lovely beach where her heart's desire had remained." These were the ballad-like longings of Mairéad the emigrant for her Irish sweetheart Pádraig, wrapped up in the visceral material elements of foreshore culture. In rich, vivid detail, Mairéad's senses are alert to the sounds of the Cora, and "in spite of the cold and wretchedness of the salt water, she felt her blood rush, something she hadn't felt for ten years." Exposure to the shore, its harshness notwithstanding, resonates with Mairéad more than anything she had experienced while abroad.[9]

Figure 8.1. Beach combing/Cnuasacht feamainne, Co. Galway, 1940. Photographer: Heinrich Becker. By permission of the National Folklore Collection, University College Dublin, Ireland.

Interspersed with these surges of confidence in her aptitude for the harvest and her sense of belonging on the foreshore, Mairéad is relentlessly confronted by the reality of her underdeveloped acumen for shore work and the impatience of the neighbors with whom they will share the harvest, Lydon and his two daughters. In an exchange with Lydon, Mairéad betrays her lack of knowledge of the great spring tide that coincides with the feast day of Ireland's patroness saint, Bridget. "With all the appearance of a bishop in whose presence a shameless blasphemy had been uttered," Lydon responds: "'The great spring tide of the feast of Saint Bridget! You're not used to the spring tides yet, my dear, you have other things on your mind.'" Lydon's ridicule is infused with the locals' deference to the forces of nature and the Catholic faith, implying that Mairéad is more concerned with the pleasures of her marital bed than with respecting the protectress of Irish womanhood. She, in turn, is acutely aware of the preconceptions around female returnees, which expose them to accusations of frivolity, immodesty, and immorality, transgressions of the frugal, practical, and faithful virtues of the women of Connemara.[10]

Navigating her new status as a returnee among her own people, Mairéad anticipates or reacts to these comments by diminishing and concealing anything that might confirm the stereotype and cast her as an outsider. In literary representations of the returned Yank, particularly of women, appraisal of American fashion is a common motif. "Floodtide" presents this interaction from the perspective of the returnee, conveying Mairéad's embarrassed attempt to downplay her mistake of wearing light American shoes, which Lydon derides as "toy toys" better suited to the streets of New York than the shingle of a beach. In a similar way, Mairéad, acutely aware of both the stereotype of the sexually awakened female emigrant and her neighbors' predilection for gossiping about the returnees in their midst, stops herself from telling the Lydon sisters about a man who had wanted to marry her in New York. "They would just end up laughing about it in all the rambling houses of the village that night. Was there ever a hussy or whore came back from America and didn't claim that some millionaire or other wanted to marry her beyond?"[11]

The arrested development of Mairéad's shore acumen presents a more pragmatic challenge: not only is she unfit for the harvest, but she is also a hindrance to the communal struggle for subsistence and survival. In a heartrending treatment of this returnee's nostalgia for the landscape and nature of her home, Mairéad's appreciation of the shore is exposed as naïve, inadequate, and frivolous, primarily by Lydon, the voice of authority on surviving on the Cora. When the sight of limpets arouses her dormant craving for roasted shellfish and offers an opportunity to appease her mother-in-law, Mairéad fashions a "bucket" from the coarse apron she is wearing over her American dress. "'Slowly but surely,' she told herself, 'I am developing some sea acumen.'" Her

Figure 8.2. Gathering seaweed, Co. Galway. Photographer: Domhnall Ó Cearbhaill. By permission of the National Folklore Collection National Folklore Collection, University College Dublin, Ireland.

sense of confidence is immediately shattered by Lydon. Frustrated that Mairéad is not concentrating on the seaweed and other essential crops, he exposes her lack of expertise on the tides and sea life: "'Don't be driving yourself daft with those limpets, Mairéad,' said Lydon. 'Top-shore limpets have twice as much meat in them as low-water ones, and besides, limpets are not right until they have had three drinks of April water.'"[12]

Written from Mairéad's perspective, the narrative voice of "Floodtide" brings into sharp relief the profound disappointment felt by a returnee whose attempts to reintegrate and refamiliarize herself with her native culture are repeatedly challenged. Battered by the unrelenting physical brutality of the seashore and the derision and lack of compassion from her neighbors, Mairéad stoically and reluctantly resolves to embrace the life she has chosen. Although she concludes that her work in the "murky heat of a narrow kitchen" in New York was comfortable compared to "crushing and scalding" and repetitive work on the beach, Mairéad is confident that she, like returnees to the shore before her, "who are as used to this slavery today as if they had never left home," possesses the fortitude to adapt to her chosen future. Her acceptance, however, is not without ambivalence. Echoing her unfinished elliptical thoughts as she luxuriated in bed that morning and considered the purpose of her ten years in New York, Mairéad thinks "she had made her bed and she would lie in it."[13]

The most acute heartbreak occurs in the story's final lines: Mairéad's repudiation by her beloved Pádraig. Out of spite toward the Lydons, she returns to the beach that has been almost entirely reclaimed by the floodtide, taking a position near Pádraig, her touchstone, who had brightened her new hearth and home just that morning. Drenched and beaten by the waves and troubled in her mind and heart, Mairéad attempts to claim whatever she can from the tide but inadvertently obstructs her husband's frenetic laboring against the incoming sea. "'Leave my way!'" shouts Pádraig in a "harsh, alien voice. A voice from a kingdom far removed from that of lonely letters, sweet nothings, and pillow talk." After a morning of compensating for his chosen and long-awaited partner's deficient contribution to the harvest, Pádraig's impatience matches that of Lydon, and Mairéad's decision to return loses its last and most important justification. Like the other daughters of Connemara that populate Ó Cadhain's *The Cloudy Drop*, Mairéad faces a future of toil and privation. In the case of this returnee, that fate is made more burdensome by the gaps in her knowledge of life on the shore and by the fact that she had experienced and decided against another path abroad. Mairéad's morning on the Cora dispels the joy and security she found in the rituals of return—the familiar hearth warmed by Pádraig and her encounters with the landscape and bounty of the Cora—that had validated her decision to return home.[14]

Eilis: Imagined Migrations

Disappointment and fear also color the initial hours of Eilis Lacey's return to her native Enniscorthy in Colm Tóibín's critically acclaimed 2009 novel *Brooklyn*. Set in the mid-1950s, the novel depicts a young woman's emigration and return in the most heartbreaking circumstances following the sudden death of her beloved older sister, Rose. Eilis, eager for sleep after an unexpectedly discomfiting reunion with her grieving mother, finds that her childhood bedroom "seemed empty of life, which almost frightened her in how little it meant to her." She had assumed that coming home after over two years in Brooklyn would be easy and natural, and she had not given any thought to what the transition would actually be like. Taking in the space around her, Eilis comes to the realization that her time in Enniscorthy, her return, will be challenging and unsettling. The unease she feels in her bedroom and her desire to return to the now familiar rooms of her life in Brooklyn "made her feel strange and guilty; she curled up in bed and closed her eyes in the hope that she might sleep."[15]

There are similarities that connect Eilis's experience with that of Mairéad despite the different circumstances and historical moments in which they make their returns. These connections reflect the familiar rituals of the returnee's encounter with home, particularly Eilis's contemplation of the environment of home, built and natural, and her deep introspection on her new place within her native community. In the course of several weeks in Enniscorthy, Eilis also experiences swings of emotion, equivocating between feeling revitalized by the familiar landscapes and people of home and enervated by the closeness and closed-mindedness of that community. She is subject to the scrutiny of her neighbors, who appraise how she has changed—her clothes, how she carries herself, and her romantic life. At various moments, Eilis either takes pleasure in how the people of Enniscorthy see her as changed or attempts to conceal the ways in which she is now marked as different from those who never left.

Eilis's return reflects another feature of return: her imagination moves between two homes, never fully belonging in either place. Her apparently ambivalent attitude toward the idea of home has been the subject of significant scrutiny by Tóibín scholars, who consider the degree to which she undertook all her migrations—to Brooklyn, to Enniscorthy, and then back to Brooklyn—reluctantly. The more decisive conclusion to John Crowley's 2015 film adaptation, in which Eilis (played by Saoirse Ronan) appears to confidently choose a life on Long Island with her Italian American husband Tony (Emory Cohen) over the Enniscorthy publican Jim Farrell (Domhnall Gleeson), has generated further analysis and debate. Rather than trying to determine Eilis's attitude to her final decision, or which of the two men she really loved, the analysis I offer here will unpack how her experience of return shaped her definition of and relationship with home.[16]

Born and raised in Enniscorthy, Colm Tóibín has spent time living in Barcelona, London, New York, and elsewhere. In interviews, he has frequently discussed the ways in which his work draws on the past and the present—both his own and that of the places and communities he has inhabited. In crafting the characters, plotlines, and emotions of *Brooklyn*, Tóibín was inspired by the local stories he absorbed as a child in 1950s Enniscorthy, by his encounters with home as a returnee, and by his observations in adulthood that elements of the individual experience of migration are universal and timeless. The novel, and the figure of Eilis specifically, was inspired by a story Tóibín overheard as a child of a local girl who had married in Brooklyn but removed her wedding ring on the journey home, afraid that the realization that she would be settling in the United States forever would break her family's hearts. Eilis's mother, Mary, likewise emerged from the real streets of Enniscorthy. As a twelve-year-old, Tóibín had listened to a visitor to his family home around the time of his father's death who talked at length about her daughter in Brooklyn. "It was almost forty years later," he wrote in 2009, "before I took what I had heard, just the bones of a story about her daughter who had gone to Brooklyn and then come home, and began making a novel from it." Tóibín has also discussed how, as a frequent migrant himself, he encounters the landscapes, sounds, and smells of home, sensory experiences that heighten his emotions and provide inspiration for his writing.[17]

Building on a theme with long precedents in Irish literature, Tóibín published *Brooklyn* in the context of renewed emigration from Ireland and the arrival of refugees and other migrants into the country, following the collapse of the "Celtic Tiger" economy. As scholars have noted, Tóibín's work is richly intertextual, drawing on a multitude of sources, stories, and literary inheritances as he crafts his writing. One such influence on *Brooklyn* was George Moore's "Homesickness," from his pathbreaking short-story collection *The Untilled Field* (1903), one of the few previous depictions of return migration in Irish literature told from the returnee's perspective, in which James Bryden's return to his native village of Duncannon after thirteen years in New York's Bowery district quickly shifts from reconnection, contentment, and belonging to disappointment, contempt, and disgust. Against this literary background, Tóibín captured the minute particulars of life in Enniscorthy and Brooklyn in the 1950s in a way that hit home with readers in the early twenty-first century because of the similarities as well as the differences between the two periods. Comparing Eilis's long-distance grief and concern for her sister and mother in 1952 to a Syrian refugee's worry for someone they left at home in 2015, Tóibín explained that "there is an element . . . [of] trying to dramatize a story to remind the world of what migration is actually like. . . . It isn't easy for anybody."[18]

As with her departure for Brooklyn, Eilis initially returned to Enniscorthy less on her own terms than she would have preferred. During her first hours at home, Eilis cannot help but feel that her mother is deliberately ignoring her profoundly transformative emigration to America. This return has been entirely reframed—and, indeed, provoked—by her sister's death. Eilis's time in Enniscorthy, which occupies only the last fifth of the novel, opens not with the returnee on a boat or train, or with her first embrace with her mother, but with Eilis and Mary Lacey standing together in the doorway to Rose's now-silent bedroom. While Eilis soon comes to understand the overwhelming depth of her mother's grief, her initial response to this lack of interest in her American life is one of disappointment. Eilis had hoped to tell her mother about her journey, show her the bookkeeping certificate she has earned from Brooklyn College, and give her a cardigan, scarf, and stockings from Bartocci's, the department store where she worked, but "her mother had not asked her one question about her time in America, or even her trip home," and "had almost absentmindedly" left the gifts aside, "saying that she would open them later." Eilis's initial experience is an inversion of a familiar returned Yank narrative in which those who stayed at home pepper the returnee with questions about life in America and appraise the luxuries and material things that the person has brought home.[19]

Eilis's transformation is the focal point of interactions with her friends and neighbors, as the natives of Enniscorthy comment on "her beautiful clothes, her sophisticated hairstyle and her suntan." The interactions rehash the familiar trope of the confident and fashion-forward

Figure 8.3. Eilis Lacey (Saoirse Ronan) in her bedroom in the Lacey family home on Priory Street, preparing to return to Brooklyn, in *Brooklyn* (dir. John Crowley, 2015).

returned female Yank. Yet from Eilis's perspective, these changes fully develop only in dialogue with those who stayed behind in Enniscorthy: Eilis is apparently unaware of her external transformation until her neighbors point it out. During her first walk in the town a day or two after her arrival home, Eilis notices "a woman studying her dress and stockings and her shoes and then her tanned skin, and she realized with amusement . . . that she must look glamorous in these streets." As she spends more time in town, socializing with childhood friend Nancy Byrne, Nancy's fiancé, George Sheridan, and his friend Jim Farrell, Eilis begins to embrace and enjoy these changes, realizing that her time in Brooklyn has indeed given her a newfound confidence, which lifts her mood and helps her find a new footing in Enniscorthy. Enjoying dinner with these friends at the Courtown Hotel, Eilis recalls the sense of social inadequacy she felt before her emigration, including being previously spurned by Jim, but "now that she was back from America, she believed, she carried something with her, something close to glamour, which made all the difference to her as she sat with Nancy watching the men talk."[20]

Eilis's most profound transformations—those that strike to the core of her perception of herself and her place in the world—remain unspoken and invisible, and she consciously conceals some of the rituals of homecoming, such as her nostalgic reencounter with the landscapes of home, from her family and friends. Returning reveals for Eilis the ways in which the experience of emigration has marked her as permanently different from those who never left. One such transformation has been underway since Eilis's initial emigration to Brooklyn—the homesickness that separates the emigrant from those left behind. Eilis endured profound anguish during some early nights in her bedroom in Mrs. Keough's Brooklyn boarding house, her sense of isolation heightened by the realization that "they would not find out about this; she would not put it into a letter. And because of this she understood that they would never know her now." This lonely experience in her Brooklyn bedroom is echoed in Eilis's first sleepless night back on Friary Street. Her renewed feelings of strangeness and fear in her childhood bedroom reflect how emigration involves an emotional transformation that can never be reversed, even by a return home. Much like Mairéad on the shorefront in Connemara, the returnee Eilis also conceals emotions that she fears might betray her sense of being an outsider, including her nostalgic reactions to the landscape. She keeps silent about the memories that come to her mind while visiting parts of her homeland that are perfectly ordinary and unremarkable to those who never left. In the car with Nancy, George, and Jim on the way to the beach at Curracloe, Eilis "almost pointed out the places she knew," landmarks, pubs, and shops that remind her of family excursions when she was a child, "but she stopped herself. She did not want to sound like someone who had come back home after a long time away." While she might not have the opportunity to enjoy such spaces again on a beautiful Sunday in the summer, "for the others it was nothing," and "she was sure that if she began to talk about her memories of this place, they would notice the difference."[21]

As Eilis repositions herself as a returnee in her native community, she finds that the social capital gained through her new clothes, skills, and sense of confidence are only part of what would allow her to fully readjust to life at home. This realization points to the deepest ambivalence that lingers as the novel comes to a close. Eilis feels pulled back and forth between Enniscorthy and Brooklyn. The strength of her sense of connection to either place is reflected in whether the people and

Figure 8.4. Eilis Lacey (Saoirse Ronan), returned from Brooklyn, looks over Curracloe Beach, Co. Wexford, alongside Jim Farrell (Domhnall Gleeson), Nancy (Eileen O'Higgins), and George Sheridan (Peter Campion) in *Brooklyn* (dir. John Crowley, 2015).

spaces are described as "vivid" or "dissolved," "filled with detail," or "no longer richly present." At the same time, the fullness of Eilis's migratory experience—of leaving and returning—reflects how the ability to imagine oneself elsewhere diminishes over time. After some weeks in Enniscorthy, Eilis realizes that everything about her secret husband Tony "seemed remote," and the spaces and people in her life in Brooklyn— her room in Mrs. Keough's, the Fiorello family's apartment, the shop floor at Bartocci's—seemed "almost dissolved" and "no longer richly present for her. . . . She went through all of it as though she were trying to recover what had seemed so filled with detail, so solid, just a few weeks before." By contrast, the rooms of her childhood home on Friary Street are "once more familiar and warm and comforting." She has found her place in Enniscorthy—a bookkeeping role and a future with Jim Farrell—and "the idea that she would leave all of this . . . [and] go back to Brooklyn and not return for a long time again frightened her now." Eilis's migratory experience raises the question of whether the migrant's capacity for imaginary return (in either direction) can withstand the passage of time and the immediacy of physical proximity and daily life over the long term.[22]

Brooklyn's closing line—Eilis's closing thought—keeps this question open. As she sits on a train traveling away from Enniscorthy, she imagines her mother telling Jim Farrell that "she has gone back to Brooklyn," a line that reflects Eilis's full understanding of the stakes of her own decision. Eilis imagines the years ahead, when her return to Brooklyn would come to mean less to Jim and more to herself, the person who chose to root herself far from her native home. As Eilis "almost" smiles at the thought of it and then tries "to imagine nothing more," she conveys once again the ambivalence with which she migrates and her unwillingness, and perhaps inability, to close down the imaginary space in which she moves between homes.

* * *

As Máirín, the emigrating daughter in Máirtín Ó Cadhain's "The Year 1912," sits atop a cart on the first leg of her journey to America, she takes a last look back at her childhood home. From this point in the road, "it, and the few houses clustered around it, would be lost from view." Máirín notices how "a line at the apex of the roof, where last year's fresh thatch met the black and withered stuff of previous years, seemed to demarcate days gone by from the days to come." Less than a mile into her journey, Máirín already has a new perspective on her home and realizes that, like so many friends and neighbors before her, she has begun her emigration. She commits to memory the landscapes and sights of her birthplace and reflects on how, in her absence, those places will continue to be marked by the passage of time. This emigrant's perspective on rituals of migration illuminates the individual and emotional elements of departure and return. For Mairéad and Eilis, these rituals reveal to them how much they have changed and now stand apart from those who remained behind. Return, in this sense, proves both as transformative and as incomplete as emigration, marking both women with a deeply ambivalent sense of place, belonging, and the location of home.[23]

9

The Visual Culture of Italian Migrant Return

Snapshots at the Crossroads of Home Visits and Touristic Itineraries

JOSEPH SCIORRA

"All photographs are a form of transport and an expression of absence."
—John Berger and Jean Mohr[1]

In December 2010, my father, Enrico Sciorra, then eighty-eight years old, mailed me a letter from his Brooklyn home to my apartment at the other end of the borough. It was a rare occasion indeed, outside of Christmas cards, to receive a handwritten note from him. Evidently, he had something important to tell me. The envelope contained two almost identical 6" x 4" photographs, one slightly cropped compared to the other, both of which were clearly scanned, although poorly, from an original physical print (see figure 9.1). My dad wrote that the source image had at some point gone missing, suggesting that he had only recently rediscovered it. The second line of the letter simply stated: "This photo was important for me because [it] was the beginning of the life in Italy." This poignant and telling autobiographic assertion references the fact that, in 1926, the year the image was created, his father, Joseph, having "made good money" as a tailor during six years in New York City, repatriated his family to his hometown, Carunchio, Chieti Province, in the region then called Abruzzi e Molise. As my father's short but detailed text conveys, thirty-year-old Joseph, his twenty-seven-year-old wife, Filomena, and their two Brooklyn-born children—four-year-old Enrico and two-month-old Gloria—set sail from New York City to Naples on July 4, 1926, on the Italian steamship *Duilio*.[2]

Figure 9.1. The repatriating Sciorra family aboard the Italian steamship *Duilio* on their way to Italy, July 10, 1926. Photograph courtesy of the author.

The formal portrait depicts six people—the family plus two unknown individuals (one a child, the other an adult). The decentered framing, with a person cut off on the left, challenges the viewer to discern if the image is a snapshot made by a nonprofessional photographer or a cropped version of a larger image created perhaps by a steamship employee for a fee. On the left is my grandmother Filomena, sporting a beatific smile as she holds her baby daughter on her lap. While not at the center of the photograph, Filomena is clearly the image's familial core. On her right shoulder is the hand of an unidentified woman, whose face and entire body in its full-length polka-dot dress is cropped at the image's edge. Another hand and arm, Enrico's, is draped on his mother's left shoulder. On the right, my grandfather, in suit and tie, sits perched on the arm of a deck chair. Occupying more than half of the image is a light-haired boy in a suit and striped tie kneeling in front of the Sciorras. This enigmatic figure holds a life preserver ring reading *Duilio*. My father dated the image on the back "July 10, 1926," the sixth day after leaving the United States toward his new life in Italy.[3]

In the historiography of the first Italian mass migration (1880s–1920s), images abound of people in transit from Italy to the United States—at Italian docks, on board steamships, and at Ellis Island and other ports. Such depictions in prints, paintings, films, and most significantly in photographs, are the iconographic representations that characterize much of how we visualize transatlantic Italian movement during the great migration. Despite this profusion of visual material concerning Italian migrant departure, arrival, and settlement, as well as the scholarly literature about the subject, we know little about the imagery of return migration, including repatriation, home visits, and heritage tourism, which often involved multiple trips and stops along the way. My father's treasured photo, which he deemed important to share with me, his eldest son, offers a starting point for reflection on Italian migrant return imagery.[4]

This chapter addresses the scholarly lacuna of the visual culture of return migration by examining a cache of family photographs assembled by a paternal granduncle Nicola "Nick" Sciorra (1902–1992) in 1930 and 1937 and my father (1922–2015) in 1957 during return visits to Italy. Their photographs document their travels to Carunchio, other towns and cities, and several touristic sites. Relying on primary sources—visual and textual information, family and official documents, oral history, and personal memory—and drawing on the rich scholarship on visual culture, material culture, and the Italian diaspora, I situate these historically constituted images of return within their original social and cultural context. The images are largely unremarkable. Mostly they conform to conventions of "snapshot photography" in subject matter and style. In keeping with Richard Chalfen's study of analog domestic photographs, my work looks at the "social process, pictorial messages, and symbolic forms" of this "home mode communication" as they pertain to Italian diasporic encounters. What do these pictorial representations illustrate about social relations and emergent identities in the context of migrant return? How are aspects of migrant return visualized and interpreted in subsequent viewings, including my own repositioning within the context of this chapter? Such information is not immediately evinced from the images themselves but requires a significant amount of personal and cultural knowledge to decipher it with any degree of accuracy. These mediated interpretations of diasporic and touristic experiences provide a visualized network of belonging, obligation, sentiment, success, and evolving identity.[5]

Given that both Nick and Enrico are deceased, the social context and motivation of these return photographs are difficult to reconstruct. Family photos constitute a "world of traces," impenetrable objects that "defy analysis by outsiders on all but the most superficial levels." For this chapter, I draw on my recollections and sensations of seeing my father's curated slideshows of 1957 Italy and the stories told about the spectral projections of distant family members. Given these familial connections and my scholarly training, I am well suited to interpret the photographs at this moment when personal memory offers opportunities for illumination, however speculative, and before that future time when they will become opaque jetsam of memory loss and family dislocation. My analysis of these images as visual culture involves an "excavatory or archaeological strategy" of contextualizing and interpreting some of the larger meanings in their production and in their dissemination.[6]

My work builds on scholarly literature on diasporas and tourism that examines the intimate, dynamic relationships between migrants (as well as their descendants) and their family in their places of origin as significant aspects of transnational mobilities. Scholars understand VFR tourism—visiting friends and relatives—as a critical part of the larger migrant experience that reveals a diasporic realm of kinship ties, intense emotions, and hybrid identities at the intersection of local and global spheres. Migration, especially for Italians, has never been unidirectional but has always been a process of transnational circularity of people, objects, and ideas. The photographs of return discussed here are postcards of a sort, documenting "emotional landscapes of migration" in which love and longing are rendered visually.[7]

This chapter documents the formation of the Sciorra photographic collection as a history of migration, obligation, and consumerism. It then focuses on three aspects of the Sciorras' visual communication of their photographed return: depictions of intimacy regarding family gatherings and the hometown; representations of tourist destinations, suggesting Italian national affiliations and cosmopolitan identities; and picturesque, exoticized depictions of people, revealing emergent migrant dispositions. These categories of intimacy, tourism, and the picturesque frame the transnational diasporic visual culture that Nick and Enrico—along with family members, *paesani* (townspeople), and American friends—created at the crossroads of the local, the national, and the transnational. These images reconcile memories of these two migrants' affiliations with place, reimagine their changing sense of self in relation to a distant homeland, and craft a visual culture that perpetuates affecting links into the future, even for those who were not part of the situations depicted. Family photographs are documentation of the people, places, and moments that came before us, inspirations for inchoate identities of affiliations, and reminders of the loss of knowledge and memory that time and distance produce.

Creating a Photographic Archive in the Diaspora

The very existence of these historical images is predicated on Italian cultural values that motivated Nick and Enrico to voyage home. Loretta Baldassar has observed that post–World War II Italian Australians' return visits to Italy involved key principles relevant to the Sciorra photographic collection: the attachment to local places (*campanilismo*), the urge to establish oneself financially and start a family (*sistemazione*), and the commitments and responsibilities to family members that include home visits. These were important considerations for these men in creating documents of Italy and for the photos' maintenance and preservation.[8]

Figure 9.2. Two photographs of Nicola Sciorra (right) and his nephew Enrico in New York City, circa 1924 and 1952. Photograph courtesy of the author.

Nick's and Enrico's images of home visits are directly connected to their intricate migration histories and mutual obligation as family members, developed over decades (see figure 9.2). Their respective sets of photographs survive owing to a web of transatlantic travel and familial duty: Enrico's father, Joseph, accompanied his eighteen-year-old brother Nicola's migration in 1920, cementing a strong bond between the two ("He was like my father. He took care of me," Nick told me in 1987); Nick, in turn, encouraged and ultimately facilitated his nephew Enrico's migration in 1952; and, finally, Enrico took his aging widower uncle (and his personal items including photographs) into his home and, along with my mother, Anna, cared for him until he died at ninety. Later I would conserve and contextualize these historical documents, realizing their importance not only as family heirlooms but as objects of twentieth-century Italian migration. My curatorial actions are in keeping with a moral sense of familial obligation.

Nick's and Enrico's home visits, like my grandfather Joseph's family re-patriation, were part and parcel of the Sciorra family's history of transatlan-tic travel for more than half a century. My family's migration experiences, involving four generations crisscrossing the Atlantic first to Argentina and later to the United States featuring multiple trips, fit a common pattern of Italian mobilities. Acknowledging my family's multigenerational and multidirectional migration, one that "acquired all the characteristics of an inheritance, a patrimony, a source that could be transmitted among family members and across generations," is crucial for contextualizing Nick's and Enrico's return visits and the images they created of them.[9]

Nicola's Italian passport and Ellis Island ship manifest list him as a *calzolaio*/shoemaker, but by 1930 he was a short-order cook in his American-born cousin's Manhattan diner, where he stayed until his re-tirement in the 1960s. In 1932, he wed Mary "Irene" Harrington (1898–1974), who had migrated from Ireland as a nurse. On May 26, 1930, the then-unmarried Nick returned to Italy as a naturalized US citi-zen. World politics disrupted his six-month stay when rumors of war between Italy and Yugoslavia began circulating and the fascist regime mobilized recruits. Nick's mother feared he would be drafted, so he left Carunchio abruptly one night, sailing from Naples on June 14. In 1937, Nick traveled one last time to Italy, with Irene, after his brother Joseph's death the previous year, staying five months. While Nick never returned, he remained in constant contact with his family through ex-tensive letter-writing and remittances (sent as late as the mid-1970s), ultimately assisting Enrico's migration and settlement after the war.

Enrico's family lived a prosperous life in Carunchio with money his father earned in the United States and his successful tailor shop. With my grandfather's illness in 1934 and his death from cancer two years later, life took a financial and emotional downturn, despite support from the extended family. In 1939, Nick wrote to his father suggesting that seventeen-year-old Enrico migrate to New York City under his care, a proposal that was rejected at the time. After the war, Enrico at-tended the University of Naples and graduated in veterinary medicine in 1951. Unable to make a living in Carunchio, he left Italy with a US passport at age twenty-nine, arriving at Ellis Island on May 5, 1952. My father's personal trajectory—born in the United States, raised in Italy, migrated after the war—bridges different eras of the ongoing streams of Italian mobilities. His history, like thousands of others, challenges conventional narratives about Italian migration to the United States as being solely a pre–World War II phenomenon. He moved in with his Uncle Nick and Aunt Irene in Manhattan, securing a job as a veterinarian with the United States Department of Agriculture. In 1954, he married Anna Annibale (1927–2022), who in 1950 had migrated from Maranola, a hamlet of Formia, Latina Province, Lazio.[10]

My birth in 1955 prompted the family visit to Italy two years later. The sense of longing across the oceanic divide during this time was expressed in my grandmother's ardent message to her family in New York City: "I don't know how to express the pain that I suffer due to your distance, especially now that dear little Joseph is born." We departed in May, my father by airplane and my mother, afraid to fly, sailing across with me. My father stayed two months; my mother and I returned to New York City in late September.[11]

The Sciorra photograph collection is a testimony to the two migrants' *sistemazione*—success in having secured jobs, created a home and family, and established themselves in the United States. The photographs are products of ethnic consumerism before and after World War II that embody the cultural values of Italian diasporic lives. While the cameras were purchased in the United States, their use in this historical period situates them as "part of transnational networks and multidirectional flows" within an Italian diasporic context. The photographic project of purchasing equipment, studying technical aspects, being the primary image makers, and (in Enrico's case) organizing and showing the images speaks to the highly gendered practice of domestic snapshot photography.[12]

Enrico took great care to organize, index, and annotate the 1957 images. The 284 Kodachrome slides are housed in eight trays, part of a larger collection of slides made between 1954 and the 1970s. It appears that Enrico organized the images more or less sequentially. He labeled his collection according to places, people, and occasions, facilitating a complete mapping of my parents' Italian itinerary. Projections of these images were part of family gatherings up to the 1970s and as a result provided me with an intimate knowledge about them.[13]

Nick's images consist of ten black-and-white and sepia-toned prints, two from 1930 and eight from 1937. All the latter photographs were originally glued into and subsequently cut out of a photo album, so there is no way to

reconstruct how they were organized. In addition, there are fifty-nine negatives, nineteen from 1930 and forty from 1937. Many of the images show
motion blur (see figure 9.9) or are under- or overexposed; one is double-
exposed, and frequently images are off-centered with people cut off. I do
not know what camera Nick used, but the 2 ½"x 4 ¼"size of the negatives
suggests it may have been the 1A Pocket Kodak: a folding camera with bel-
lows first manufactured in 1926 and, at eighteen dollars, costing a hefty sum
for a migrant short-order cook on the eve of the Great Depression.

Unlike Nick's photographs, Enrico's slides, in their deep Kodachrome colors, are, for the most part, properly exposed, well framed,
and visually legible. This may be a result in part of his 35mm German-
made Voigtländer Vito II, a lightweight, versatile folding camera that
cost approximately fifty-five dollars when he purchased it around 1954.
Enrico's interest in technical advancements, added to his studiousness
in photographic technique, may also have contributed to the photographs' quality. His personal library contained several midcentury
Kodak-published booklets as well as the nine-volume *The Complete
Photographer: An Encyclopedia of Photography* (1949), which offered
technical and aesthetic tips for better photo making.

Carunchio and the Intimacies of Place

The camera does not merely document the emotional event but by
its presence also confirms its significance. The home visit's exceptional
nature warrants the presence of a camera to mark its distinctiveness
from everyday life and to "sanctify experience." The camera, along with
the subsequent photograph, is an inherent element in the visit, one of
the essential things packed for the journey and an expected appearance
that is sometimes welcomed and sometimes considered intrusive. The
presence of the camera and the photographer are a "significant catalyst
of events," and this is most evident in posed stances (see figure 9.3).
Azriella Azoulay suggests that the "event of photography," as distinct
from the "photographed event," does not merely document a specific
moment or the photographer's omnipotence but rather points to a situation in which "no-one is the sole signatory." This line of inquiry helps
us understand Nick's and Enrico's home-visit images as involving not
only the returning migrant but also family, friends, and *paesani*. The

Figure 9.3. A group of men and children pose in Carunchio's Piazza Vittorio Emanuele, 1930. The author's grandfather, Joseph Sciorra, is the second man on the right, and his son, Enrico, is standing in front of him. Photograph courtesy of the author.

symbiotic "visual event" happens when the social relations and mutual obligations existing between those who have left and those who stayed are first created as an event of photography and then rendered into a tangible object for future reflection.[14]

Several of Enrico's images highlight the significance of home return in documenting moments of family and social gatherings that constitute parts of the 1957 journey. The opening five photographs in the first slide tray were made in Manhattan on board Anna's ship and feature her extended family, who came to see her off (see figure 9.4). This family sendoff and its photographic documentation were an integral part of the Italian home visit—mirror images of those made at Italian ports—and they illustrate the web of obligations and emotions that these occasions entail.

Our arrival in Carunchio occasioned a celebration involving the immediate family and a larger group of family members and *paesani*. Local musicians performed the song "Paisà, bone arrivate" (Welcome, Paisan), written in the local dialect to the melody of the Neapolitan tune "Funiculì, funiculà" in honor of "Enriche, llu duttore de Carugne" (Enrico, the doctor of Carunchio; see figure 9.5). Lyrics include:

Figure 9.4. Anna Sciorra (center in white hat) and family members on board the *Cristo-foro Colombo* in New York City harbor, 1957. Color slide original. Photograph courtesy of the author.

"Enrico, the doctor of Carunchio/ He left contently for America/ This mountainous land has not forgotten him/ And has followed his success/ Finally he's arrived/ Paisà, welcome home." The song acknowledges that the townspeople are aware and proud of his *sistemazione* with work and a family in the United States.

The song's personified geography—the land that remembers—points to the deep-seated sense of place with one's hometown that operates prominently within the Italian diaspora. *Campanilismo*, stemming from the Italian word for "bell tower," is a topographically grounded and emotionally charged sensibility and identity tied to cultural affiliations and family obligations. For Italian migrants, this place-based sentience constantly evolves, and home visits are part of a negotiation and reformulation of individual and ethnic identities. Enrico's first photographs of Italy are of Carunchio from afar, its surrounding valley, and the town's campanile (see figure 9.6). This early placement in the collection contextualizes the images of family and *paesani* that follow. *Campanilismo*'s visual allure had a powerful

Figure 9.5. Musicians perform on the occasion of Enrico's return visit to Carunchio, 1957. Color slide original. Photograph courtesy of the author.

Figure 9.6. Panorama of the Abruzzese hill town Carunchio, 1957. Color slide original. Photograph courtesy of the author.

Figure 9.7. Cousins Mariapina Farina and Joseph Sciorra, Carunchio, 1957. Color slide original. Photograph courtesy of the author.

influence throughout Enrico's life as images of Carunchio permeated his domestic sphere. Two noteworthy examples were displayed on his bedside nightstand and on his car dashboard like a religious icon. Carunchio was the place my father woke up to each morning and the one he was continually driving toward all his life.[15]

The sentimental hometown connection is fundamentally linked to the bonds of affection for and obligation to family. Family-based *campanilismo* is visually manifested in the large number of portraits of relatives in the Sciorra collection. The Carunchio images depict intimate family scenes with smiling friends and townspeople grouped together and touching, posing for the camera (see figure 9.3). Some images bring together family from both sides of the Atlantic to highlight the bonds of affiliation and love, like a snapshot of my grandmother bathing me when

Figure 9.8. Enrico Sciorra's cousin Italia Ciavatta surrounded by friends on her wedding day, Carunchio, 1957. Color slide original. Photograph courtesy of the author.

I was two. Children—the new family members not fully known to the photographers and their US relatives—are given special attention in both sets of images. They are used as props in a sense to simulate and reinforce overseas bonds when they are brought together to awkwardly kiss and embrace (see figure 9.7). These choreographies between the photographer, the subject, and those outside the frame are scenarios of transatlantic affection that were revisited with each viewing. Both impromptu and staged portraits were up-to-date documents to be shared with relatives in New York City upon returning.

The migrant's return was often timed to coincide with rites of passage such as a birth, a marriage, or a death. Enrico turned his camera four times to his cousin Olga's newborn son, Giuseppe. Eight photographs were taken of Enrico's cousin Italia's marriage and two of Anna's cousin Maria's wedding reception in Formia (see figure 9.8). Nick's 1937 visit with Irene was prompted by the death of his older brother, Joseph, and the images of relatives are noticeably more somber than those made seven years earlier. The importance of transnational family ties and obligations is evident in the three images of the decorated grave of Nick's brother Umberto, a return migrant and Italian soldier who died from the Great Influenza pandemic a month after the Armistice of 1918. The fact that Nick visited and photographed the burial site in the Veneto region reveals the power of familial commitment involving both the living and the dead.

Touring Migrants

Nick and Enrico did more than visit family in Carunchio; they also traveled to noteworthy tourist locales around Italy. These larger migrant journeys linked Carunchio (and New York City) with the Amalfi Coast, Pompeii, and Venice as part of an ever-shifting notion of Italianness (see figure 9.9). Migrant tourism, as Sabine Marschall notes, is "instrumental in negotiating one's sense of belonging, identity and self-construal." Nick's and Enrico's photographed travels mapped their changing senses of self, no longer bound by a Carunchio–New York City *campanilismo* but tied to a more capacious and national cosmopolitan *italianità* (Italianness). The touristic enactment combined local intimacies and national locales of cultural capital to refashion and reinforce their emerging Italian *and* American selves.[16]

Figure 9.9. Nick Sciorra feeding pigeons in Piazza San Marco, Venice, 1937. The image's motion blur is found in several of Nick's photographs. Photograph courtesy of the author.

The images show once-impecunious interwar and postwar migrants now successful and with sufficient economic stability to engage in leisurely travel and document it. Home visits and return tourism point to the "crucial role that consumption has had in shaping the diasporic identities of Italians in America." These diasporic tours offered returning migrants opportunities to reimagine their relationship to the country of their childhood and their adopted homeland. The visual documents position the image makers, the individuals pictured, and subsequent viewers in a dialogue about spatial identities and affinities.[17]

Both collections reproduce a series of conventional images of the Italian landscape, a style that Giorgio Bertellini calls "classicism" or "antiquarianism." Roman ruins, Renaissance buildings, and an assortment of churches and monuments figure prominently in the 1937 black-and-white negatives and 1957 color slides. Most conform in subject matter and framing to those found on postcards both men brought home with them to New York City. The fact that Enrico and Anna drove in a relative's borrowed car, unlike Nick and Irene, who traveled by train, allowed them opportunities to stop and photograph unpeopled mountain vistas and seascapes that replicated the "ethereal beauty of the panorama" that had long come to represent an archetypal southern Italy.[18]

A few images in the collections suggest encounters with Italy's more troubling aspects: fascism and World War II. One photograph shows Irene standing in the Stadium of Marbles, with the Fascist School of Physical Education in the background, both part of the Foro Mussolini in Rome, the sports complex inaugurated in 1932. The fascist regime touted the forum as a triumph of architectural design and urban infrastructure, part of the city's vast modernization project. But why would Nick and Irene venture far from the centrally located sites of the Vatican and the Victor Emmanuel II National Monument, which they also visited and photographed? Did they travel to this site simply because they were in Rome the very month the regime inaugurated the large-scale black-and-white mosaics heralding the fascist achievements at the forum? Alternately, Enrico's visual documentation of the fascist legacy included two places associated with the devastating 1944 Battle of Monte Cassino. While he created thirteen photographs of the abbey and cathedral, he made none at the nearby Polish Military Cemetery, which he visited on behalf of a Polish migrant and fellow veterinarian who had fought in the campaign. Instead, he brought home postcards of the memorial park. In these two instances, both photographers focused on the more immediate landscapes of then contemporary and recent Italian history as opposed to those of the distant past.[19]

Nick's 1937 and Enrico's 1957 photographs conform to a large degree to the American tourist's view of Italy. Yet their itineraries and consumption also visualize specifically Italian ethnic sensibilities and Roman Catholic proclivities. Photographing churches did not merely document historical buildings; it also affirmed religious affiliation. This visual assertion is perhaps most evident in the images both men made at the Sanctuary of the Madonna of the Rosary in Pompei, a site of historically fervent popular veneration. Photographs also depict the Sanctuary of the Madonna della Civita in Itri and the procession to St. Michael in Maranola, sites of local religious devotion in the Lazio region that held personal meaning for Anna. In turn, Anna purchased miniature shrines at Pompei and Itri that she kept all her life. But even secular souvenirs the couple brought back—a painted jug from Maranola and a ceramic wall hanging featuring an irreverent adage—suggest the evolving hybrid ethnic identities that the visit helped stimulate.[20]

Framing the Picturesque and Cultural Distancing

Amid the slide trays of Enrico's images made outside of Carunchio, two startling photographs disrupt the repetition of scenic vistas and historical buildings. These images of unknown Italians render the local picturesque, replicating and perpetuating a visual othering. Dean MacCannell characterizes sightseeing as a "ritual performed to the differentiations of society," the tourist's attraction to people and places signifying an authenticity that establishes a distancing of the viewer from people deemed economically, culturally, and politically different. The tourist's exoticizing gaze searches for local color to confirm a desired unique experience, and the photograph offers a "truth marker," validating the encounter with the "real." For the visiting urban Italian American, such experiences and reproductions confirmed and enhanced the photographers' positions as modern cosmopolitans distanced from their former selves.[21]

Figure 9.10. Two boys in Naples, 1957. Color slide original. Photograph courtesy of the author.

The first image (in a tray marked "Naples and environs") is a portrait of two boys posing in a congested cityscape. The thin children are barefoot and clothed in matching bathing suits (or perhaps simply underwear; see figure 9.10). Their ribs are notably visible, their legs marked with scrapes, their feet dirty. They stand at a metal pole in a comradely shoulder embrace. This singular snapshot, out of a series of near peopleless touristic landscapes, depicts a classic Neapolitan type, that of *scugnizzi* (street urchins), a subject of local color and "plebeian street scenes" long established in paintings, photography, and film. It serves as a cultural marker, an authentication of uniqueness of place, situating the photographer's presence in a specific milieu. No proceeding or following image provides context for this photographic moment. The image suggests Enrico's position as an (Italian) American tourist, one with the means to travel through an Italy still contending with the war's aftereffects.[22]

The second image contrasts the premodern and modern, revealing the photographer's sensibilities (see figure 9.11). On a sidewalk in the foreground, a man wearing a red plaid shirt, salmon-colored pants, and a striped knit cap sits astride a miniature donkey festooned with bells and red-and-white ribbons. To his left, a green Fiat 600 is parked on the side of the road. My mother sits on the passenger side. The background consists of a mountainous wall of rock on which a placard advertises a Sorrento campground. It is possible that the man was a sort of a living advertisement pointing with his mallet to the campsite sign. Like the image of the two boys, this photograph documents an encounter made along Enrico and Anna's driving expedition. One can easily imagine Enrico sighting the man on the side of the road and stopping abruptly to pop out of the car to take a photograph. The juxtaposition of the car's green and the man's reddish hues accentuates the two transportation modes—the new fastback sedan introduced in 1955 and the agres-

Figure 9.11. The modern and agrarian juxtaposed on the road to Sorrento, 1957. Color slide original. Photograph courtesy of the author.

Figure 9.12. Enrico Sciorra's sister Gloria (center) and other girls preparing food outdoors, Carunchio, 1937. Photograph courtesy of the author.

tic work animal. This somewhat comical image validates the couple's presence as cosmopolitan tourists themselves just a few years removed from agrarian existence.

While Nick's 1937 collection does not exhibit the intentional featuring of strangers outside Carunchio, a visual othering is evident in his depictions of some family members. One example is an image of nine girls—several identifiable as relatives—standing around an outdoor table who, temporarily stopping their work, peer at the camera (see figure 9.12). At the center, rolling dough, is Nick's niece Gloria, an apron covering her black mourning clothing. Around her, others hold kitchen utensils such as plates and a mortar and pestle. The image has an ethnographic quality to it, as if documenting a quaint rural practice. Like Enrico's images of *scugnizzi* and the donkey rider, it is an emblem of a premodern Italy, one remembered from the returning migrant's recent past life but no longer part of his urban American self. Its symbolic import of Italian rural practices in an American context profoundly evokes the image maker's rendering of his hometown, seventeen years after his departure.

Figure 9.13. Anna Sciorra, a model of her past and present selves, Maranola, 1957. Color slide original. Photograph courtesy of the author.

The most intriguing of the picturesque images are two of Anna in her hometown—former and current lives portrayed in a single photograph (see figure 9.13). In a full-body portrait, Anna stands erect with a decorated two-handled terracotta jug (*cannata* in the local dialect) balanced on her head. What is arresting is her attire—a short-sleeved white dress with polka dots, a double-strand bead necklace with matching earrings, and open-toe high-heels. She stands on cobblestones; a pile of hay and an olive tree are behind her, and a mountain looms in the background. Anna's urbane elegance amid her hometown's rural setting suggests a fashion photo shoot, an enacted display of male fantasy. But her splayed fingers pressed against the base of jug, the most telling aspect of the image, reveal her familiarity with the work of transporting water, muscle memory called back into action in the snapshot's staged performance, knowledge not erased after seven years abroad.[23]

Diasporic Visual Futures

Writing on diasporic visual culture, Nicholas Mirzoeff, citing Homi Bhabha's work on hybrid identities, says migrant subjectivities emerge not solely in an engagement with the past but also in the "creation of multiple diaspora futures, futures forged from memory and experience but not dependent on them." Framed in this way, the diasporic image operates continually at a past–present–future intersection, incipient objects constantly being reinterpreted and remade. Nick's and Enrico's Italian images were created at the crossroads of their Italian pasts and their present lives in the United States. These images were not static; they involved display and narration and constant reseeing and retelling as they and their makers moved into the future. The photos collectively produced an "intervisuality . . . of multiple visual and intellectual associations," bridging multiple temporal and spatial spheres while recalibrating and reimagining migrant selves.[24]

These images were not confined to Nick and Enrico but always involved an expansive audience of family, *paesani*, friends, neighbors, and sometimes strangers. Duplicates were mailed back to Italy and displayed in a photo album and as part of domestic slideshows. For the next generation, including my siblings and me, the images took on different meanings that contributed to knowledge of distant relatives and antecedents and of Italian life and culture. Over the years, they have been touchstones of conveyed memory, instilled belonging, and emotional connection to others beyond our immediate world. In a revealing example, copies of Nick's 1937 photograph of a desolate Pompeiian street now hang in the homes of all of Enrico and Anna's four children, a testimony to its lingering influence and appreciation. The multiple viewings and accompanying narrations contributed to an ethnic awareness, diasporic sensibilities, and subsequent Italian visits. Their influence is evident in my own reclamation of the subject matter for this scholarly inquiry and my renewed interpretation, which is in part an effort to stem the tide of family memory loss and the conceivable abandonment of these cultural objects to flea-market piles of curios. For now, these snapshots of return continue to retain historical grounding and familial relevance and make a small but not insignificant contribution to our understanding of Italian mobility and diasporic visual culture.[25]

Acknowledgments

I wish to thank those who reviewed drafts of this article and offered their invaluable comments, helping improve the work significantly: Giorgio Bertellini, Siân Gibby, Loredana Polezzi, Laura E. Ruberto, Joan Saverino, Pasquale Verdicchio, the editors Kevin Kenny and Maddalena Marinari, and my fellow contributors to this book, who offered their insightful comments during a workshop organized at Glucksman Ireland House, New York University, in May 2023. I am grateful to my cousin Mariapina Farina and to Kathleen Valentine and Vittorio Romano Valentini for providing aspects of family and Carunchiese history, Megi Abazaj for transcribing family letters, and Rosangela Briscese and Peter Mantione for their work on the digitized images.

Epilogue

KEVIN KENNY AND MADDALENA MARINARI

In Matteo Garrone's *Io Capitano* (2023), Seydou and Moussa, two Senegalese teenagers, decide to leave Dakar for Italy. In a final, desperate attempt, Seydou's mother begs him to stay, but he decides to leave, hoping to escape poverty and give his family a better life. Before leaving, Seydou and Moussa visit a local holy man who tells them they must go to the local cemetery to seek their ancestors' blessing. They then depart on their arduous journey without telling their families. Garrone's film powerfully captures how migration today has become much more dangerous, less predictable, and more violent. Racism suffuses every step of Seydou and Moussa's journey. At the same time, the film shows how people on the move continue to exorcise fear on the eve of departure, make sense of uncertainty during their journey, and find hope on arrival.[1]

Many of today's rituals of migration are reminiscent of earlier Irish and Italian practices. Like Italian immigrants celebrating their hometowns' patron saints during festas in their new countries, for example, thousands of Shia Muslims meet in the streets of present-day Copenhagen to take part in the annual procession of Ashura. Like the Italian women who were left behind at the turn of the twentieth century, many Indian women today, to quote a *New York Times* report in 2023, feel abandoned "by men working overseas, leaving them trapped in their in-laws' homes and often defrauded of dowry money." Overall, though, women are much more likely to emigrate today than a century ago and, especially among the undocumented women, are often the breadwinners, reluctantly leaving family behind. New kinds of migration are also emerging, triggered by climate change, religious and ethnic conflicts, and corrupt or oppressive political regimes. Migrant journeys are becoming harder and deadlier, particularly for refugees, asylum seekers, and the undocumented. Deportation and removal are also much more common than in the past, causing untold hardships and pain and often leading to family separation. These kinds of migration have their own grim rites of passage.[2]

As in the past, migrants today continue to carry objects with them that provide security, comfort, and hope. The Undocumented Migration Project captures the continued importance of these objects—including love letters, rosaries, spices, Bibles, family photographs, and diaries—amid journeys far more perilous than those endured by earlier Italian or Irish migrants. Because Europeans did not need passports or visas to enter the United States until World War I, most Irish and Italian immigrants faced far fewer restrictions than migrants do today. With barriers to international mobility higher than ever before, migrants carefully collect, store, and carry documents that can determine their future and their chances of gaining entry and seeking refuge. As the lines among economic migrants, refugees, and asylum seekers continue to blur, migrants bring with them special pouches to protect their passports, identification cards, birth certificates, vaccination records, driver's licenses, and marriage certificates, clinging to the hope that these documents could make admission and acceptance more likely. Because most migrants today are people of color, they also face barriers to acceptance higher than either of the groups explored in this book. At the same time, new technologies and cheaper travel make it easier to remain connected to family and friends back home.[3]

We chose to focus in this book on the Italians and the Irish, two of the largest migrant groups in modern history, in the hope that scholars and students of other migrant groups might find our approach suggestive. Amid a global resurgence of xenophobic attacks against migrants and intensified efforts to curtail human mobility, *Rituals of Migration* places migrants and their families front and center. Focusing on rituals uncovers aspects of the migrant experience that might otherwise go unnoticed. We hope this book will inspire similar studies of other migrant groups, both past and present.

ACKNOWLEDGMENTS

Kevin Kenny would like to thank Owen Crocitto Kenny for reading a draft of the Introduction, as well as Rosanna Crocitto Kenny, Michael Crocitto Kenny, Prasannan Parthasarathi, and Virginia Reinburg for their comments on various aspects of the project. Maddalena Marinari wishes to thank her families on both sides of the Atlantic for their support and good cheer throughout her work on this volume. We are also very grateful to Nick Wolf for his expert editing and advice, Peter Hession for his work on the bibliography, Clara Platter, Ainee Jeong, and Brianna Jean at New York University Press, and all the contributors. The opportunity to hold a workshop at Glucksman Ireland House at New York University helped us frame the book and created a vibrant sense of intellectual community as we all worked together on *Rituals of Migration*.

NOTES

INTRODUCTION

1 Maria Messina, *Piccoli gorghi* (Palermo: Sellerio Editore, 1997); Maria Messina, *Behind Closed Doors: Her Father's House and Other Stories of Sicily*, translated with an introduction by Elise Magistro (New York: Feminist Press of the City University of New York, 2007); Máirtín Ó Cadhain, *The Road to Brightcity*, translated with an introduction by Eoghan Ó Tuairisc (Dublin: Poolbeg Press, 1981); *Rocco e i suoi fratelli* (*Rocco and His Brothers*), directed by Luchino Visconti, Italy, 1960; *Nuovomondo* (*Golden Door*), directed by Emanuel Crialese, (Italy/USA, 2006); *The Field*, directed by Jim Sheridan, Ireland, 1990. The success and critical acclaim of *Minari* (2020), a movie about a Korean American family moving to an Arkansas farm, and of *Crying in H-Mart*, a memoir about the author's efforts to reconnect with her Korean heritage in the wake of a family tragedy, shows the power that migration retains in film and literature. *Minari*, directed by Lee Isaac Chung, United States, 2020; *Crying in H-Mart* (New York: Knopf, 2021).

2 On theories of ritual, see notes 11, 12, and 13 below. On migration rituals, see Marianne Hold Pedersen and Mikkel Rytter, "Rituals of Migration, an Introduction," *Journal of Ethnic and Migration Studies* 44, no. 16 (2018), 2603–16; Elaine Chase, Nando Sigona, and Dawn Chatty, eds., *Becoming Adult on the Move: Migration Journeys, Encounters and Life Transitions* (Cham, Switzerland: Palgrave Macmillan, 2023). We discovered Pedersen and Rytter's article, the introduction to a special issue, about two years into our project, after we had edited the first drafts of the chapters in this book. The six ethnographic articles in the special issue examine formal religious rituals—a theme we do not focus on—among Christian, Hindu, and Muslim immigrants in contemporary Scandinavia. The collection edited by Chase, Sigona, and Chatty consists of sociological, anthropological, and policy articles that examine young immigrants from Afghanistan, Albania, Eritrea, and Vietnam in the contemporary United Kingdom and, to a lesser extent, the European Union (especially Italy), revealing the importance of migration in the transition to adulthood in both the sending and the receiving countries.

3 Hasia Diner, *Hungering for America: Italian, Irish, and Jewish Foodways in the Age of Migration* (Cambridge, MA: Harvard University Press, 2003); Simone Cinotto, *The Italian American Table: Food, Family, and Community in New York City* (Champaign: University of Illinois Press, 2013); Donna Gabaccia, *We are What We Eat: Ethnic Food and the Making of Americans* (Cambridge, MA: Harvard University Press, 2000); Robert Orsi, *The Madonna of 115th Street: Faith and Community in Italian Harlem,*

1880–1950 (New Haven: Yale University Press, 1988). On rites of passage, see note 12 below.

4 Piero Bevilacqua, Andreina De Clementi, and Emilio Franzina, eds., *Storia dell'emigrazione italiana: Partenze* (Rome: Donzelli Editore, 2001).

5 Donna Gabaccia, *Italy's Many Diasporas* (London: UCL Press, 2000); Piero Bevilacqua, Andreina De Clementi, and Emilio Franzina, eds., *Storia dell'emigrazione italiana: Arrivi* (Rome: Donzelli Editore, 2002); Donna R. Gabaccia and Fraser M. Ottanelli, *Italian Workers of the World: Labor Migration and the Formation of Multiethnic States* (Urbana: University of Illinois Press, 2005); Linda Reeder, *Widows in White: Migration and the Transformation of Rural Italian Women, Sicily, 1880–1920* (Toronto: University of Toronto Press, 2003); Danielle Battisti, *Whom We Shall Welcome: Italian Americans and Immigration Reform, 1945–1965* (New York: Fordham University Press, 2019); Thomas Guglielmo, *White on Arrival: Italians, Race, Color, and Power in Chicago, 1890–1945* (New York: Oxford University Press, 2000); Maddalena Marinari, *Unwanted: Italian and Jewish Mobilization against Restrictive Immigration Laws, 1882–1965* (Chapel Hill: University of North Carolina Press, 2020); Samuel L. Baily, *Immigrants in the Lands of Promise: Italians in Buenos Aires and New York City, 1870–1914* (Ithaca: Cornell University Press, 1999); Mark I. Choate, *Emigrant Nation: The Making of Italy Abroad* (Cambridge, MA: Harvard University Press, 2008); Roberta Pergher, *Mussolini's Nation-Empire: Sovereignty and Settlement in Italy's Borderlands, 1922–1943* (Cambridge: Cambridge University Press, 2017).

6 Laura Ruberto and Joseph Sciorra, eds., *New Italian Migrations to the United States*, 2 vols, vol. 1: *Politics and History since 1945*, vol. 2: *Art and Culture since 1945* (Champaign: University of Illinois Press, 2017); Bevilacqua, De Clementi, and Franzina, eds., *Storia dell'emigrazione italiana*; Marinari, *Unwanted*, 98–150; Sandro Rinauro, *Il cammino della speranza: L'emigrazione clandestina degli italiani nel secondo dopoguerra* (Turin: Giulio Einaudi Editore, 2009); Michele Colucci, *Storia dell'immigrazione straniera in Italia. Dal 1945 ai giorni nostri* (Bologna: Carocci Editore, 2018); Eleanor Paynter, "Creating Crises: Risk, Racialization, and the Migration-Security Nexus in Italy and the US," in *Managing Migration in Italy and the United States*, ed. Lauren Braun-Strumfels, Maddalena Marinari, and Daniele Fiorentino (Berlin: DeGruyter, 2023), 55–78; Tony Paganoni, "Italian Emigration after the Second World War," *International Migration Review* 37 (January 2003), Supplement: 85–96; "Italiani all'estero, sempre più giovani e settentrionali," *La Repubblica*, October 6, 2015, www.repubblica.it, Stefano Casini, "Sono circa 80 million glib oriundi italiani nel mondo," *Gente d'Italia*, February 4, 2020, www.genteditalia.org. The number of Italians abroad rose from 3,106,251 in 2006 to 4,636,647 in 2015. See Register of Italian Residents Abroad (AIRE), Ministero degli Affari Esteri e della Cooperazione Internazionale, www.esteri.it.

7 Kevin Kenny, "Irish Emigrations in a Comparative Perspective," in *The Cambridge Social History of Modern Ireland*, ed. Eugenio F. Biagini and Mary Daly (Cambridge: Cambridge University Press, 2017), 405–22.

8 Kerby Miller, *Emigrants and Exiles: Ireland and the Irish Exodus to North America* (New York: Oxford University Press, 1985); Kevin Kenny, "Diaspora and Comparison: The Global Irish as a Case Study," *Journal of American History* 90 (June 2003): 134–62; Donald H. Akenson, *The Irish Diaspora: A Primer* (Dublin: P. D. Meany, 1993); Malcolm Campbell, *Ireland's New Worlds: Immigrants, Politics, and Society in the United States and Australia, 1815–1922* (Madison: University of Wisconsin Press, 2008); Malcolm Campbell, *Ireland's Farthest Shores: Mobility, Migration, and Settlement in the Pacific World* (Madison: University of Wisconsin Press, 2022); David Fitzpatrick, *The Americanisation of Ireland: Migration and Settlement, 1841–1925* (Cambridge: Cambridge University Press, 2020).

9 Kevin Kenny, "Irish Emigration, ca. 1845–1900," in *The Cambridge History of Ireland*, 4 vols, gen. ed., Thomas Bartlett, *Vol. 3. 1730–1880*, ed. James Kelly (Cambridge: Cambridge University Press, 2018); David Fitzpatrick, *Irish Emigration, 1801–1921* (Dundalk: Economic and Social History Society of Ireland, 1984), 7–8, 11; Miller, *Emigrants and Exiles*, 345–554.

10 Kenny, "Irish Emigration, ca. 1845–1900," 681; Miller, *Emigrants and Exiles*, 380–402; Arnold Schrier, *Ireland and the American Emigration, 1850–1900* (Minneapolis: University of Minnesota Press, 1958), 105; Fitzpatrick, *Irish Emigration, 1801–1921*, 37–41; J. H. Senner, "Immigration from Italy," *North American Review* 162 (1896): 649–57.

11 Emile Durkheim, *The Elementary Forms of Religious Life*, trans. Karen E. Fields (*Les formes élémentaires de la vie réligieuse*, 1912; New York: Free Press, 1995); Barry Stephenson, *Ritual: A Very Short Introduction* (Oxford: Oxford University Press, 2015), 1–3, 7–8; David I. Kertzer, *Ritual, Politics, and Power* (New Haven, CT: Yale University Press, 1989); Robbie Davis-Floyd and Charles D. McLaughlin, *Ritual: What It Is, How It Works, and Why* (New York: Berghahn Books, 2022).

12 Arnold Van Gennep, *The Rites of Passage*, 2nd ed., trans. Monika B. Vizedom and Gabrielle L. Caffee (Chicago: University of Chicago Press, 2019), 15–20, 25, 28, 35–36.

13 Van Gennep, *The Rites of Passage*; Barbara M. Myerhoff, "Rites of Passage: Process and Paradox," in *Celebration: Studies in Festivity and Ritual*, ed. Victor Turner (Washington, DC: Smithsonian Institute Press, 1982), 109–35; Victor and Edith Turner, "Religious Celebrations," in Turner, ed., *Celebration*, 202–03; Stephenson, *Ritual*, 42, 54–59, 76, 87, 95, 99; Daniel de Coppet, ed., *Understanding Rituals* (London: Routledge, 2022), 12–15, 18. Van Gennep criticized Durkheim for depicting aboriginal societies as simple and unevolved on the basis of miscellaneous written accounts rather than fieldwork (and was ostracized by Durkheim and his nephew, Marcel Mauss, as a result) but proceeded to use similarly eclectic sources in his own depictions of "semi-civilized" societies.

14 Leonie Hannan and Sarah Longair, *History through Material Culture* (Manchester: University of Manchester Press, 2017), 1 (quote), 6, 29; Laura Auslander, "Beyond Words," *American Historical Review* 110 (October 2005), 1017–19; Anne Gerritsen and Giorgio Riello, eds., *Writing Material Culture History*, 2nd ed. (London: Bloomsbury Academic, 2021), 3–5, 8–10, 13; Harvey Green, "Cultural History and

the Material(s) Turn," *Cultural History* 1, no. 1 (2012), 61–62, 77; Tiya Miles, *All That She Carried: The Journey of Ashley's Sack, a Black Family Keepsake* (New York: Random House, 2021), 16; Daniel Miller, *Stuff* (London: Polity Press, 2010); James Deetz, *In Small Things Forgotten: An Archaeology of Early American Life* (New York: Knopf, 1996); Laura Ruberto and Joseph Sciorra, "Italian American Stuff: A Survey of Material Culture, Migration, and Ethnicity," *SOAR: The Society of Americanists Review* 3 (2021–2022): 1–84.

15 On frog bread, see chapter 1 in this volume by Bernadette Whelan.

16 Máirtín Ó Cadhain, "The Year 1912," *Irish Pages* 2. The Earth Issue (Autumn/Winter, 2004): 255–67 (quotes 255).

17 Ó Cadhain, "The Year 1912," 256, 262–63.

18 Annette B. Weiner and Jane Schneider, eds., *Cloth and Human Experience* (Washington, DC: Smithsonian Institution Press, 1989), 2–3, 25; Jane Schneider, "Trousseau as Treasure: Some Contradictions of Late Nineteenth-Century Change in Sicily," in *Beyond the Myths of Culture: Essays in Cultural Materialism*, ed. Eric B. Ross (San Francisco: Academic Press, 1980); Sophie Cooper, "Something Borrowed: Women, Limerick Lace and Community Heirlooms in the Australian Irish Diaspora," *Social History* 45, no. 3 (2020): 304–27; Miles, *All That She Carried*, 14–16. Cloth is also a common metaphor for society, as in references to the social fabric or the connecting threads of social relations.

19 Adam McKeown, "Ritualization of Regulation: The Enforcement of Chinese Exclusion in the United States and China," *American Historical Review* 108 (April 2003): 377–403; Amy L. Fairchild, *Science at the Borders: Immigrant Medical Inspection and the Shaping of the Modern Industrial Labor Force* (Baltimore: Johns Hopkins University Press, 2003).

20 William Ian Miller, "Getting a Fix on Violence," in William Ian Miller, *Humiliation and Other Essays on Honor, Social Discomfort, and Violence* (Ithaca and London: Cornell University Press, 1993), 53–92; McKeown, "Ritualization of Regulation."

21 On return migration as a form of secular pilgrimage, see Loretta Baldassar, "The Return Visit as Pilgrimage: Secular Redemption and Cultural Renewal in the Migration Process," in *The Australian Immigrant in the Twentieth Century: Searching Neglected Sources*, ed. Eric Richards and Jacqueline Templeton (Canberra: Division of Historical Studies and Centre for Immigration and Multicultural Studies, Research School of Social Sciences, Australian National University, 1998), 127–56.

I. LEAVING FOR AMERICA

1 National Folklore Collection (hereafter NFC), University College Dublin (hereafter UCD), MS 1410, Mícheál Mac Éinrí, Barony of Erris, County Mayo, 35.

2 Patrick J. Duffy, "Assisted Emigration from the Shirley Estate, 1843–54," *Clogher Record*, 14:2 (1992): 7–62.

3 Harriet Martineau, *Letters from America* (London: John Chapman, 1852), 60–61.

4 Quoted in Anne O'Connell, "Assisted Female Emigration: Vere Foster's Scheme, 1880–1896" (PhD thesis, University of Limerick, 1998), 78; Arnold Schrier, *Ireland and the American Emigration, 1850–1900* (Wymossing, PA: Dufour Editions, 1997), 151; Peig Sayers, *Peig* (1935; Dublin: Comhleacht Oideachas na hÉireann, 2003), 123, 165.

5 Friends Historical Library, Dublin, Ireland, "Journal of Margaret Boyle Harvey, 1786–1832," 26; *Reports of the Immigration Commission. Volume 1. Abstracts of Reports of the Immigration Commission* (New York: Arno and the New York Times, 1970), 590, 591.

6 NFC, UCD, MS 1410, Mícheál Mac Éinrí, Barony of Erris, County Mayo, 30.

7 NFC, UCD, School Radharc na Céile, roll no. 14156, "Famine Times," Collector Eileen Curtin, 152–53, www.duchas.ie/en/cbes/4921989/4915814/4945904 (accessed January 20, 2023).

8 Ulster American Folk Museum, Northern Ireland (hereafter UAFM), *Bad Bridget Exhibition*; NFC, UCD, MS 1407 Munster Tadhg Ó Murchadha, An Coiréan, Co. Chiarraí, 6–7. See Vere Foster, *Work and Wages; or, the Penny Emigrant's Guide to the United States for Female Servants, Laborers, Mechanics, Farmers, &c.*, 6th ed. (London: W. and F. G. Cash, 1855); Alex. J. Peyton, *The Emigrant's Friend; or Hints on Emigration to the United States of America Addressed to the People of Ireland* (Cork: J. O'Brien, 1853), 8–9.

9 M. A. Cusack, *Advice to Irish Girls in America* (New York: J. A. McGee, 1876), 12–13.

10 NFC, UCD, MS 1409, Ciarán Bairéad, County Galway, 121; NFC, UCD, MS 1407, Tadhg Ó Murchadha, An Coiréan, Co. Chiarraí, 10.

11 NFC, UCD, MS 1408, Transcription in Matthew Byrne, Edenderry, Co. Offaly, pp. 169–71; Sullivan Beara Collection, Special Collections, University College Cork, Denis O'Sullivan to "Dear friends," April 20, 1876.

12 *Reports of the Immigration Commission. Volume 1*, 182; Asenath Nicholson, *Ireland's Welcome to the Stranger: On an Excursion through Ireland in 1844 & 1845, for the Purpose of Personally Investigating the Condition of the Poor* (New York: Bakker and Scrivner, 1847), 88, 334–35; US State Department, National Archives and Records Administration, US, US Cork vol. 9, roll 9, T196, Enclosure in Piatt to Davis, July 20, 1884; NFC, UCD, MS 1408, Transcription in Matthew Byrne, Edenderry, Co. Offaly, 169–71; Sullivan Beara Collection, Special Collections, University College Cork, Denis O'Sullivan to "Dear friends," April 20, 1876; NFC, UCD, MS 1407, Tadhg Ó Murchadha, An Coiréan, Co. Chiarraí, 3.

13 New York Public Library, Emigrant Savings Bank Records, reel 59, Report of Agent at Ellis Island for May, September, November 1927.

14 Ulster Folk Museum, Northern Ireland, list of objects considered for inclusion in *Bad Bridget Exhibition*; NFC, UCD, MS 1407, Tadhg Ó Murchadha, An Coiréan, Co. Chiarraí, 35; Joseph Guinan, *Scenes and Sketches in an Irish Parish, or Priest and People of Doon by a Country Curate*, 3rd ed. (Dublin: M. H. Gill, 1903), 35.

15 Ulster-American Folk Park Museum, Northern Ireland, "The Presbyterian Meeting House Mountjoy Exhibition Notice"; NFC, UCD, MS 1411, Mrs. John Byrne, Malin Town, Co. Donegal to Conall C. O'Beirn, Co. Donegal, 227.

16 See many references to these terms in NFC, UCD, MS 1407–11, particularly Conall C. O'Beirn, Co. Donegal, MS 1411, 43.

17 Guinan, *Scenes and Sketches*, 35; Fr. Albert Bibby, OFSC, "American Wake," October–December 1906, available at Capuchin Archives, "An 'American Wake,' County Galway, 1906," *Facebook*, July 25, 2019, www.facebook.com/Capuchin-ArchivesIreland/posts/an-american-wake-county-galway-1906a-reference-to-the-practice-of-the-american-w/2310472839043495; NFC, UCD, MS 1407, Tadhg Ó Murchadha, An Coiréan, Co. Chiarraí, 10; NFC, UCD, MS 1409, Ciarán Bairéad, Co. Galway, 6, 61; NFC, UCD, MS 1410, Mícheál Mac Éinrí, Barony of Erris, Co. Mayo, 32.

18 Martineau, *Letters from America*, 140–41. Wakes could also be occasions of violence. See *Ballina Herald*, June 19, 1930.

19 NFC, UCD, MS 1407, Tadhg Ó Murchadha, An Coiréan, Co. Chiarraí, 8–9, 311; NFC, UCD, MS 1409, Ciarán Bairéad, Co. Galway, 7; NFC, UCD, MS 1408, Matthew Byrne, Edenderry, Co. Offaly, 9; NFC, UCD, MS 1410, Mícheál Mac Éinrí, Barony of Erris, Co. Mayo, 116; NFC, UCD, MS 1411, Conall C. O'Beirn, Co. Donegal, 90; NFC, UCD, MS 1409, Ciarán Bairéad, County Galway, 49–50; NFC, UCD, The Schools Collection, Cnuicín na hAbhann, www.duchas.ie (accessed September 19, 2022); Tomás Ó Criomhthain, *Allagar na hInise* (Baile Átha Cliath: An Gúm, 1997), 34–35.

20 NFC, UCD, The Schools Collection, Tobar Pádraig, Patrickswell, Co. Limerick, roll no. 4764, informant Thomas Mahony, 110, www.duchas.ie (accessed September 19, 2022); NFC, UCD, MS 1410, Mícheál Mac Éinrí, Barony of Erris, Co. Mayo, 201; NFC, UCD, MS 1407, Tadhg Ó Murchadha, An Coiréan, Co. Chiarraí, 9–10, 11, 12; NFC, UCD, MS 1409, Ciarán Bairéad, Co. Galway, 6, 7, 76, 77, 121; NFC, UCD, MS 1407, Tadhg Ó Murchadha, An Coiréan, Co. Chiarraí, 11; NFC, UCD, MS 1410, Mícheál Mac Éinrí, Barony of Erris, Co. Mayo, 32, 35, 86, 115, 117; NFC, UCD, MS 1407, Tadhg Ó Murchadha, An Coiréan, Co. Chiarraí, 330; NFC, UCD, MS 1409, Ciarán Bairéad, Co. Galway, 47; NFC, UCD, MS 1411, Conall C. O'Beirn, Co. Donegal, 90.

21 University of Limerick Oral History Project, 2001. For more on the project, see Bernadette Whelan, "The 'Idea of America' in the New Irish State, 1922–1960," in *The Irish in the Atlantic World*, ed. David T. Gleeson (Columbia: University of South Carolina Press, 2013), 76–109.

22 NFC, UCD, MS 1410, Mícheál Mac Éinrí, Barony of Erris, Co. Mayo, 201; NFC, UCD, MS 1407, Tadhg Ó Murchadha, An Coiréan, Co. Chiarraí, 9–10, 11, 12; NFC, UCD, MS 1409, Ciarán Bairéad, Co. Galway, 6, 7, 76, 77, 121; NFC, UCD, MS 1407, Tadhg Ó Murchadha, An Coiréan, Co. Chiarraí, 11; NFC, UCD, MS 1410, Mícheál Mac Éinrí, Barony of Erris, Co. Mayo, 32, 35, 86, 115, 117; NFC, UCD, MS 1407, Tadhg Ó Murchadha, An Coiréan, Co. Chiarraí, 330; NFC, UCD, MS 1409,

Ciarán Bairéad, Co. Galway, 47; NFC, UCD, MS 1411, Conall C. O'Beirn, Co. Donegal, 90.

2. LA PARTENZA

1 Angelo Mosso, *Vita moderna degli italiani* (Milan: Fratelli Treves, 1912), 11–12; Salvatore Salomone-Marino, *Customs and Habits of the Sicilian Peasants*, edited and translated by Rosalie N. Norris (Rutherford, NJ: Fairleigh Dickinson University Press, 1981), 207–15.

2 The sense of loss comes through clearly in letters. See Sonia Cancian, *Families, Lovers, and Their Letters: Italian Postwar Migration to Canada* (Winnipeg: University of Manitoba Press, 2010); Sonia Cancian, *With Your Words in My Hands: The Letters of Antonietta Petris and Loris Palma* (Montreal: McGill-Queen's Press, 2021).

3 Linda Reeder, *Widows in White: Migration and the Transformation of Rural Italian Women, Sicily, 1880–1920* (Toronto: University of Toronto Press, 2003); Donna Gabaccia et al., eds., *Gender and Migration Revisited* (New York: Center for Migration Studies, 2006); Marlou Schrover and Eileen Yeo, eds., *Gender, Migration, and the Public Sphere, 1850–2005* (New York: Routledge, 2010); Katharine M. Donato and Donna R. Gabaccia, *Gender and International Migration* (New York: Russell Sage Foundation, 2015); Caroline B. Brettell, *Gender and Migration* (Hoboken, NJ: John Wiley & Sons, 2017).

4 Marcelo J. Borges, Sonia Cancian, and Linda Reeder, eds., *Emotional Landscapes: Love, Gender, and Migration* (Urbana: University of Illinois Press, 2021); Loretta Baldassar and Donna R. Gabaccia, *Intimacy and Italian Migration: Gender and Domestic Lives in a Mobile World* (New York: Fordham University Press, 2011).

5 Meridee L. Bailey and Katie Barclay, eds., *Emotion, Ritual and Power in Europe, 1200–1920: Family, State and Church* (Cham, Switzerland: Springer International Publishing, 2021), 4–5.

6 Bailey and Barclay, *Emotion, Ritual and Power*, 1; Katie Barclay, *Love, Intimacy and Power: Marriage and Patriarchy in Scotland, 1650–1850* (Manchester: Manchester University Press, 2014), 2.

7 Broughton Brandenburg, "Imported Americans: The Overflow," *Frank Leslie's Popular Monthly* 57, no. 4 (February 1904), 408–9.

8 Istat, *Serie Storiche*, Popolazione, "Espatri e rimpatri per regione e ripartizione geografica—Anni 1876–2014." The South reported a 40 percent overall return rate between 1905 and 1915.

9 Maria Messina, "Le Scarpette," *Piccoli gorghi*, repr. ed. (Palermo: Sellerio Editore, 1988), 138–44. The original was published in 1911.

10 Charlotte Gower Chapman, *Milocca: A Sicilian Village* (London: Allen and Unwin, 1973); Vito Teti, "Noti sui comportamenti delle donne sole degli 'americani' durante la prima emigrazione in Calabria," *Studi Emigrazione* 24 (1987): 13–46.

11 Messina, "La Mèrica, 1911," *Piccoli gorghi*, 127–37.

12 Linda Reeder, "Men of Honor and Honorable Men: Migration and Italian Migration to the United States from 1880–1930," *Italian Americana* 28, no. 1 (2010): 18–35; Chapman, *Milocca*, 108.

13 Dino Taruffi, Leonello de Nobili, and Pasquale Villari, *La questione agraria e l'emigrazione in Calabria: Note statistiche ed economiche* (Florence: G. Barbèra, 1908), 878–79; Giovanni Lorenzoni, *Inchiesta parlamentare sulle condizioni dei contadini nelle province meridionali e nella Sicilia.* Vol. 6/1/2 (Rome: Tip. Naz. G. Bertero, 1910), 309–10, 362; Francesco Coletti, *Dell' emigrazione italiana* (Milan: Hoepli, 1912), 250.

14 Paolo Orano, "Per una psicologia del popolo Italiano," *Rivista politica e letteraria* (Rome: Stab. Tip. della Tribuna, 1900), 135; Chapman, *Milocca.*

15 Messina, "Nonna Lidda," *Piccoli gorghi,* 145–58.

16 Taruffi, de Nobili, and Villari, *La questione agraria,* 842.

17 Anthony Mangano, "Effect of Emigration upon Italy," *Charities and the Commons: A Weekly Journal of Philanthropy and Social Advance* 9 (January 4, 1908): 1337.

18 Taruffi, de Nobili, and Villari, *La questione agraria,* 841.

19 Angelo Mosso, "Gli Emigranti," *Nuova antologia di lettere, scienze ed arti* (Rome: Direzione della Nuova Antologia, 1905), 202.

20 Jane Schneider, ed., *Italy's "Southern Question": Orientalism in One Country* (New York: Berg, 1998); Silvana Patriarca, *Numbers and Nationhood: Writing Statistics in Nineteenth-Century Italy* (Cambridge: Cambridge University Press, 2003); Nelson Moe, *The View from Vesuvius: Italian Culture and the Southern Question* (Berkeley: University of California Press, 2006).

21 Alfredo Niceforo, *Italiani del nord e italiani del sud* (Turin: Fratelli Bocca, 1901), 148–49, 293–352; Chapman, *Milocca*; Alfredo Niceforo, *L'Italia barbara contemporanea: Studi ed appunti* (Milan and Palermo: Remo Sandron, 1898); Giuseppe Sergi, *La decadenza delle nazioni latine* (Turin: Fratelli Bocca, 1900), 252–53.

22 Dolores Freda, *Governare i migranti: La legge sull'emigrazione del 1901 e la giurisprudenza del Tribunale di Napoli* (Turin: Giappichelli, 2018); Lauren Braun-Strumfels, *Partners in Gatekeeping: How Italy Shaped US Immigration Policy over Ten Pivotal Years, 1891–1901* (Athens: University of Georgia Press, 2023).

23 Linda Reeder, *Widows in White: Migration and the Transformation of Rural Italian Women, Sicily, 1880–1920* (Toronto: University of Toronto Press, 2003), 72–102.

24 Salvatore Coco, *Sulle macerie di Mascali, memorie della mia vita: Diario di un siciliano emigrato in Argentina (1888–1929)* (independently published, 2018), 93–94; Mosso, *Vita moderna degli italiani*; Amy A. Bernardy, *Italia randagia attraverso gli Stati Uniti* (Turin: Fratelli Bocca, 1913), 1–2.

25 Brandenburg, "Imported Americans," 404.

26 Brandenburg, "Imported Americans," 405.

27 For the importance of food among Italian migrants, see Simone Cinotto, *The Italian American Table: Food, Family, and Community in New York City* (Champaign: University of Illinois Press, 2013); Simone Cinotto, *Making Italian America: Consumer Culture and the Production of Ethnic Identities* (New York: Fordham University Press, 2014).

28 Chapman, *Milocca,* 220.

29 Marcelo J. Borges, "What's Love Got to Do with It? Language of Transnational Affect in the Letters of Portuguese Migrants," in Borges, Cancian, and Reeder, eds., *Emotional Landscapes*, 25–52; Reeder, *Widows in White*, 64–95; Marcelo J. Borges and Sonia Cancian, eds., *Migrant Letters: Emotional Language, Mobile Identities, and Writing Practices in Historical Perspective* (New York: Routledge, 2019).

30 Paolo Bignami, "I partiti politici nelle diverse regioni d'Italia," *Nuova antologia*, Sesta Serie, vol. CCIV (February 16, 1920), 416.

31 Mangano, "Effect of Emigration upon Italy," 1481. For a general discussion of letters see Borges, "What's Love Got to Do with It?," 25–52.

32 Mangano, "Effect of Emigration upon Italy," 1479.

33 On the gendered dimension of transnational migration, see Reeder, *Widows in White*; Victoria Calabrese, *Italian Women in Basilicata: Staying Behind but Moving Forward during the Age of Mass Emigration, 1876–1914* (Lanham, MD: Rowman & Littlefield, 2022).

3. TROUSSEAU TEXTILES

1 "A ritual is a patterned, repetitive, and symbolic enactment of cultural (or individual) beliefs and values." Robbie Davis-Floyd and Charles D. Laughlin, *Ritual: What It Is, How It Works, and Why* (New York: Berghahn, 2022), 6. Rituals surrounding marriage, often elaborate and symbolically complex, vary cross-culturally and change over time.

2 Joan Saverino, "Embroidery as Inscription in the Life of a Calabrian Immigrant Woman," in *Embroidered Stories: Interpreting Women's Domestic Needlework from the Italian Diaspora*, ed. Edvige Giunta and Joseph Sciorra (Jackson: University of Mississippi Press, 2014), 281–312.

3 Jane Schneider, "Of Vigilance and Virgins: Honor, Shame and Access to Resources in Mediterranean Societies," *Ethnology* 10, no. 1 (1971): 18, 22.

4 Anna Maria Ratti, "The Italian Migration Movements," in *International Migrations, Vol. II: Interpretations*, ed. Walter F. Willcox and Imre Ferenczi (Washington, DC: National Bureau of Economic Research, 1931), 440–70.

5 Mario Badagliacca with Derek Duncan, *Italy Is Out* (Liverpool: Liverpool University, 2021), 23, 37, 39, 41, 73; Francesca Canadé Sautman, "Between Divestment and Migration: Clothing Artifacts and Identity among Italian Immigrant Women, 1880s–1920s," *Italian American Review* 8, no. 2 (2018): 157–58.

6 Jane Schneider, "Trousseau as Treasure: Some Contradictions of Late Nineteenth Century Change in Sicily," in *Behind the Myth of Culture*, ed. Eric Ross (New York: Academic Press, 1980), 323–59.

7 Anna and Stan Carbone, interview by Joan Saverino, February 19, 2023.

8 Saverino, fieldnotes, June 19, 2018.

9 Domenico Caruso, personal communication, April 11, 2023.

10 Family genealogy hints at the origin of uncertainties in the provenance card, as discussed below.

11 Gabaccia pieced together the Chicago story of the Bastiani family from census listings and other records compiled from Ancestry.com.
12 Mary Ellen's father, Vincenzo—always called James—Mancina, had emigrated from San Giovanni in Fiore to Minnesota's Iron Range mining district.
13 "Black Parents Demand Bar Sbarboro Principal," *Chicago Tribune* October 28, 1970; Brenda Stone, "Kellberg Must Go," *Chicago Tribune*, August 6, 1972; "Principals: New Victims of Protests," *Chicago Tribune*, February 11, 1973. Batinich saved clippings on the ousters: Mary Ellen Batinich Collection, University of Minnesoota, Minneapolis, MN. Immigration History Research Center, box 40, folder 4, "Sbarboro Ousting Eavesdropping Case 1968–1970."
14 The Casa Italia / Italian Cultural Center website is available at https://casaitaliachicago.org/library-museums.
15 Vittoria Lopez was the mother of Stan Carbone of Winnipeg, Canada. Saverino interviewed Stan and his wife, Anna Girimonte Carbone.
16 Anna and Stan Carbone, interview by Joan Saverino, February 19, 2023. The remainder of this section and all direct quotations are extracted from this interview.
17 Joan Saverino, "*Ozaturù, 'Ncullerata and Rituortu*: Deeply Local Textiles, Identity, and Diasporic Connections," in *Teorizzare la diaspora italiana: Saggi 2017–2020*, ed. Marco Gatto and Annamaria Scorza (Saveria Mannelli: Rubettino, 2021), 117.
18 P. De Simonis, A. Falassi, A. Fornari, S. Guerrini, I. Moretti, and R. Stopani, *Cultura contadina in Toscana* (Florence: Bonechi, 1982–2004); see especially volume 1, *Il lavoro. I prodotti della terra*; volume 2, *La casa. Gli animali*; and volume 3, *Il paesaggio. La vita quotidiana*.
19 Maddalena Tirabassi, "Bourgeois Men, Peasant Women: Rethinking Domestic Work and Morality in Italy," in *Women, Gender, and Transnational Lives: Italian Workers of the World*, ed. Donna Gabaccia and Franca Iacovetta (Toronto: University of Toronto Press, 2002), 109.
20 Tirabassi, "Bourgeois Men, Peasant Women," 109.
21 Email correspondence, Anna Zurzolo, May 17, 2013.

4. SABBATH ON THE OCEAN

1 Samuel Harvey journal, 1849 [hereafter, Harvey journal] (T3258/66/8, 7, 13, 7, 5, Public Record Office of Northern Ireland).
2 Marcus Rediker, *Outlaws of the Atlantic: Sailors, Pirates, and Motley Crews in the Age of Sail* (Boston: Beacon Press, 2014); Michael A. Schoeppner, *Moral Contagion: Black Atlantic Sailors, Citizenship, and Diplomacy in Antebellum America* (Cambridge: Cambridge University Press, 2019); Nicholas Frykman, *The Bloody Flag: Mutiny in the Age of Atlantic Revolution* (Oakland: University of California Press, 2020); David Cressy, *Coming Over: Migration and Communication between England and New England in the Seventeenth Century* (Cambridge: Cambridge University Press, 1987), 145; Stephen R. Berry, *A Path in the Mighty Waters: Shipboard Life and Atlantic Crossings*

to the New World (New Haven: Yale University Press, 2015), 6. The "city afloat" quote appears in *Liverpool Mercury*, April 29, 1853.

3 Harvey journal (T3258/66/1–5, 16). It is worth noting that Samuel Harvey was a certain kind of Protestant: probably Presbyterian. Throughout the seventeenth and eighteenth centuries, Presbyterians were treated as theological dissenters by the Anglican elite and subjected to various sanctions. By the mid-nineteenth century, however, Irish Anglicans and Presbyterians had found common cause in a twin campaign to oppose Roman Catholicism and maintain Ireland's political union with Great Britain.

4 *Sailors' Magazine and Nautical Intelligencer* (London) [hereafter, *Sailors' Magazine* (London)] 9, no. 106 (October 1847): 227; 8, no. 88 (April 1846): 73, 74; 9, no. 107 (November 1847): 253; *Sailor's Magazine and Naval Journal* (New York) [hereafter, *Sailor's Magazine* (New York)] 19, no. 8 (April 1847): 227.

5 John Wiley and George Putnam, *Wiley & Putnam's Emigrant's Guide* (London: Wiley & Putnam, 1845), 66.

6 *Liverpool Mercury*, July 26, 1853; April 29, 1853; *Sailor's Magazine* (New York) 23, no. 3 (November 1850): 92.

7 Harvey journal (T3258/66/13, 3, 7).

8 Harvey journal (T3258/66/6, 8). The Orange Order was a fraternal organization founded in Ireland in 1795, predicated on the belief that Roman Catholicism constituted a threat to the political and constitutional rights granted to Protestants by the Glorious Revolution of 1688.

9 *Sailors' Magazine* (London) 9, no. 97 (January 1847): 21–23.

10 *Sailor's Magazine* (New York) 20, no. 12 (August 1848): 371.

11 *Sailor's Magazine* (New York) 20, no. 12 (August 1848): 371; 27, no. 7 (March 1855): 196–97.

12 *Galway Vindicator*, April 5, 1851; Harvey journal (T3258/66/4); James Duncan diary, 1846–1848 (MssColl 859, New York Public Library).

13 *Sailor's Magazine* (New York) 20, no. 8 (April 1848): 235; 18 no. 6 (February 1846): 171; 18, no. 8 (April 1846): 234; 21, no. 6 (February 1849): 172.

14 Harvey journal (T3258/66/19–20).

15 *Sailor's Magazine* (New York) 18, no. 8 (April 1846): 234; 20, no. 8 (April 1848): 233–34.

16 *Sailors' Magazine* (London) 8, no. 87 (March 1846): 46–48; *Emigrant Ship "Washington." Copy of a Letter from Lord Hobart to the Colonial Land and Emigration Commissioners*, 437–38, H.C. 1851 (198), xl. 433.

17 *Sailors' Magazine* (London) 8, no. 87 (March 1846): 46–48; *Emigrant Ship "Washington." Copy of a Letter from Lord Hobart to the Colonial Land and Emigration Commissioners*, 437–38, H.C. 1851 (198), xl. 433; *Sailors' Magazine* (London) 10, no. 109 (January 1848): 7–8. In traditional Irish Catholic "wake" practices, dead bodies were cleaned, dressed, and laid out in their homes for a few days before burial. Friends, family, and neighbors spent that time both praying over the corpse and engaging in social activities that usually included games, storytelling, and singing. For more on

the subject, see Gearóid Ó Crualaoich, "The 'Merry Wake,'" in *Irish Popular Culture, 1650–1850*, ed. James S. Donnelly Jr. and Kerby A. Miller (Dublin: Irish Academic Press, 1999), 173–200.

18 Harvey journal (T3258/66/18).

19 Harvey journal (T3258/66/18, 19, 23).

20 Harvey journal (T3258/66/29, 32).

21 Washington Irving, *The Sketch Book of Geoffrey Crayon, Gent.*, 2 vols. (London: John Murray 1824), 1:7–8.

5. "WILD GIRLS" AT SEA

1 William B. Neville journal, 1848–1849, State Library-New South Wales (hereafter SL-NSW), DLMSQ 148 (CY Reel 3562).

2 William B. Neville journal, 1848–1849, SL-NSW, DLMSQ 148 (CY Reel 3562); George E. Binsted diary, 1848–1849, SL-NSW, DLMS 137 (CY Reel 3562).

3 Virginia Crossman, "The New Ross Workhouse Riot of 1887: Nationalism, Class and the Irish Poor Laws," *Past & Present* 179 (May 2003): 135–58; Anna Clark, "Wild Workhouse Girls and the Liberal Imperial State in Mid-Nineteenth Century Ireland," *Journal of Social History* 39 (Winter 2005): 389–409; Ciara Breathnach, "Even 'Wilder Workhouse Girls,'" *Journal of Imperial and Commonwealth History* 39 (December 2011): 771–94.

4 William Ian Miller, "Getting a Fix on Violence," in *Humiliation and Other Essays on Honor, Social Discomfort, and Violence* (Ithaca and London: Cornell University Press, 1993), 53–92; Adam McKeown, "Ritualization of Regulation: The Enforcement of Chinese Exclusion in the United States and China," *American Historical Review* 108 (April 2003): 377–403.

5 T. W. C. Murdoch, C. Alexander Wood, and Frederic Rogers to Colonial Secretary Earl Grey, May 17, 1848, *Eighth General Report of the Colonial Land and Emigration Commissioners*, pp. 8, 12 [961] [961-II], H.C. 1847–48, xxvi.1, 41; Rebecca Abbott, "The Earl Grey Orphan Scheme, 1848–1850, and the Irish Diaspora in Australia," in *Women and the Great Hunger*, ed. Christine Kinealy, Jason King, and Ciaran O'Reilly (Hamden, CT: Quinnipiac University Press, 2016), 202.

6 Robin F. Haines, *Emigration and the Labouring Poor: Australian Recruitment in Britain and Ireland, 1831–60* (Houndmills, UK: Palgrave Macmillan, 1997), 152–54; Robin F. Haines, "Workhouse to Gangplank: Mobilising Irish Pauper Women and Girls Bound for Australia in the Mid-Nineteenth Century," in *Irish-Australian Studies: Papers Delivered at the Eighth Irish-Australian Conference*, ed. Richard Davis, Jennifer Livett, Anne-Maree Whitaker, and Peter Moore (Sydney: Crossing Press, 1996), 169–70; "Despatch from the Right Honourable Earl Grey to Governor Sir Charles A. Fitz Roy, July 18, 1849, with 5 enclosures," printed in *Barefoot and Pregnant? Irish Famine Orphans in Australia*, documents and register compiled and introduced by Trevor McClaughlin (Melbourne, Australia: The Genealogical Society of Victoria Inc., 1991), 64; Belfast Union Workhouse Minutes, March 17, 1848, Public Records Office of Northern Ireland, BG/7/A/7; Cian T. McMahon, *The Coffin Ship: Life and*

Death at Sea during the Great Irish Famine (New York: New York University Press, 2021), 62; Gerard Moran, *Sending Out Ireland's Poor: Assisted Emigration to North America in the Nineteenth Century* (Dublin: Four Courts Press, 2004), 131.

7   Clark, "Wild Workhouse Girls," 390; McMahon, *Coffin Ship*, 109–10.

8   T. W. Murdoch and Frederic Rogers to Herman Merivale, February 29, 1849, The National Archives (hereafter TNA), CO 201/406; "The Commissioners of Colonial Lands and Emigration to the Under Secretary for the Colonial Department," T. W. Murdoch and Frederic Rogers to Herman Merivale, February 17, 1848, National Archives of Ireland (hereafter NAI), CSORP 1849, Box 1574, O6808; "Memorandum" enclosed with "The Commissioners of Colonial Lands and Emigration to the Under Secretary for the Colonial Department," T. W. Murdoch and Frederic Rogers to Herman Merivale, February 17, 1848, NAI, CSORP 1849, Box 1574, O6808.

9   Report of the Orphan Immigration Committee respecting the Female Orphans who arrived in the "Earl Grey," New South Wales State Archives & Records (hereafter NSW State Archives), 4/4702 (AO Reel 2852). This report was also printed for Parliament. See Enclosure 2 in No. 1: Report of the Orphan Immigration Committee respecting the Female Orphans who arrived in the "Earl Grey," *Emigration. Papers Relative to the Emigration to the Australian Colonies*, 1850 No. 1163, 2–4; Arthur Moore to T. N. Redington, July 14, 1849, TNA, CO 201/423.

10   Arthur Moore to T. N. Redington, July 14, 1849, TNA CO 201/423; William B. Neville journal, 1848–1849, SL-NSW, DLMSQ 148 (CY Reel 3562); Legislative Assembly, New South Wales, *Report from the Select Committee on Irish Female Immigrants* (1858–59).

11   Clark, "Wild Workhouse Girls," 391; Andrew August, "'A Horrible Looking Woman': Female Violence in Late-Victorian East London," *Journal of British Studies* 54 (October 2015), 855, 857–58; William B. Neville journal, 1848–1849, SL-NSW, DLMSQ 148 (CY Reel 3562).

12   "Minutes of Evidence of the Orphan Immigration Committee," October 12, 1848 (Copy), Enclosed with C. Fitz Roy to Earl Grey, December 19, 1848, NAI, CSORP, Box 1574, O9048.

13   "Minutes of Evidence of the Orphan Immigration Committee," October 12, 1848 (Copy), Enclosed with C. Fitz Roy to Earl Grey, December 19, 1848, NAI, CSORP, Box 1574, O9048.

14   "Report of the Immigration Board on the complaints recorded by the Surgeon Superintendent of the Ship *Digby* against the Master of that Vessel, respecting his treatment of the Passengers during the Voyage," NSW State Archives, 4/4702 (AO Reel 2852); William B. Neville journal, 1848–1849, SL-NSW, DLMSQ 148 (CY Reel 3562); George E. Binsted diary, 1848–1849, SL-NSW, DLMS 137 (CY Reel 3562).

15   William B. Neville journal, 1848–1849, SL-NSW, DLMSQ 148 (CY Reel 3562); George E. Binsted diary, 1848–1849, SL-NSW, DLMS 137 (CY Reel 3562); Miller, "Getting a Fix on Violence," 74.

16   August, "A Horrible Looking Woman," 852; "Minutes of Evidence of the Orphan Immigration Committee," October 12, 1848 (Copy), Enclosed with C. Fitz Roy to

Earl Grey, December 19, 1848, NAI, CSORP, Box 1574, O9048; George E. Binsted diary, 1848–1849, SL-NSW, DLMS 137 (CY Reel 3562).

17 "Minutes of Evidence of the Orphan Immigration Committee," October 12, 1848 (Copy), Enclosed with C. Fitz Roy to Earl Grey, December 19, 1848, NAI, CSORP, Box 1574, O9048.

18 "Minutes of Evidence of the Orphan Immigration Committee," October 12, 1848 (Copy), Enclosed with C. Fitz Roy to Earl Grey, December 19, 1848, NAI, CSORP, Box 1574, O9048.

19 "Minutes of Evidence of the Orphan Immigration Committee," October 12, 1848 (Copy), Enclosed with C. Fitz Roy to Earl Grey, December 19, 1848, NAI, CSORP, Box 1574, O9048.

20 McMahon, *Coffin Ship*, 110–11; Elaine Farrell, *Women, Crime and Punishment in Ireland: Life in the Nineteenth-Century Convict Prison* (Cambridge: Cambridge University Press, 2020), 77, 79; Miller, "Getting a Fix on Violence," 74.

21 "Minutes of Evidence of the Orphan Immigration Committee," October 12, 1848 (Copy), Enclosed with C. Fitz Roy to Earl Grey, December 19, 1848, NAI, CSORP, Box 1574, O9048; William B. Neville journal, 1848–1849, SL-NSW, DLMSQ 148 (CY Reel 3562); George E. Binsted diary, 1848–1849, SL-NSW, DLMS 137 (CY Reel 3562); McMahon, *Coffin Ship*, 144.

22 Jan Gothard, *Blue China: Single Female Migration to Colonial Australia* (Melbourne: Melbourne University Press, 2001), 141–42; "Minutes of Evidence of the Orphan Immigration Committee," October 12, 1848 (Copy), Enclosed with C. Fitz Roy to Earl Grey, 19 December 1848, NAI, CSORP, Box 1574, O9048.

23 George E. Binsted diary, 1848–1849, SL-NSW, DLMS 137 (CY Reel 3562); "Minutes of Evidence of the Orphan Immigration Committee," October 12, 1848 (Copy), Enclosed with C. Fitz Roy to Earl Grey, December 19, 1848, NAI, CSORP, Box 1574, O9048.

24 George E. Binsted diary, 1848-1849, SL-NSW, DLMS 137 (CY Reel 3562); William B. Neville journal, 1848–1849, SL-NSW, DLMSQ 148 (CY Reel 3562).

25 Enclosure 1 in No. 1: Surgeon Superintendent, Henry Douglas, to Colonial Secretary, Edward D. Thompson, October 7, 1848, *Emigration. Papers Relative to the Emigration to the Australian Colonies*, 1850, No. 1163, 1–2.

26 William B. Neville journal, 1848–1849, SL-NSW, DLMSQ 148 (CY Reel 3562).

27 William B. Neville journal, 1848–1849, SL-NSW, DLMSQ 148 (CY Reel 3562).

6. ON THE BORDER IN NEW ORLEANS

1 Mary Grace Quackenbos, Report to the Attorney General, December 28, 1907, Department of Justice Record Group 60, folder 4, file 100937, page 13, National Archives and Records Administration, College Park, MD.

2 Quackenbos Report, letters and list of questions, 15–18 (description of Dell'Orto's business, 11).

3 Adam McKeown, "Ritualization of Regulation: The Enforcement of Chinese Exclusion in the United States and China," *American Historical Review* 108 (April 2003): 379.

4 A total of 951,227 people entered the United States from all ports of entry—by sea and by land—in 1903. Percentages calculated from exhibit at Ellis Island National Historical Park, observed by Lauren Braun-Strumfels on October 14, 2022. Dell'Orto reported on November 12, 1904, to the *Daily Picayune* that NGI had carried 3,209 Italians to the city since January 1 of that year. Clipping in box 143, folder 3161, Rappresentanze diplomatiche e consolari, Ambasciata d'Italia a Washington 1901–1909, Archivio storico diplomatico del Ministero degli Affari Esteri, Rome, Italy. Subsequent box and folder numbers abbreviated b., f.

5 US Census Bureau, "Historical Census Statistics on the Foreign-Born Population of the United States: 1850 to 2000." Census.gov, February 1, 2006. www.census. gov; Guido Bonsaver and Alice Gussoni, "From Sicily to Louisiana: Early Migration and Historiographical Issues," in *Managing Migration in Italy and the United States*, ed. Lauren Braun-Strumfels, Maddalena Marinari, and Daniele Fiorentino (Berlin: DeGruyter, 2024): 171–83 (see map on page 179). Preliminary research reveals a connection between the cities and towns where emigration agents were active and high rates of migration.

6 Mae Ngai, *The Lucky Ones: One Family and the Extraordinary Invention of Chinese America* (Princeton, NJ: Princeton University Press, 2010), 28–30, 74.

7 "Transfer of Station," *Times-Democrat*, March 8, 1907, b. 144, f. 3169.

8 Edmondo Mayor Des Planches, *Attraverso gli Stati Uniti* (Turin: Unione tipografico-editrice torinese, 1913), 133–34. See also McKeown, "Ritualization of Regulation"; John Torpey, *The Invention of the Passport: Citizenship, Surveillance, and the State* (New York: Cambridge University Press, 2018).

9 Augusta Molinari, "Porti, trasporti, compagnie," in *Storia dell'emigrazione Italiana: Partenze*, ed. Piero Bevilaqua, Andreina De Clementi, and Emilio Franzina (Rome: Donzelli, 2001), 237–39; Amoreno Martellini, "Il commercio dell'emigrazione: Intermediari e agenti," in *Storia dell'emigrazione italiana*, 297 (on "the job of the intermediary," 298–300).

10 Ngai, *The Lucky Ones*, 28; Tara Zahra, *The Great Departure: Mass Migration from Eastern Europe and the Making of the Free World* (New York: W. W. Norton, 2016), 38–39; George Pozzetta, "Italian Migration: From Sunnyside to the World," in *Shadows over Sunnyside: An Arkansas Plantation in Transition, 1830–1945*, ed. Jeannie Whayne (Fayetteville: University of Arkansas, 1993), 97–98.

11 McKeown, "Ritualization of Regulation," 401.

12 *Times-Democrat* (New Orleans), September 21, 1904. See also Arturo Dell'Orto to Senator Murphy J. Foster, November 1904, b. 143, f. 3161. For more on Sargent's visits to immigration stations as part of a larger campaign to increase the effectiveness of the Bureau of Immigration, see McKeown, "Ritualization of Regulation," 384.

13 Dell'Orto to Des Planches, April 22, 1905, b. 144, f. 3167.

14 Dell'Orto to Foster, b. 143, f. 3161 ("erroneously detained" and "ordered deported"); Bragging, Dell'Orto to Des Planches, April 22, 1905, b. 144, f. 3167. On exclusion rates, see Mae Ngai, *Impossible Subjects: Illegal Aliens and the Making of Modern America* (Princeton, NJ: Princeton University Press, 2004), Table A.1: Immigration

to the United States, 1820–2000, 273; Lauren Braun-Strumfels, "Binational Gate-keepers: The Italian Government and US Border Enforcement in the 1890s," *Labor* 18, (March 2021): 11–37; *Daily Picayune* (New Orleans), November 12, 1904, b. 143, f. 3161 (quote by Dell'Orto).

15 Dell'Orto to Des Planches, April 22, 1905, b. 144, f. 3167.

16 Villari to Reynaudi, October 10, 1906, b. 144, f. 3169.

17 Villari to Reynaudi, October 10, 1906, b. 144, f. 3169.

18 Dell'Orto Des Planches, April 22, 1905, b. 144, f. 3167.

19 Undersecretary of State to Des Planches, February 2, 1907, b. 144, f. 3169; "Will Inspect Station," *Times-Democrat*, March 7, 1907. Clipping and letter, Scelsi to Luigi Dell'Orto Ltd., January 10, 1907, b. 144, f. 3169; Dell'Orto to Foster, b. 143, f. 3161. See also Martellini, "Il commercio dell'emigrazione," 295–96.

20 *Times-Democrat* clippings dated March 7, 8, 10, 1907, b. 144, f. 3169; Scelsi to Reynaudi, March 20, 1907, b. 144, f. 3169.

21 Scelsi to Reynaudi, March 20, 1907, page 2, b. 144, f. 3169 ("artificially provoked"); Scelsi to Catalani, 19 March 1907, box 2, folder 4, acc. no. Z/ 0209.003/5, Percy Family Papers, Manuscript Collection, Archives and Library Division, Mississippi Department of Archives and History, Jackson MS. LeRoy Percy, part owner of Sunnyside, had directed Catalani to recruit the families.

22 Scelsi to Reynaudi, March 20, 1907, b. 144, f. 3169.

23 Rossi to Des Planches, February 27, 1905, b. 144, f. 3167. On Sargent's push, see McKeown, "Ritualization of Regulation," 384.

24 Quackenbos Report, 11 (text of Dell'Orto's letter copied by other agencies).

25 Gunther Peck, *Reinventing Free Labor: Padrones and Immigrant Workers in the North American West, 1880–1930* (Cambridge: Cambridge University Press, 2000), 23 (quote on Missler); Quackenbos Report, 11.

26 Scelsi to Reynaudi, March 20, 1907, b. 144, f. 3169; McKeown, "Ritualization of Regulation," 383–84. Extensive coaching was becoming an entrenched practice among Chinese migrants who had to secure residence certificates under pain of deportation.

27 Scelsi to Reynaudi, March 20, 1907, b. 144, f. 3169; Reynaudi to Des Planches, June 25, 1905, b. 144, f. 3167.

7. STRANGERS IN THE HOMELAND

Earlier versions of some of the material in this chapter appeared in Hidetaka Hirota, *Expelling the Poor: Atlantic Seaboard States and the Nineteenth-Century Origins of American Immigration Policy* (New York: Oxford University Press, 2017).

1 Inmate Case Histories, Reel 2, Volume 6, Tewksbury State Almshouse Records, Massachusetts Archives; *Annual Report of the Commissioners for Administering the Laws for Relief of the Poor in Ireland, Including the Twenty-Third Report under the 10 & 11 Vic., c. 90, and the Eighteenth Report under the 14 & 15 Vic., c. 68; with Appendices*, p. 74 [C.156], H.C. 1870, xxxvi.1, 36; *Cork Constitution*, December 10, 1868.

2 Hirota, *Expelling the Poor*. Massachusetts immigration officials never published any statistics about the gender ratio among deportees, but many of them were women. This was not a random outcome but a reflection of women's particular economic vulnerability in the nineteenth-century United States. Compared to men, women could easily lose sources of income and become dependent on public relief for gender-related reasons, such as pregnancy, abandonment, widowhood, or husbands' temporary absence for seasonal employment away from home. Irish immigrant women were picked up for deportation within this gendered structure of poverty and dependency.

3 On the removal of Irish paupers under the British Poor Law, see Christine Kinealy, *This Great Calamity: The Irish Famine, 1845–52* (Boulder, CO: Roberts Rinehart, 1995); Frank Neal, *Black '47: Britain and the Famine Irish* (London: Newsham Press, 1998); Lewis Darwen, Donald MacRaild, Brian Gurrin, and Liam Kennedy, "'Unhappy and Wretched Creatures': Charity, Poor Relief and Pauper Removal in Britain and Ireland during the Great Famine," *English Historical Review* 134, no. 568 (2019): 589–619.

4 Inmate Case Histories, Reel 2, Volume 8, Tewksbury State Almshouse Records; *Freeman's Journal* (Dublin), February 27, 1854; Adam McKeown, "Ritualization of Regulation: The Enforcement of Chinese Exclusion in the United States and China," *American Historical Review* 108 (April 2003): 377–403.

5 Linda K. Kerber, "The Stateless as the Citizens' Other: A View from the United States," *American Historical Review* 112 (February 2007): 13.

6 John Belchem, *Irish, Catholic and Scouse: The History of the Liverpool-Irish, 1800–1939* (Liverpool: Liverpool University Press, 2007), 1, 3–6, 56–60, 73–74.

7 Massachusetts, *Thirty-Sixth Annual Report of the Trustees of the State Lunatic Hospital, at Worcester, 1868*, Public Doc. 23, 13–14; *Freeman's Journal* (Dublin), September 27, 1858; *Quebec Mercury*, October 18, 1858.

8 Neal, *Black '47*, 53, 61, 139, 240–41, 249; J. Matthew Gallman, *Receiving Erin's Children: Philadelphia, Liverpool, and the Irish Famine Migration, 1845–1855* (Chapel Hill: University of North Carolina Press, 2000), 67.

9 October 11, 1855, Workhouse Committee Minute Book, 1855–57, 353SEL/10/4, Records of the Liverpool Board of Guardians, Liverpool Records Office; *Liverpool Daily Post*, June 4, 1858; *Liverpool Mercury*, June 4, September 15, September 18, October 24, November 12, 1858; *Freeman's Journal* (Dublin), September 27, 1858. The deportation of the Irish poor from the United States to Liverpool continued throughout the 1850s, 1860s, and 1870s. Between 1859 and 1860, the Liverpool authorities led the UK Foreign Office to investigate the practice through British consuls in Boston and New York, but the investigation did not result in any diplomatic action about it. Hirota, *Expelling the Poor*, 163–65.

10 *Freeman's Journal* (Dublin), March 5, 1855; *Liverpool Daily Post*, August 20, 1858; *Liverpool Mercury*, September 30, 1859; Herbert S. Klein, *A Population History of the United States* (New York: Cambridge University Press, 2004), 115.

11 Virginia Crossman, *Local Government in Nineteenth-Century Ireland* (Belfast: The Queen's University of Belfast for the Ulster Society of Irish Historical Studies, 1994), 48; *Boston Daily Advertiser*, June 7, 1855; *Freeman's Journal* (Dublin), March 5, 1855; Admission and Discharge, BG78/13, Records of the North Dublin Poor Law Union, National Archives of Ireland. On the nineteenth-century Irish asylum system for people with mental illness, see Catherine Cox, *Negotiating Insanity in the Southeast of Ireland, 1820–1900* (Manchester: Manchester University Press, 2012).

12 Deirdre M. Mageean, "Emigration from Irish Ports," *Journal of American Ethnic History* 13 (Fall 1993): 24–26; *Irish Examiner* (Cork), April 7, 1864; *Irish Times*, October 29, 1867.

13 Cox, *Negotiating Insanity in the Southeast of Ireland*, 18; *Cork Constitution*, December 10, 1868; *Freeman's Journal* (Dublin), July 21, 1864.

14 *Cork Constitution*, May 27, 1869; *Cork Examiner*, December 24, 1868.

15 Frank Neal, "Lancashire, the Famine Irish and the Poor Laws: A Study in Crisis Management," *Irish Economic and Social History* 22 (1995): 26–28.

16 *Liverpool Mercury*, May 14, 1847; Neal, *Black '47*, 220–22, 227; John Crowley, William J. Smyth, and Mike Murphy, eds., *Atlas of the Great Irish Famine* (New York: New York University Press, 2012), 505; *Freeman's Journal* (Dublin), July 14, 1847; Indoor Relief Register, 1854–1857, BG69/A9, Records of the Cork Poor Law Union Cork City and County Archives.

17 *Cork Examiner*, January 1, 1855; *Belfast News-Letter*, June 18, 1851; *New York Citizen*, March 28, 1857.

18 Neal, *Black '47*, 220–21; Darwen, MacRaild, Gurrin, and Kennedy, "'Unhappy and Wretched Creatures,'" 592–93, 610.

19 Frank Neal, "Liverpool, the Irish Steamship Companies and the Famine Irish," *Immigrants & Minorities* 5 (1986): 52; Darwen, MacRaild, Gurrin, and Kennedy, "'Unhappy and Wretched Creatures,'" 608–9; *Belfast Morning News*, January 8, 1858; *Belfast News-Letter*, July 4, 1857.

20 Cormac Ó Gráda, *Black '47 and Beyond: The Great Irish Famine in History, Economy, and Memory* (Princeton, NJ: Princeton University Press, 1999), 174.

21 Virginia Crossman, *The Poor Law in Ireland, 1838–1948* (Dublin: Dundalgan Press, 2006), 10; Kinealy, *This Great Calamity*, 25–26, 334–41; April 16, 1856, Board of Guardians Minute Books, BG69/A22, Records of the Cork Poor Law Union; April 30, 1856, Board of Guardians Minute Books, Roll 347, Item 5, Records of the North Dublin Poor Law Union; *Kerry Evening Post*, October 12, 1856; *New York Citizen*, September 4, 1869; *Belfast News-Letter*, May 12, 1863. On the return of deported paupers to Britain, see Darwen, MacRaild, Gurrin, and Kennedy, "'Unhappy and Wretched Creatures,'" 612–17.

22 *Freeman's Journal* (Dublin), January 5, 1854; *Belfast News-Letter*, January 21, 1858; *Freeman's Journal* (Dublin), July 21, 1864; *Cork Examiner*, January 1, 1855.

23 *Cork Examiner*, December 24, 1868; *Cork Examiner*, December 24, 1868 (parentheses original); *Annual Report of the Commissioners for Administering the Laws for Relief of the Poor in Ireland*, 77.

24 Emily Mark-Fitzgerald, Ciarán McCabe, and Ciarán Reilly, eds., *Dublin and the Great Irish Famine* (Dublin: University College Dublin Press, 2022), 57; *Liverpool Mercury*, January 7, 1848; *Liverpool Mercury*, September 30, 1859.

25 *Cork Examiner*, May 20, 1869; *Freeman's Journal* (Dublin), February 27, 1854; Darwen, MacRaild, Gurrin, and Kennedy, "Unhappy and Wretched Creatures," 617.

26 James S. Donnelly Jr., *The Great Irish Potato Famine* (Phoenix Mill, UK: Sutton Publishing, 2001), 130; Virginia Crossman, *Poverty and the Poor Law in Ireland, 1850–1914* (Liverpool: Liverpool University Press, 2013), 12–32, 198–225.

8. FEELING STRANGE ON THE SHORE

1 Colm Tóibín, *Brooklyn: A Novel* (New York: Scribner, 2009), 213.

2 Philip O'Leary, "Yank Outsiders: Irish Americans in Gaelic Fiction and Drama of the Irish Free State, 1922–1939," in *New Perspectives on the Irish Diaspora*, ed. Charles Fanning (Carbondale and Edwardsville: Southern Illinois University Press, 2000), 259.

3 On the extant historical evidence of experiences of return, Ann Schofield has shown that while the questionnaire on returned migrants included in the 1955 Irish Folklore Commission's yields some useful memories of "Returned Yanks," the framing of the questionnaire fed into existing stereotypes. See Ann Schofield, "The Returned Yank as Site of Memory in Irish Popular Culture," *Journal of American Studies* 47 (November 2013), 1175–95. For analysis of the influence of the "Returned Yank" on Irish society, see especially Sinead Moynihan, *Ireland, Migration and Return Migration: The "Returned Yank" in the Cultural Imagination, 1952 to Present* (Liverpool: Liverpool University Press, 2019).

4 Moynihan, *Ireland, Migration and Return Migration*, 88.

5 Máirtín Ó Cadhain, "Floodtide," in Máirtín Ó Cadhain, *The Quick and the Dead: Selected Stories*, ed. Louis De Paor, trans. Katherine Duffy (New Haven: Yale University Press, 2021), 55–56.

6 For a fuller discussion of Ó Cadhain's political outlook, see Steve Coleman, "Sí Teanga na Muintire a Shlánós an Mhuintir: Ó Cadhain, Rhetoric, and Immanence," in *Tropological Thought and Action: Essays on the Poetics of Imagination*, ed. Marko Živković, Jamin Pelkey, and James W. Fernandez (New York and Oxford: Berghahn Books, 2021), 183–208. For more on the influence of Connemara on Ó Cadhain's writing, see Louis de Paor, "Introduction," in Ó Cadhain, *Quick and the Dead*, vii–ix.

7 Máirtín Ó Cadhain, "The Year 1912," in *Quick and the Dead*, 43, 47.

8 Ó Cadhain, "Floodtide," 57–58.

9 Ó Cadhain, "Floodtide," 62–63.

10 Ó Cadhain, "Floodtide," 57.

11 Ó Cadhain, "Floodtide," 60.

12 Ó Cadhain, "Floodtide," 61.

13 Ó Cadhain, "Floodtide," 57, 64–66.

14 Ó Cadhain, "Floodtide," 67.

15 Tóibín, *Brooklyn*, 212–13.

16 Kathleen Costello-Sullivan and Julie Grossman, "Plagues of Silence: Adaptation and Agency in Colm Tóibín's and John Crowley's Brooklyns," in *Screening Contemporary Irish Fiction and Drama*, ed. Marc C. Connor, Julie Grossman, and R. Barton Palmer (Cham, Switzerland: Springer International Publishing AG, 2022), 181–98. See also Kathleen Costello-Sullivan, *Mother/Country: Politics of the Personal in the Fiction of Colm Tóibín* (Bern: Peter Lang, 2012), 189–219; Ellen McWilliams, *Women and Exile in Contemporary Irish Fiction* (London and New York: Palgrave MacMillan, 2013), 156–83.

17 McWilliams, *Women and Exile in Contemporary Irish Fiction*, 169. On the inspiration for *Brooklyn*, see Colm Tóibín, interviewed by Kirsty Young for Desert Island Discs (BBC), January 3, 2016.

18 Moynihan, *Ireland, Migration and Return Migration*, 21; George Moore, *The Untilled Field* (1903; Buckinghamshire: Colin Smythe Ltd., 2000); Colm Tóibín, interviewed by Krishnan Guru-Murthy, Channel 4 News, February 5, 2016.

19 Tóibín, *Brooklyn*, 211–13.

20 Tóibín, *Brooklyn*, 216–17, 220, 236.

21 Tóibín, *Brooklyn*, 73, 229.

22 Tóibín, *Brooklyn*, 240–41.

23 Ó Cadhain, "The Year 1912," 52.

9. THE VISUAL CULTURE OF ITALIAN MIGRANT RETURN

1 John Berger and Jean Mohr, *A Seventh Man: A Book of Images and Words about the Experience of Migrant Workers in Europe* (1975; London: Writers and Readers, 1982), 13.

2 I do not cite personal documents in this chapter due to space limitations.

3 A similar family photo aboard the *Duilio* circa 1924 is available online at Grand Rapids Historical Society, "Italian Liner Duilio," *History Grand Rapids.org*, n.d., www.historygrandrapids.org/photo/3986/italian-liner-duilio (accessed February 16, 2024).

4 For a recent study of an Italian American's photographic documentation of his stay in Italy during the 1950s, see Loredana Polezzi, "Translating, Repositioning, Reframing: On the Transatlantic Routes of Objects and Memories" *Forum Italicum* 57, no. 2 (2023): 462–75. See, also, the exhibit catalogues by Paola Agosti and Maria Rosaria Ostuni, *L'Italia fuori d'Italia* (Rome: Ministero degli Affari Esteri, 1990); Rosangela Briscese and Joseph Sciorra, eds., *Reframing Italian America: Historical Photographs and Immigrant Representations* (New York: John D. Calandra Italian American Institute, 2015). For discussion of Italian migrations and visual culture, see Giorgio Bertellini, *Italy in Early American Cinema: Race, Landscape, and the Picturesque* (Bloomington: Indiana University Press, 2010); Pasquale Verdicchio, *Looters, Photographers, and Thieves: Aspects of Italian Photographic Culture in the Nineteenth and Twentieth Centuries* (Madison, NJ: Fairleigh Dickinson University Press, 2011).

5 Richard Chalfen, *Snapshot Versions of Life* (Bowling Green, KY: Bowling Green State University Press, 1987), 4, 8. Scholars and journalists who write about nonprofes-

sional photography in the analog era have used various interchangeable names to categorize it: amateur, folk, Kodak culture, mass photography, ordinary, vernacular.

6 James C. A. Kaufman, "Learning from the Fotomat," *American Scholar* 49 (Spring 1980): 245; Julia Adeney Thomas, "The Evidence of Sight," *History and Theory* 48 (December 2009): 152.

7 Loretta Baldassar, *Visits Home: Migrations Experiences between Italy and Australia* (Melbourne: Melbourne University Press, 2001); Tim Coles and Dallen J. Timothy, eds., *Tourism, Diasporas and Space* (New York: Routledge, 2004); Natalia Bloch and Kathleen M. Adams, eds., *Intersections of Tourism, Migration, and Exile* (New York: Routledge, 2023); Marcelo J. Borges, Sonia Cancian, and Linda Reeder, "Introduction," in *Emotional Landscapes: Love, Gender, and Migration*, ed. Marcelo J. Borges, Sonia Cancian, and Linda Reeder (Urbana: University of Illinois Press, 2021), 2.

8 Baldassar, *Visits Home*, 13.

9 Donna R. Gabaccia, *Italy's Many Diasporas* (Seattle: University of Washington Press, 2000), 81–105; Laura Cuppone, "Get Skilled and Get Out: Post-WWII Italian Emigrants and Transnational Training" (PhD dissertation, Michigan State University, 2014), 205. For a more in-depth account of the Sciorra family's known transatlantic migrations, see Joseph Sciorra, "'Don't Forget You Have Relatives Here': Transnational Intimacy and Acoustic Communities of WOV-AM's *La Grande Famiglia*," in *New Italian Migrations to the United States, Vol. 2: Art and Culture since 1945*, ed. Laura E. Ruberto and Joseph Sciorra (Urbana: University of Illinois Press, 2017), 32–64.

10 Laura E. Ruberto and Joseph Sciorra, "Introduction: Real Italians, New Immigrants," in *New Italian Migrations to the United States, Vol. 1: Politics and History since 1945*, ed. Laura E. Ruberto and Joseph Sciorra (Urbana: University of Illinois Press, 2017), 1–58.

11 About this and similar messages, see Sciorra, "'Don't Forget You Have Relatives Here.'"

12 Simone Cinotto, "All Things Italian: Italian American Consumers, the Transnational Formation of Taste, and the Commodification of Difference," in *Making Italian America: Consumer Culture and the Production of Ethnic Identities*, ed. Simone Cinotto (New York: Fordham University Press, 2014), 1–3; Laura E. Ruberto and Joseph Sciorra, "Italian American Stuff: A Survey of Material Culture, Migration, and Ethnicity," *SOAR: The Society of Americanists Review* 3 (2021–2022): 14.

13 There are also two hundred-foot reels of 8mm film footage from the 1957 trip that I will not analyze here.

14 Kaufman, "Learning from the Fotomat," 244; Ariella Azoulay, "Photography: The Ontological Question," *Mafte'akh: Lexical Review of Political Thought* 2 (2011): 70; Nicholas Mirzoeff, "The Multiple Viewpoint: Diaspora and Visual Culture," in *The Visual Culture Reader*, ed. Nicholas Mirzoeff (New York: Routledge, 2002), 6; Baldassar, *Visits Home*, 21.

15 Baldassar, *Visits Home*, 112.

16 Sabine Marschall, "Tourism and Memories of Home: Introduction," in *Tourism and Memories of Home: Migrants, Displaced People, Exiles and Diasporic Communities*, ed. Sabine Marschall (Bristol, UK: Channel View Publications, 2017), 2.

17 Cinotto "All Things Italian," 1. With his 1957 trip, Enrico became a lifelong member of the Italian Touring Club, receiving maps and publications that fueled his imagination and aided his subsequent Italian visits.

18 Bertellini, *Italy in Early American Cinema*, 36, 48.

19 Valentina Fallo, "The Power of Images in the Age of Mussolini" (PhD dissertation, University of Pennsylvania, 2013), vii.

20 Joseph Sciorra, "Sending a Telegram to the Pope," *i-Italy.org [Joseph Sciorra's Blog]*, August 20, 2008, https://bloggers.iitaly.org/node/3951 (accessed August 12, 2023).

21 Dean MacCannell, *The Tourist: A New Theory of the Leisure Class* (New York: Schocken Books, 1976), 13, 137–41.

22 Bertellini, *Italy in Early American Cinema*, 60.

23 I used one of these two photographs on the poster for the John D. Calandra Italian American Institute's 2009 conference on the theme of "The Land of Our Return: Diasporic Encounters with Italy."

24 Mirzoeff, "The Multiple Viewpoint," 209.

25 In 1999, my children and I claimed our Italian citizenship.

EPILOGUE

1 Matteo Garrone, *Io Capitano*, directed by Matteo Garrone, Italy, 2023.

2 Caroline B. Brettell, *Men Who Migrate, Women Who Wait: Population and History in a Portuguese Parish* (Princeton, NJ: Princeton University Press, 1987); Sameer Yasir, "They Married for a Life Abroad. But They Never Saw Their Husbands Again," *New York Times*, June 13, 2023, www.nytimes.com, Marianne Hold Pedersen and Mikkel Rytter, "Rituals of Migration, an Introduction," *Journal of Ethnic and Migration Studies* 44, no. 16 (2018): 2603.

3 Migration Policy Institute, "Top 35 Diasporas in the United States, 2021," www.migrationpolicy.org.

BIBLIOGRAPHY

This bibliography contains all of the secondary sources cited in the endnotes, along with a wide range of additional readings. It does not include unpublished primary sources.

Abbott, Rebecca. "The Earl Grey Orphan Scheme, 1848–1850, and the Irish Diaspora in Australia." In *Women and the Great Hunger*, edited by Christine Kinealy, Jason King, and Ciaran O'Reilly, 201–10. Hamden, CT: Quinnipiac University Press, 2016.

Agosti, Paola, and Maria Rosaria Ostuni. *L'Italia fuori d'Italia*. Rome: Ministero degli Affari Esteri, 1990.

Akenson, Donald H. *The Irish Diaspora: A Primer*. Dublin: P. D. Meany, 1993.

Anbinder, Tyler. "From Famine to Five Points: Lord Lansdowne's Irish Tenants Encounter North America's Most Notorious Slum." *American Historical Review* 107 (April 2002): 351–87.

Anbinder, Tyler. "Networks and Opportunities: A Digital History of Ireland's Great Famine Refugees in New York." *American Historical Review* 124 (December 2019): 1591–629.

Anbinder, Tyler. *Plentiful Country: The Great Potato Famine and the Making of Irish New York*. New York: Little, Brown & Company, 2024.

Anderson, Virginia DeJohn. *New England's Generation: The Great Migration and the Formation of Society and Culture in the Seventeenth Century*. New York: Cambridge University Press, 1991.

Arrighi, Giovanni, and Fortunata Piselli. "Capitalist Development in Hostile Environments: Feuds, Class Struggles, and Migrations in a Peripheral Region of Southern Italy." *Review—Fernand Braudel Center for the Study of Economies, Historical Systems, and Civilizations* 10, no. 4 (1987): 649–751.

Audenino, Patrizia, and Maddalena Tirabassi. *Migrazioni Italiane. Storia e storie dall'Ancien régime a oggi*. Milan: Arnoldo Mondadori Editore, 2008.

August, Andrew. "'A Horrible Looking Woman': Female Violence in Late-Victorian East London." *Journal of British Studies* 54 (October 2015): 844–68.

Auslander, Laura. "Beyond Words." *American Historical Review* 110 (October 2005): 1015–45.

Azoulay, Ariella. "Photography: The Ontological Question." *Mafte'akh: Lexical Review of Political Thought* 2e (2011): 65–80.

Badagliacca, Mario, with Derek Duncan. *Italy Is Out*. Liverpool: Liverpool University, 2021.

Bailey, Merridee L., and Katie Barclay, eds. *Emotion, Ritual and Power in Europe, 1200–1920: Family, State and Church*. New York: Palgrave Macmillan, 2017. Cham, Switzerland: Springer International Publishing, 2021.

Baily, Samuel. *Immigrants in the Lands of Promise: Italians in Buenos Aires and New York City, 1870–1914*. Ithaca: Cornell University Press, 2004.

Baldassar, Loretta. "The Return Visit as Pilgrimage: Secular Redemption and Cultural Renewal in the Migration Process." In *The Australian Immigrant in the Twentieth Century: Searching Neglected Sources*, edited by Eric Richards and Jacqueline Templeton, 127–56. Canberra: Division of Historical Studies and Centre for Immigration and Multicultural Studies, Research School of Social Sciences, Australian National University, 1998.

Baldassar, Loretta. *Visits Home: Migrations Experiences between Italy and Australia*. Melbourne: Melbourne University Press, 2001.

Baldassar, Loretta, and Donna R. Gabaccia, eds. *Intimacy and Italian Migration: Gender and Domestic Lives in a Mobile World*. New York: Fordham University Press, 2011.

Barbata Jackson, Jessica. *Dixie's Italians: Sicilians, Race, and Citizenship in the Jim Crow Gulf South*. Baton Rouge: Louisiana State University Press, 2020.

Barclay, Katie. *Love, Intimacy and Power: Marriage and Patriarchy in Scotland, 1650–1850*. Manchester: Manchester University Press, 2011.

Batinich, Mary Ellen. *Italian Voices: Making Minnesota Our Home*. St. Paul: Minnesota Historical Society, 2007.

Battisti, Danielle. *Whom We Shall Welcome: Italian Americans and Immigration Reform, 1945–1965*. New York: Fordham University Press, 2019.

Beier, A. L., and Paul Ocobock, eds. *Cast Out: Vagrancy and Homelessness in Global and Historical Perspective*. Athens: Ohio University Press, 2008.

Belchem, John. *Irish, Catholic and Scouse: The History of the Liverpool-Irish, 1800–1939*. Liverpool: Liverpool University Press, 2007.

Berger, John, and Jean Mohr. *A Seventh Man: A Book of Images and Words about the Experience of Migrant Workers in Europe*. London: Writers and Readers, 1975.

Berger, John, and Jean Mohr. *Another Way of Telling*. New York: Pantheon Books, 1982.

Bernardy, Amy A. *Italia randagia attraverso gli Stati Uniti*. Turin: Fratelli Bocca, 1913.

Berry, Stephen R. *A Path in the Mighty Waters: Shipboard Life and Atlantic Crossings to the New World*. New Haven: Yale University Press, 2015.

Bertellini, Giorgio. *Italy in Early American Cinema: Race, Landscape, and the Picturesque*. Bloomington: Indiana University Press, 2010.

Bevilacqua, Piero, Andreina De Clementi, and Emilio Franzina, eds. *Storia dell'emigrazione italiana: Arrivi*. Rome: Donzelli Editore, 2002.

Bevilacqua, Piero, ed. *Verso l'America: L'emigrazione italiana e gli Stati Uniti*. Rome: Donzelli Editore, 2005.

Bianco, Carla. *The Two Rosetos*. Bloomington: Indiana University Press, 1974.

Bignami, Paolo. "I partiti politici nelle diverse regioni d'Italia." *Nuova antologia*, Sesta Serie, vol. CCIV (February 16, 1920), 406–24.

Bloch, Natalia, and Kathleen M. Adams, eds. *Intersections of Tourism, Migration, and Exile*. New York: Routledge, 2023.

Bonifazi, Corrado. *L'Italia delle migrazioni*. Milan: Il Mulino, 2013.

Bonsaver, Guido, and Alice Gussoni, "From Sicily to Louisiana: Early Migration and Historiographical Issues." In *Managing Migration in Italy and the United States*, edited by Lauren Braun-Strumfels, Maddalena Marinari, and Daniele Fiorentino, 171–83. Berlin: DeGruyter, 2024.

Borges, Marcelo J. "What's Love Got to Do with It? Language of Transnational Affect in the Letters of Portuguese Migrants." In *Emotional Landscapes: Love, Gender, and Migration*, edited by Marcelo J. Borges, Sonia Cancian, and Linda Reeder, 25–52. Urbana: University of Illinois Press, 2021.

Borges, Marcelo J., and Sonia Cancian, eds. *Migrant Letters: Emotional Language, Mobile Identities, and Writing Practices in Historical Perspective*. New York: Routledge, 2019.

Borges, Marcelo J., Sonia Cancian, and Linda Reeder, eds. *Emotional Landscapes: Love, Gender, and Migration*. Urbana: University of Illinois Press, 2021.

Borges, Marcelo J., Sonia Cancian, and Linda Reeder, "Introduction." In *Emotional Landscapes: Love, Gender, and Migration*, edited by Marcelo J. Borges, Sonia Cancian, and Linda Reeder, 1–17. Urbana: University of Illinois Press, 2021.

Brandenburg, Broughton. "Imported Americans: The Overflow." *Frank Leslie's Popular Monthly* 57, no. 4 (February 1904): 399–413.

Brandenburg, Broughton. *Imported Americans: The Story of the Experiences of a Disguised American and His Wife Studying the Immigration Question*. New York: F. A. Stokes, 1904.

Braun-Strumfels, Lauren. "Binational Gatekeepers: The Italian Government and US Border Enforcement in the 1890s." *Labor* 18 (March 2021): 11–37.

Braun-Strumfels, Lauren. *Partners in Gatekeeping: How Italy Shaped US Immigration Policy over Ten Pivotal Years, 1891–1901*. Athens: University of Georgia Press, 2023.

Braun-Strumfels, Lauren, Maddalena Marinari, and Daniele Fiorentino, eds. *Managing Migration in Italy and the United States*. Berlin: DeGruyter, 2023.

Breathnach, Ciara. "Even 'Wilder Workhouse Girls.'" *Journal of Imperial and Commonwealth History* 39 (December 2011): 771–94.

Brettell, Caroline B. *Gender and Migration*. New York: John Wiley & Sons, 2016. Cambridge: Polity Press, 2017.

Brettell, Caroline B. *Men Who Migrate, Women Who Wait: Population and History in a Portuguese Parish*. Princeton, NJ: Princeton University Press, 1987.

Briscese, Rosangela, and Joseph Sciorra, eds. *Reframing Italian America: Historical Photographs and Immigrant Representations*. New York: John D. Calandra Italian American Institute, 2015.

Brown, Thomas N. *Irish-American Nationalism, 1870–1890*. Philadelphia: Lippincott, 1966.

Brundage, David. *Irish Nationalists in America: The Politics of Exile, 1798–1998*. New York: Oxford University Press, 2017.

Cacciarru, Angela. "The Agrarian Reform in Italy: Historical Analysis and Impact on Access to Land and Social Class Composition." *Europe Now. Council for European Studies*

(CES). (November 10, 2020). www.europenowjournal.org/2020/11/09/historical-analysis-of-the-agrarian-reform-in-italy-impact-on-access-to-land-and-social-class-composition.

Calabrese, Victoria. *Italian Women in Basilicata: Staying Behind but Moving Forward during the Age of Mass Emigration, 1876–1914*. Lanham, MD: Rowman & Littlefield, 2022.

Campbell, Malcolm. *Ireland's Farthest Shores: Mobility, Migration, and Settlement in the Pacific World*. Madison: University of Wisconsin Press, 2022.

Campbell, Malcolm. *Ireland's New Worlds: Immigrants, Politics, and Society in the United States and Australia, 1815–1922*. Madison: University of Wisconsin Press, 2008.

Canadé Sautman, Francesca. "Between Divestment and Migration: Clothing Artifacts and Identity among Italian Immigrant Women, 1880s-1920s." *Italian American Review* 8 (July 2018): 157–58.

Cancian, Sonia. *Families, Lovers, and Their Letters: Italian Postwar Migration to Canada*. Winnipeg: University of Manitoba Press, 2010.

Cancian, Sonia. *With Your Words in My Hands: The Letters of Antonietta Petris and Loris Palma*. Montreal: McGill-Queen's Press, 2021.

Carper, Katherine. "The Migration Business and the Shift from State to Federal Immigration Regulation." *Journal of the Civil War Era* 11 (September 2021): 340–60.

Cary, Meredith. "Going Home: The 'Returned Yank' in Irish and Irish-American Fiction." *Colby Quarterly* 29 (March 1993): 57–67.

Chalfen, Richard. *Snapshot Versions of Life*. Bowling Green, KY: Bowling Green State University Press, 1987.

Chapman, Charlotte Gower. *Milocca: A Sicilian Village*. London: Allen and Unwin, 1973.

Chase, Elaine, Nando Sigona, and Dawn Chatty, eds. *Becoming Adult on the Move: Migration Journeys, Encounters and Life Transitions*. Cham, Switzerland: Palgrave Macmillan, 2023.

Choate, Mark I. *Emigrant Nation: The Making of Italy Abroad*. Cambridge, MA: Harvard University Press, 2008.

Cinotto, Simone. "All Things Italian: Italian American Consumers, the Transnational Formation of Taste, and the Commodification of Difference." In *Making Italian America: Consumer Culture and the Production of Ethnic Identities*, edited by Simone Cinotto, 1–31. New York: Fordham University Press, 2014.

Cinotto, Simone. *The Italian American Table: Food, Family, and Community in New York City*. Champaign: University of Illinois Press, 2013.

Cinotto, Simone, ed. *Making Italian America: Consumer Culture and the Production of Ethnic Identities*. New York: Fordham University Press, 2014.

Clark, Anna. "Wild Workhouse Girls and the Liberal Imperial State in Mid-Nineteenth Century Ireland." *Journal of Social History* 39 (Winter 2005): 389–409.

Coco, Salvatore, *Sulle macerie di Mascali, memorie della mia vita: Diario di un siciliano emigrato in Argentina (1888–1929)*. Independently published, 2018.

Cohn, Raymond L. *Mass Migration under Sail: European Immigration to the Antebellum United States*. Cambridge: Cambridge University Press, 2008.

Coleman, Steve. "Sí Teanga na Muintire a Shlánós an Mhuintir: Ó Cadhain, Rhetoric, and Immanence." In *Tropological Thought and Action: Essays on the Poetics of*

Imagination, edited by Marko Živković, Jamin Pelkey, and James W. Fernandez, 183–208. New York and Oxford: Berghahn Books, 2021.

Coles, Tim, and Dallen J. Timothy, eds. *Tourism, Diasporas and Space*. New York: Routledge, 2004.

Coletti, Francesco. *Dell' emigrazione italiana*. Milan: Hoepli, 1912.

Colucci, Michele. *Storia dell'immigrazione straniera in Italia. Dal 1945 ai giorni nostri*. Bologna: Carocci Editore, 2018.

Connell, William, and Fred Gardaphé, eds. *Anti-Italianism: Essays on Prejudice*. New York: Palgrave Macmillan, 2010.

Connell, William J., and Stanislao G. Pugliese, eds. *The Routledge History of Italian Americans*. New York: Routledge, 2017.

Connolly, Sean. *On Every Tide: The Making and Remaking of the Irish World*. New York: Basic Books, 2021.

Cooper, Sophie. "Something Borrowed: Women, Limerick Lace and Community Heirlooms in the Australian Irish Diaspora." *Social History* 45 (2020): 304–27.

Costello-Sullivan, Kathleen. *Mother/Country: Politics of the Personal in the Fiction of Colm Tóibín*. Bern: Peter Lang, 2012.

Costello-Sullivan, Kathleen, and Julie Grossman, "Plagues of Silence: Adaptation and Agency in Colm Tóibín's John Crowley's *Brooklyns*." In *Screening Contemporary Irish Fiction and Drama*, edited by Marc C. Conner, Julie Grossman, and R. Barton Palmer, 181–98. Cham, Switzerland: Springer International Publishing AG, 2022.

Cox, Catherine. *Negotiating Insanity in the Southeast of Ireland, 1820–1900*. Manchester: Manchester University Press, 2012.

Cressy, David. *Coming Over: Migration and Communication between England and New England in the Seventeenth Century*. New York: Cambridge University Press, 1987.

Crossman, Virginia. *Local Government in Nineteenth-Century Ireland*. Belfast: Queen's University of Belfast for the Ulster Society of Irish Historical Studies, 1994.

Crossman, Virginia. "The New Ross Workhouse Riot of 1887: Nationalism, Class and the Irish Poor Laws." *Past & Present* 179 (May 2003): 135–58.

Crossman, Virginia. *The Poor Law in Ireland, 1838–1948*. Dublin: Dundalgan Press, 2006.

Crossman, Virginia. *Poverty and the Poor Law in Ireland, 1850–1914*. Liverpool: Liverpool University Press, 2013.

Crossman, Virginia, and Peter Gray, eds. *Poverty and Welfare in Ireland, 1838–1948*. Dublin: Irish Academic Press, 2011.

Crowley, John, William J. Smyth, and Mike Murphy, eds. *Atlas of the Great Irish Famine*. New York: New York University Press, 2012.

Cuppone, Laura. "Get Skilled and Get Out: Post-WWII Italian Emigrants and Transnational Training." PhD diss., Michigan State University, 2014.

Cusack, M. A. *Advice to Irish Girls in America*. New York: J. A. McGee, 1876.

D'Agostino, Peter. *Rome in America: Transnational Catholic Ideology from the Risorgimento to Fascism*. Chapel Hill: University of North Carolina Press, 2005.

Darwen, Lewis, Donald MacRaild, Brian Gurrin, and Liam Kennedy, "'Unhappy and Wretched Creatures': Charity, Poor Relief and Pauper Removal in Britain and Ireland during the Great Famine." *English Historical Review* 134, no. 568 (2019): 589–619.

Davis-Floyd, Robbie, and Charles D. McLaughlin. *Ritual: What It Is, How It Works, and Why*. New York: Berghahn Books, 2022.

De Coppet, Daniel, ed. *Understanding Rituals*. London: Routledge, 2022.

Deetz, James. *In Small Things Forgotten: An Archaeology of Early American Life*. Knopf: New York, 1996.

Delaney, Enda. "Our Island Story? Towards a Transnational History of Late Modern Ireland." *Irish Historical Studies* 37 (November 2011): 599–621.

Delaney, Enda. *Demography, State and Society: Irish Migration to Britain, 1921–71*. Montreal and Kingston: McGill-Queen's University Press, 2000.

Delaney, Enda. *Irish Emigration since 1921*. Dundalk: Economic and Social History Society of Ireland, 2002.

Delaney, Enda. *The Irish in Post-War Britain*. New York: Oxford University Press, 2007.

Delaney, Enda, and Donald MacRaild, eds. *Irish Migration, Networks and Ethnic Identities since 1750*. London: Routledge, 2015.

DeSimone, Francesco. *L'Arte della tessitura a Longobucco*. Paludi: Ferrari, 2008.

De Simonis, Paolo, et al. *Cultura contadina in Toscana. Il lavoro dell'uomo. Vol. I: Il lavoro. I prodotti della terra. Vol. II: La casa. Gli animali. Vol. III: Il paesaggio. La vita quotidiana*. Florence: Bonechi, 1982–2004.

Dillon, Niamh. *Homeward Bound: Return Migration from Ireland and India at the End of the British Empire*. New York: New York University Press, 2022.

Diner, Hasia. *Hungering for America: Italian, Irish, and Jewish Foodways in the Age of Migration*. Cambridge, MA: Harvard University Press, 2003.

Diner, Hasia. *Erin's Daughters in America: Irish Immigrant Women in the Nineteenth Century*. Baltimore: Johns Hopkins University Press, 1983.

Donato, Katherine, and Donna R. Gabaccia. *Gender and International Migration: From the Slavery Era to the Global Age*. New York: Russell Sage Foundation, 2015.

Donnelly, James S., Jr. *The Great Irish Potato Famine*. Phoenix Mill: Sutton Publishing, 2001.

Driver, Felix. *Power and Pauperism: The Workhouse System, 1834–1884*. Cambridge: Cambridge University Press, 1993.

Duffy, Patrick J. "Assisted Emigration from the Shirley Estate, 1843–54." *Clogher Record* 14, no. 2 (1992): 7–62.

Durkheim, Emile. *The Elementary Forms of Religious Life (Les formes élémentaires de la vie réligeuse)*. Translated by Karen E. Fields. New York: Free Press, 1995.

Fairchild, Amy L. *Science at the Borders: Immigrant Medical Inspection and the Shaping of the Modern Industrial Labor Force*. Baltimore: Johns Hopkins University Press, 2003.

Fallo, Valentina. "The Power of Images in the Age of Mussolini." PhD diss., University of Pennsylvania, 2013.

Farrell, Elaine. *Women, Crime and Punishment in Ireland: Life in the Nineteenth-Century Convict Prison*. Cambridge: Cambridge University Press, 2020.

Finlay, Victoria. *Fabric: The Hidden History of the Material World.* New York: Pegasus Books, 2022.

Fitzpatrick, David. *The Americanisation of Ireland: Migration and Settlement, 1841–1925.* Cambridge: Cambridge University Press, 2020.

Fitzpatrick, David. *Irish Emigration, 1801–1921.* Dundalk: Economic and Social History Society of Ireland, 1984.

Fitzpatrick, David, ed. *Oceans of Consolation: Personal Accounts of Irish Emigration.* Ithaca: Cornell University Press, 1994.

Fitzgerald, Patrick, and Brian Lambkin. *Migration in Irish History, 1607–2007.* London: Palgrave Macmillan, 2008.

Folassi, Alessandro, ed. *Time Out of Time: Essays on the Festival.* 1987. Albuquerque: University of New Mexico Press, 2005.

Foster, Vere. *Work and Wages; or, the Penny Emigrant's Guide to the United States for Female Servants, Laborers, Mechanics, Farmers, &c.* 6th ed. London: W. and F. G. Cash, 1855.

Foxhall, Katherine. *Health, Medicine, and the Sea: Australian Voyages, c. 1815–1860.* Manchester: Manchester University Press, 2012.

Franzina, Emilio. *Gli italiani al Nuovo mondo. L'emigrazione in America, 1492–1942.* Milan: Arnoldo Mondadori Editore, 1995.

Fraser, Derek, ed. *The New Poor Law in the Nineteenth Century.* New York: St. Martin's Press, 1976.

Freda, Dolores. *Governare i migranti: La legge sull'emigrazione del 1901 e la giurisprudenza del Tribunale di Napoli.* Turin: Giappichelli, 2018.

Freda, Dolores. "La legislazione sulle migrazioni italiane fino al 1901." *Studi Emigrazione* 56, no. 215 (2019): 379–92.

Frykman, Nicholas. *The Bloody Flag: Mutiny in the Age of Atlantic Revolution.* Oakland: University of California Press, 2020.

Gabaccia, Donna R. *Foreign Relations: American Immigration in Global Perspective.* Princeton, NJ: Princeton University Press, 2012.

Gabaccia, Donna R. *From Sicily to Elizabeth Street: Housing and Social Change among Italian Immigrants, 1880–1930.* Albany: State University of New York Press, 1984.

Gabaccia, Donna R. *From the Other Side: Women, Gender, and Immigrant Life in the U.S., 1820–1990.* Bloomington: Indiana University Press, 1995.

Gabaccia, Donna R. ed. *Gender and Migration Revisited.* New York: Center for Migration Studies of New York, 2006.

Gabaccia, Donna R. *Italy's Many Diasporas.* London: University College London Press, 2000.

Gabaccia, Donna R. *Militants and Migrants: Rural Sicilians Become American Workers.* New Brunswick: Rutgers University Press, 1988.

Gabaccia, Donna R. *We Are What We Eat: Ethnic Food and the Making of Americans.* Cambridge, MA: Harvard University Press, 2000.

Gabaccia, Donna R., and Franca Iacovetta, eds. *Women, Gender, and Transnational Lives: Italian Workers of the World.* Toronto: University of Toronto Press, 2002.

Gabaccia, Donna R., and Fraser M. Ottanelli. *Italian Workers of the World: Labor Migration and the Formation of Multiethnic States*. Urbana: University of Illinois Press, 2005.

Gallagher, Joseph, ed. *Material Culture of Donegal Communities Abroad. Donegal Heritage Series 2*. Donegal: Donegal County Council, 2014.

Gallman, J. Matthew. *Receiving Erin's Children: Philadelphia, Liverpool, and the Irish Famine Migration, 1845–1855*. Chapel Hill: University of North Carolina Press, 2000.

Gattey, Emma. "The Migration of Religion to New Zealand in the Shipboard Diaries of Scottish Presbyterians." *Journal of Migration History* 9, no. 1 (2023): 78–105.

Gennari, John. *Flavor and Soul: Italian America at Its African American Edge*. Chicago: University of Chicago Press, 2017.

Gentile, Vincenzo. *La Calabria strappata*. Milan: LibrAre, 2009.

Gerritsen, Anne, and Giorgio Riello, eds. *Writing Material Culture History*. Second edition. London: Bloomsbury Academic, 2021.

Giunta, Edvige, and Joseph Sciorra, eds. *Embroidered Stories: Interpreting Women's Domestic Needlework from the Italian Diaspora*. Jackson: University Press of Mississippi, 2014.

Giunta, Edvige, and Mary Anne Tasciatti. *Talking to the Girls: Intimate and Political Essays on the Triangle Shirtwaist Factory Fire*. New York: New York University Press, 2022.

Glassie, Henry H. *Material Culture*. Bloomington: Indiana University Press, 1999.

Goody, Jack. "Against 'Ritual': Loosely Structured Thoughts on a Loosely Defined Topic." *Cambridge Journal of Anthropology* 2 (February 1975): 32–43.

Gothard, Jan. *Blue China: Single Female Migration to Colonial Australia*. Melbourne: Melbourne University Press, 2001.

Green, David R. *Pauper Capital: London and the Poor Law, 1790–1870*. Burlington, UK: Ashgate, 2010.

Green, Harvey. "Cultural History and the Material(s) Turn." *Cultural History* 1, no. 1 (2012): 61–82.

Groarke, Vona. *Hereafter: The Telling Life of Ellen O'Hara*. New York: New York University Press, 2022.

Guglielmo, Jennifer. *Living the Revolution: Italian Women's Resistance and Radicalism in New York City, 1880–1945*. Chapel Hill: University of North Carolina Press, 2010.

Guglielmo, Jennifer, and Salvatore Salerno, eds. *Are Italians White? How Race Is Made in America*. London: Routledge, 2003.

Guglielmo, Thomas. *White on Arrival: Italians, Race, Color, and Power in Chicago, 1890–1945*. New York: Oxford University Press, 2000.

Guinan, Joseph. *Scenes and Sketches in an Irish Parish, or Priest and People of Doon by a Country Curate*. 3rd ed. Dublin: M. H. Gill, 1903.

Haines, Robin F. *Doctors at Sea: Emigrant Voyages to Colonial Australia*. Basingstoke: Palgrave Macmillan, 2005.

Haines, Robin F. *Emigration and the Labouring Poor: Australian Recruitment in Britain and Ireland, 1831–60*. Houndmills, UK: Palgrave Macmillan, 1997.

Haines, Robin F. "Workhouse to Gangplank: Mobilising Irish Pauper Women and Girls bound for Australia in the Mid-Nineteenth Century." In *Irish-Australian Studies: Papers Delivered at the Eighth Irish-Australian Conference*, edited by Richard Davis,

Jennifer Livett, Anne-Maree Whitaker, and Peter Moore, 166–78. Sydney: Crossing Press, 1996.

Hallissy, Margaret. "But Come Ye Back: The Yank." In *Understanding Contemporary Irish Fiction and Drama*, edited by Margaret Hallissy, 155–73. Columbia: University of South Carolina Press, 2016.

Hannan, Leonie, and Sarah Longair. *History through Material Culture*. Manchester: Manchester University Press, 2017.

Harling, Philip. "Assisted Emigration and the Moral Dilemmas of the Mid-Victorian Imperial State." *Historical Journal* 59, no. 4 (2016): 1027–49.

Harlow, Mary, and Marie-Louise Nosch, eds. *Greek and Roman Textiles and Dress: An Interdisciplinary Anthology*. Oxford and Philadelphia: Oxbow Books, 2014.

Hassam, Andrew. *No Privacy for Writing: Shipboard Diaries, 1852–1879*. Melbourne: Melbourne University Press, 1995.

Hirota, Hidetaka. *Expelling the Poor: Atlantic Seaboard States and the Nineteenth-Century Origins of American Immigration Policy*. New York: Oxford University Press, 2017.

Hobsbawm, Eric. *Nations and Nationalism since 1780: Programme, Myth, Reality*. Cambridge: Cambridge University Press, 1990.

Irving, Washington. *The Sketch Book of Geoffrey Crayon, Gent.* 2 vols. London: John Murray 1824.

Iuliano, Luigia Angela. *Lungo il filo di Aracne: Fili, trame e tinte Calabria mediterranea*. Soveria Mannelli: Rubbettino, 2010.

Juliani, Richard N. *Building Little Italy: Philadelphia's Italians before Mass Migration*. University Park: Penn State University Press, 1998.

Kaufman, James C. A. "Learning from the Fotomat." *American Scholar* 49, (Spring, 1980): 244–46.

Kenny, Kevin. *The American Irish: A History*. New York: Longman, 2000. New York: Routledge, 2014.

Kenny, Kevin. "Diaspora and Comparison: The Global Irish as a Case Study." *Journal of American History* 90 (June 2003): 134–62.

Kenny, Kevin. *Diaspora: A Very Short Introduction*. New York: Oxford University Press, 2013.

Kenny, Kevin, ed. *Ireland and the British Empire: The Oxford History of the British Empire Companion Series*. New York: Oxford University Press, 2004.

Kenny, Kevin. "Irish Emigration, ca. 1845–1900." In *The Cambridge History of Ireland, Vol. 3. 1730–1880*, edited by James Kelly, 666–87. Thomas Bartlett, gen. ed. 4 vols. Cambridge: Cambridge University Press, 2018.

Kenny, Kevin. "Irish Emigrations in a Comparative Perspective." In *The Cambridge Social History of Modern Ireland*, edited by Eugenio F. Biagini and Mary Daly, 405–22. Cambridge: Cambridge University Press, 2017.

Kenny, Kevin. *Making Sense of the Molly Maguires*. 25th anniversary edition. New York: Oxford University Press, 2023.

Kenny, Kevin. *The Problem of Immigration in a Slaveholding Republic: Policing Mobility in the Nineteenth-Century United States*. New York: Oxford University Press, 2023.

Kenny, Kevin. "Two Diasporic Moments in Irish Emigration History: The Famine Generation and the Contemporary Era." *Studi irlandesi* 9, no. 9 (2019): 43–65.

Kerber, Linda K. "The Stateless as the Citizens' Other: A View from the United States." *American Historical Review* 112 (February 2007): 1–34.

Kertzer, David I., and Richard P. Saller, eds. *The Family in Italy: From Antiquity to the Present*. New Haven: Yale University Press, 1991.

Kertzer, David I. *Ritual, Politics, and Power*. New Haven, CT: Yale University Press, 1989.

Kinealy, Christine. *This Great Calamity: The Irish Famine, 1845–52*. Boulder, CO: Roberts Rinehart, 1995.

Klein, Herbert S. *A Population History of the United States*. New York: Cambridge University Press, 2004.

Levi, Carlo. "Il mito dell'America." In *Le mille patrie, uomini, fatti, paesi d'Italia*, edited by Gigliola De Donato. Rome: Donzelli Editore, 2000.

Lorenzoni, Giovanni. *Inchiesta parlamentare sulle condizioni dei contadini nelle province meridionali e nella Sicilia*. Vol. 6/1/2. Rome: Tip. Naz. G. Bertero, 1910.

Luconi, Stefano. *From Paesani to White Ethnics: The Italian Experience in Philadelphia*. Albany: SUNY Press, 2001.

Luconi, Stefano, and Matteo Pretelli. *L'immigrazione negli Stati Uniti*. Milan: Il Mulino, 2008.

MacCannell, Dean. *The Tourist: A New Theory of the Leisure Class*. New York: Schocken Books, 1976.

MacRaild, Donald M. *The Irish Diaspora in Britain, 1750–1939*. New York: Palgrave Macmillan, 2011.

Mageean, Deirdre M. "Emigration from Irish Ports." *Journal of American Ethnic History* 13 (Fall 1993): 6–30.

Mangano, Anthony. "Effect of Emigration upon Italy." *Charities and the Commons: A Weekly Journal of Philanthropy and Social Advance* 9 (January 4, 1908), 1329–38.

Marinari, Maddalena. *Unwanted: Italian and Jewish Mobilization against Restrictive Immigration Laws, 1882–1965*. Chapel Hill: University of North Carolina Press, 2020.

Marinari, Maddalena, and María Cristina García, eds. *Whose America? U.S. Immigration Policy since 1980*. Champaign: University of Illinois Press, 2023.

Marinari, Maddalena, María Cristina García, and Madeline Hsu, eds. *A Nation of Immigrants Reconsidered: U.S. Society in an Age of Restriction, 1924–1965*. Champaign: University of Illinois Press, 2019.

Mark-Fitzgerald, Emily, Ciarán McCabe, and Ciarán Reilly, eds. *Dublin and the Great Irish Famine*. Dublin: University College Dublin Press, 2022.

Marschall, Sabine. "Tourism and Memories of Home: Introduction." In *Tourism and Memories of Home: Migrants, Displaced People, Exiles and Diasporic Communities*, edited by Sabine Marschall, 1–31. Bristol: Channel View Publications, 2017.

Martineau, Harriet. *Letters from America*. London: John Chapman, 1852.

Mayor Des Planches, Edmondo. *Attraverso gli Stati Uniti*. Turin: Unione tipografico-editrice torinese, 1913.

McCabe, Ciarán. *Begging, Charity and Religion in Pre-Famine Ireland*. Liverpool: Liverpool University Press, 2016.

McCarthy, Angela. "The Irish in Australia and New Zealand." In *The Cambridge Social History of Modern Ireland*, edited by Eugenio F. Biagini and Mary E. Daly, 478–96. Cambridge: Cambridge University Press, 2017.

McClaughlin, Trevor. *Barefoot and Pregnant? Irish Famine Orphans in Australia*. 2 vols. Melbourne: Genealogical Society of Victoria, 1991, 2001.

McKeown, Adam. "Ritualization of Regulation: The Enforcement of Chinese Exclusion in the United States and China." *American Historical Review* 108 (April 2003): 377–403.

McMahon, Cian T. *The Coffin Ship: Life and Death at Sea during the Great Irish Famine*. New York: New York University Press, 2021.

McMahon, Cian T. *The Global Dimensions of Irish Identity: Race, Nation, and the Popular Press, 1840–1880*. Chapel Hill: University of North Carolina Press, 2015.

McMahon, Cian T. "'That City Afloat': Maritime Dimensions of Ireland's Great Famine Migration." *American Historical Review* 127 (March 2022): 100–28.

McWilliams, Ellen. *Women and Exile in Contemporary Irish Fiction*. London: Palgrave MacMillan, 2013.

Meagher, Timothy J. *Becoming Irish American: The Making and Remaking of a People from Roanoke to JFK*. New Haven: Yale University Press, 2023.

Meagher, Timothy J. *The Columbia Guide to Irish American History*. New York: Columbia University Press, 2005.

Meaney, Gerardine, Mary O'Dowd, and Bernadette Whelan. *Reading the Irish Woman: Studies in Cultural Encounter and Exchange, 1714–1960*. Liverpool: Liverpool University Press, 2013.

Meligrana, Francesco Saverio. "Donne, oro e monili in un universo contadino." In *Donne e società: Atti del IV congresso internazionale di studi antropologici siciliani*, edited by Janne Vibaek, 395–412. Palermo: Faculty of Letters and Philosophy, University of Palermo, 1982.

Messina, Maria. *Behind Closed Doors: Her Father's House and Other Stories of Sicily*. Translated with an introduction by Elise Magistro. New York: Feminist Press of the City University of New York, 2007.

Messina, Maria. *Piccoli gorghi*. Palermo: Sellerio Editore, 1997.

Metress, Eileen. "The American Wake of Ireland: Symbolic Death Ritual." *OMEGA Journal of Death and Dying* 21 (1990): 147–53.

Migration Policy Institute, "Top 35 Diasporas in the United States, 2021." www.migrationpolicy.org/programs/data-hub/charts/top-diaspora-groups-united-states-2021.

Miles, Tiya. *All That She Carried: The Journey of Ashley's Sack, a Black Family Keepsake*. New York: Random House, 2021.

Miller, Daniel. *Materiality*. Durham, NC: Duke University Press, 2005.

Miller, Daniel. *Stuff*. London: Polity Press, 2010.

Miller, Kerby A. *Emigrants and Exiles: Ireland and the Irish Exodus to North America*. New York: Oxford University Press, 1985.

Miller, Kerby A., Bruce Boling, and David N Doyle. "Emigrants and Exiles: Irish Cultures and Irish Emigration to North America." *Irish Historical Studies* 22 (September 1980): 97–125.

Miller, Kerby A., et al., eds. *Irish Immigrants in the Land of Canaan: Letters and Memoirs from Colonial and Revolutionary America, 1675–1815*. Oxford: Oxford University Press, 2003.

Miller, William Ian. "Getting a Fix on Violence." In *Essays on Honor, Social Discomfort, and Violence: Humiliation and Other*, edited by William Ian Miller, 53–92. Ithaca: Cornell University Press, 1993.

Minicuci, Maria. "Notes on the Condition of Women in a Southern Italian Village." In *Women of the Mediterranean*, edited by Monique Gadant, 170–77. Translated from the French by A. M. Berrett. London and New Jersey: Zed Books, 1986.

Mirzoeff, Nicholas. "The Multiple Viewpoint: Diaspora and Visual Culture." In *The Visual Culture Reader*, edited by Nicholas Mirzoeff, 204–14. New York: Routledge, 2002.

Moe, Nelson. *The View from Vesuvius: Italian Culture and the Southern Question*. Berkeley: University of California Press, 2006.

Molinari, Augusta. "Porti, trasporti, compagnie." In *Storia dell'emigrazione Italiana: Partenze*, edited by Piero Bevilaqua, Andreina De Clementi, and Emilio Franzina, 237–39. Rome: Donzelli, 2001.

Moore, George. *The Untilled Field*. Buckinghamshire, UK: Colin Smythe Ltd., 2000.

Mora, Juan Ignacio. "Managing the Migration: Latino Intermediaries and the Expansion of United States Migratory Labor from World War I through the Bracero Program." *Journal of American Ethnic History* 42 (April 2023): 103–29.

Moran, Gerard. *Sending Out Ireland's Poor: Assisted Emigration to North America in the Nineteenth Century*. Dublin: Four Courts Press, 2004.

Mosso, Angelo. "Gli Emigranti." *Nuova antologia di lettere, scienze ed arti*. Rome: Direzione della Nuova Antologia, 1905.

Mosso, Angelo. *Vita moderna degli italiani*. Milan: Fratelli Treves, 1912.

Moynihan, Sinead. *Ireland, Migration and Return Migration: The "Returned Yank" in the Cultural Imagination, 1952 to Present*. Liverpool: Liverpool University Press, 2019.

Neal, Frank. *Black '47: Britain and the Famine Irish*. London: Newsham Press, 1998.

Neal, Frank. "Lancashire, the Famine Irish and the Poor Laws: A Study in Crisis Management," *Irish Economic and Social History* 22, no. 1 (1995): 26–28.

Neal, Frank. "Liverpool, the Irish Steamship Companies and the Famine Irish." *Immigrants & Minorities* 5 (March 1986): 87–111.

Ngai, Mae. *Impossible Subjects: Illegal Aliens and the Making of Modern America*. Princeton, NJ: Princeton University Press, 2004.

Ngai, Mae. *The Lucky Ones: One Family and the Extraordinary Invention of Chinese America*. Princeton, NJ: Princeton University Press, 2010.

Niceforo, Alfredo. *Italiani del nord e italiani del sud*. Turin: Fratelli Bocca, 1901.

Niceforo, Alfredo. *L'Italia barbara contemporanea: Studi ed appunti*. Milan and Palermo: Remo Sandron, 1898.

Nicholson, Asenath. *Ireland's Welcome to the Stranger: On an Excursion through Ireland in 1844 & 1845, for the Purpose of Personally Investigating the Condition of the Poor.* New York: Bakker and Scrivner, 1847.

Nystrom, Justin. *Creole Italian: Sicilian Immigrants and the Shaping of New Orleans Food Culture.* Athens: University of Georgia Press, 2018.

Ó Cadhain, Máirtín. *The Quick and the Dead: Selected Stories.* Edited by Louis De Paor. Translated by Katherine Duffy. New Haven: Yale University Press, 2021.

Ó Cadhain, Máirtín. *The Road to Brightcity.* Translated by Eoghan Ó Tuairisc. Dublin: Poolbeg Press, 1981.

Ó Cadhain, Máirtín. *Selected Stories.* Edited by Louis De Paor. Translated by Úna Ní Chonchúir. New Haven: Yale University Press, 2021.

Ó Cathasaigh, Aindrias. "A Vision to Realise: Ó Cadhain's Politics." *Canadian Journal of Irish Studies* 34 (Spring 2008): 18–27.

O'Connell, Anne. "Assisted Female Emigration: Vere Foster's Scheme, 1880–1896." Unpublished PhD diss., University of Limerick, 1998.

Ó Criomhthain, Tomás. *Allagar na hInise.* Baile Átha Cliath: An Gúm, 1997.

Ó Crualaoich, Gearóid. "The 'Merry Wake.'" In *Irish Popular Culture, 1650–1850,* edited by James S. Donnelly Jr. and Kerby A. Miller, 173–200. Dublin: Irish Academic Press, 1999.

Ó Gráda, Cormac. *Black '47 and Beyond: The Great Irish Famine in History, Economy, and Memory.* Princeton, NJ: Princeton University Press, 1999.

O'Leary, Philip. *Irish Interior: Keeping Faith with the Past in Gaelic Prose, 1940–1951.* Dublin: University College Dublin Press, 2010.

O'Leary, Philip. "Yank Outsiders: Irish Americans in Gaelic Fiction and Drama of the Irish Free State, 1922–1939." In *New Perspectives on the Irish Diaspora,* edited by Charles Fanning, 253–65. Carbondale and Edwardsville: Southern Illinois University Press, 2000.

Orano, Paolo. "Per una psicologia del popolo Italiano." *Rivista politica e letteraria.* Rome: Stab. Tip. della Tribuna, 1900.

Orsi, Robert. *The Madonna of 115th Street: Faith and Community in Italian Harlem, 1880–1950.* New Haven: Yale University Press, 1988.

Paganoni, Tony. "Italian Emigration after the Second World War." *International Migration Review* 37 (January 2023), Supplement: 85–96.

Parker, Rosika. *The Subversive Stitch: Embroidery and the Making of the Feminine.* New York: Routledge, 1984.

Patriarca, Silvana. *Numbers and Nationhood: Writing Statistics in Nineteenth-Century Italy.* Cambridge: Cambridge University Press, 2003.

Paynter, Eleanor. "Creating Crises: Risk, Racialization, and the Migration-Security Nexus in Italy and the US." In *Managing Migration in Italy and the United States,* edited by Lauren Braun-Strumfels, Maddalena Marinari, and Daniele Fiorentino, 55–76. Berlin: DeGruyter, 2023.

Peck, Gunther. *Reinventing Free Labor: Padrones and Immigrant Workers in the North American West, 1880–1930.* New York: Cambridge University Press, 2000.

Pedersen, Marianne Hold, and Mikkel Rytter. "Rituals of Migration, an Introduction." *Journal of Ethnic and Migration Studies* 44, no. 16 (2018): 2603–16.

Pergher, Roberta. *Mussolini's Nation-Empire: Sovereignty and Settlement in Italy's Borderlands, 1922–1943*. Cambridge: Cambridge University Press, 2017.

Perlmann, Joel. *Italians Then, Mexicans Now: Immigrant Origins and the Second-Generation Progress, 1890–2000*. New York: Russell Sage Foundation, 2007.

Petrusewicz, Marta. *Latifundium: Moral Economy and Material Life in a European Periphery*. Ann Arbor: University of Michigan Press, 1989.

Peyton, Alex. J. *The Emigrant's Friend; or Hints on Emigration to the United States of America Addressed to the People of Ireland*. Cork: J. O'Brien, 1853.

Polezzi, Loredana. "Translating, Repositioning, Reframing: On the Transatlantic Routes of Objects and Memories." *Forum Italicum* 57, no. 2 (2023): 462–75.

Pozzetta, George. "Italian Migration: From Sunnyside to the World." In *Shadows over Sunnyside: An Arkansas Plantation in Transition, 1830–1945*, edited by Jeannie Whayne, 95–102. Fayetteville: University of Arkansas, 1993.

Pretelli, Matteo, and Donatella Izzo, eds. *Il ritorno della "diaspora": Migranti italiani di ritorno dagli Stati Uniti del novecento*. Naples: La scuola di Pitagora editrice, 2023.

Ratti, Anna Maria. "The Italian Migration Movements." In *International Migrations, Vol. II: Interpretations*, edited by Walter F. Willcox and Imre Ferenczi, 440–70. Washington, DC: National Bureau of Economic Research, 1931.

Read, Charles. *The Great Famine in Ireland and Britain's Financial Crisis*. Woodbridge: Boydell Press, 2022.

Rediker, Marcus. *Outlaws of the Atlantic: Sailors, Pirates, and Motley Crews in the Age of Sail*. Boston: Beacon Press, 2014.

Redmond, Jennifer. *Moving Histories: Irish Women's Emigration to Britain from Independence to Republic*. Liverpool: Liverpool University Press, 2018.

Reeder, Linda. *Italy in the Modern World: Society, Culture, and Identity*. London: Bloomsbury Academic, 2019.

Reeder, Linda. "Men of Honor and Honorable Men: Migration and Italian Migration to the United States from 1880–1930." *Italian Americana* 28, no. 1 (2010): 18–35.

Reeder, Linda. *Widows in White: Migration and the Transformation of Rural Italian Women, Sicily, 1880–1920*. Toronto: University of Toronto Press, 2003.

Reid, Richard E. *Farewell My Children: Irish Assisted Emigration to Australia, 1848–1870*. Sydney: Anchor Books Australia, 2011.

Reilly, Ciarán, ed. *The Famine Irish: Emigration and the Great Hunger*. Dublin: History Press Ireland, 2016.

Ricci, Elisa. "Women's Crafts." In *Peasant Art in Italy*, edited by Charles Holmes, 17–32. New York: The Studio, Ltd., 1913.

Rinauro, Sandro. *Il cammino della speranza: L'emigrazione clandestina degli italiani nel secondo dopoguerra*. Turin: Giulio Einaudi Editore, 2009.

Rose, Michael E., ed. *The Poor and the City: The English Poor Law in Its Urban Context, 1834–1914*. New York: St. Martin's Press, 1985.

Ross, Eric B., ed. *Beyond the Myths of Culture: Essays in Cultural Materialism.* San Francisco: Academic Press, 1980.

Ruberto, Laura E. and Joseph Sciorra. "Introduction: Real Italians, New Immigrants." In *New Italian Migrations to the United States, Vol. 1: Politics and History since 1945,* edited by Laura E. Ruberto and Joseph Sciorra, 1–58. Urbana: University of Illinois Press, 2017.

Ruberto, Laura E., and Joseph Sciorra. "Italian American Stuff: A Survey of Material Culture, Migration, and Ethnicity." *SOAR: The Society of Americanists Review* 3 (2021–2022): 1–82.

Ruberto, Laura E., and Joseph Sciorra, eds. *New Italian Migrations to the United States.* 2 vols. *Vol. 1: Politics and History since 1945. Vol. 2: Art and Culture since 1945.* Urbana: University of Illinois Press, 2017.

Salomone-Marino, Salvatore. *Customs and Habits of the Sicilian Peasants.* 1879. Madison, NJ: Fairleigh Dickinson University Press, 1981.

Salvetti, Patrizia. *Rope and Soap: Lynchings of Italians in the United States.* New York: Bordighera Press, 2017.

Sanfilippo, Matteo, ed. *Emigrazione e storia d'Italia.* Cosenza: Luigi Pellegrini Editore, 2003.

Sautier, Albert. *Tappeti rustici italiani.* Milan: Valcarenghi, 1922.

Saverino, Joan. "Embroidery as Inscription in the Life of a Calabrian Immigrant Woman." In *Embroidered Stories: Interpreting Women's Domestic Needlework from the Italian Diaspora,* edited by Edvige Giunta and Joseph Sciorra, 281–312. Jackson: University of Mississippi Press, 2014.

Saverino, Joan. "*Ozaturù, 'Ncullerata and Rituortu*: Deeply Local Textiles, Identity, and Diasporic Connections." In *Teorizzare la diaspora italiana: Saggi, 2017–2020,* edited by Marco Gatto and Annamaria Scorza, 85–118. Saveria Mannelli: Rubettino, 2021.

Sayers, Peig. *Peig.* Dublin: Comhleacht Oideachas na hÉireannn, 1935.

Scally, Robert J. *The End of Hidden Ireland: Rebellion, Famine, and Emigration.* New York: Oxford University Press, 1995.

Scally, Robert J. "Liverpool Ships and Irish Emigrants in the Age of Sail." *Journal of Social History* 17 (Autumn 1983): 5–30.

Schneider, Jane. *Cloth and Human Experience.* Washington, DC: Smithsonian Institution Press, 1989.

Schneider, Jane, ed. *Italy's "Southern Question": Orientalism in One Country.* New York: Berg, 1998.

Schneider, Jane. "Of Vigilance and Virgins: Honor, Shame and Access to Resources in Mediterranean Societies," *Ethnology* 10, no. 1 (1971): 1–24.

Schneider, Jane. "Trousseau as Treasure: Some Contradictions of Late Nineteenth-Century Change in Sicily." In *Beyond the Myths of Culture: Essays in Cultural Materialism,* edited by Eric B. Ross, 323–56. San Francisco: Academic Press, 1980.

Schoeppner, Michael A. *Moral Contagion: Black Atlantic Sailors, Citizenship, and Diplomacy in Antebellum America.* Cambridge: Cambridge University Press, 2019.

Schofield, Ann. "The Returned Yank as Site of Memory in Irish Popular Culture." *Journal of American Studies* 47 (November 2013): 1175–95.

Schrier, Arnold. *Ireland and the American Emigration, 1850–1900*. Minneapolis: University of Minnesota Press, 1958.

Schrover, Marlou, and Eileen Yeo. *Gender, Migration, and the Public Sphere, 1850–2005*. New York: Routledge, 2010.

Sciascia, Leonardo. "Il lungo viaggio." In Leonardo Sciascia. *Il mare colore del vino*. Turin: 1973.

Sciascia, Leonardo. "The Long Journey." In *The Wine-dark Sea*, edited by Leonardo Sciascia, translated by Avril Bardoni, 19–26. Manchester, UK: Carcanet, 1985.

Sciorra, Joseph. *Built with Faith: Italian American Imagination and Catholic Material Culture in New York City*. Knoxville: University of Tennessee Press, 2015.

Sciorra, Joseph. "'Don't Forget You Have Relatives Here': Transnational Intimacy and Acoustic Communities of WOV-AM's *La Grande Famiglia*." In *New Italian Migrations to the United States, Vol. 2: Art and Culture since 1945*, edited by Laura E. Ruberto and Joseph Sciorra, 32–64. Urbana: University of Illinois Press, 2017.

Sciorra, Joseph, ed. *Italian Folk: Vernacular Culture in Italian-American Lives*. New York: Fordham University Press, 2011.

Sciorra Joseph. "Sending a Telegram to the Pope." *Joseph Sciorra's Blog*, August 20, 2008. https://bloggers.iitaly.org/bloggers/3951/sending-telegram-pope.

Senner, J. H. "Immigration from Italy," *North American Review* 162 (June 1896): 649–57.

Sergi, Giuseppe. *La decadenza delle nazioni latine*. Turin: Fratelli Bocca, 1900.

Snell, K. D. M. *Parish and Belonging: Community, Identity and Welfare in England and Wales, 1700–1950*. Cambridge: Cambridge University Press, 2006.

Stanger-Ross, Jordan. *Staying Italian: Urban Change and Ethnic Life in Postwar Toronto and Philadelphia*. Chicago: University of Chicago Press, 2009.

Stephenson, Barry. *Ritual: A Very Short Introduction*. Oxford: Oxford University Press, 2015.

Strong, Rowan. *Victorian Christianity and Emigrant Voyages to British Colonies, c. 1840–c. 1914*. London: Oxford University Press, 2017.

Taruffi, Dino, Leonello de Nobili, and Pasquale Villari. *La questione agraria e l'emigrazione in Calabria: Note statistiche ed economiche*. Florence: G. Barbèra, 1908.

Teti, Vito. "Noti sui comportamenti delle donne sole degli 'americani' durante la prima emigrazione in Calabria." *Studi Emigrazione* 24, no. 85 (1987): 13–46.

Thomas, Julia Adeney. "The Evidence of Sight." *History and Theory* 48 (December 2009): 151–68.

Tilley, Christopher Y., Webb Keane, and Susanne Kuechler et al., eds. *Handbook of Material Culture*. London: SAGE, 2006.

Tirabassi, Maddalena. "Bourgeois Men, Peasant Women: Rethinking Domestic Work and Morality in Italy." In *Women, Gender, and Transnational Lives: Italian Workers of the World*, edited by Donna Gabaccia and Franca Iacovetta, 106–30. Toronto: University of Toronto Press, 2002.

Tóibín, Colm. *Brooklyn: A Novel*. New York: Scribner, 2009.

Torpey, John. *The Invention of the Passport: Citizenship, Surveillance, and the State*. New York: Cambridge University Press, 2018.

Tsing, Anna L. *Friction: An Ethnography of Global Connection.* Princeton, NJ: Princeton University Press, 2005.

Turner, Victor. "Betwixt and Between: The Liminal Period in Rites de Passage." In *The Forest of Symbols: Aspects of Ndembu Ritual,* edited by Victor Turner, 93–111. Ithaca, NY: Cornell University Press, 1967.

Turner, Victor ed. *Celebration: Studies in Festivity and Ritual.* Washington, DC: Smithsonian Institute Press, 1982.

Turner, Victor, and Edith Turner. "Religious Celebrations." In *Celebration: Studies in Festivity and Ritual,* edited by Victor Turner, 202–3. Washington, DC: Smithsonian Institute Press, 1982.

Van Gennep, Arnold. *Rites de Passage.* Paris: A. et J. Picard, 1909.

Van Gennep, Arnold. *The Rites of Passage.* Second edition, translated by Monika B. Vizedom and Gabrielle L. Caffee. Chicago: University of Chicago Press, 2019.

Vanni, Illaria. "Oggetti Spaesati, Unhomely Belongings: Objects, Migrations and Cultural Apocalypses." *Cultural Studies Review* 19 (September 2013): 150–74.

Verdicchio, Pasquale. *Looters, Photographers, and Thieves: Aspects of Italian Photographic Culture in the Nineteenth and Twentieth Centuries.* Madison, NJ: Fairleigh Dickinson University Press, 2011.

Weiner, Annette B., and Jane Schneider, eds. *Cloth and Human Experience.* Washington, DC: Smithsonian Institution Press, 1989.

Whelan, Bernadette. *American Government in Ireland, 1790–1913: A History of the US Consular Service.* Manchester: Manchester University Press, 2010.

Whelan, Bernadette. *De Valera and Roosevelt: Irish and American Diplomacy in Times of Crisis, 1932–1939.* Cambridge: Cambridge University Press, 2020.

Whelan, Bernadette. "The 'Idea of America' in the New Irish State, 1922–1960." In *The Irish in the Atlantic World,* edited by David Gleeson, 76–109. Columbia: University of South Carolina Press, 2013.

Whelehan, Niall. *Changing Land: Diaspora Activism and the Irish Land War.* New York: New York University Press, 2021.

Wiley, John, and George Putnam. *Wiley & Putnam's Emigrant's Guide.* London: Wiley & Putnam, 1845.

Wills, Clair. *Lovers and Strangers: An Immigrant History of Post-War Britain.* New York: Allen Lane, 2017.

Wills, Clair. *The Best Are Leaving: Emigration and Post-War Irish Culture.* New York: Cambridge University Press, 2015.

Wokeck, Marianne S. "Irish Immigration to the Delaware Valley before the American Revolution." *Proceedings of the Royal Irish Academy: Archaeology, Culture, History, Literature* 96c, no. 5 (1996): 103–35.

Yasir, Sameer. "They Married for a Life Abroad. But They Never Saw Their Husbands Again," *New York Times,* June 13, 2023. www.nytimes.com/2023/06/13/world/asia/india-brides-women.html.

Zahra, Tara. *The Great Departure: Mass Migration from Eastern Europe and the Making of the Free World.* New York: W. W. Norton, 2016.

ABOUT THE EDITORS

KEVIN KENNY is Glucksman Professor of History at New York University. He is the author of *Making Sense of the Molly Maguires* (1998; 25th anniversary edition, 2023); *The American Irish: A History* (2000); *Peaceable Kingdom Lost: The Paxton Boys and the Destruction of William Penn's Holy Experiment* (2009); *Diaspora: A Very Short Introduction* (2013); *The Problem of Immigration in a Slaveholding Republic: Policing Mobility in the Nineteenth-Century United States* (2023); and articles on migration in the *Journal of American History*, the *Journal of American Ethnic History*, *Irish Historical Studies*, and *Studi Irlandesi*. Professor Kenny is a past president of the Immigration and Ethnic History Society.

MADDALENA MARINARI is Professor of History at Gustavus Adolphus College. She is the author of *Unwanted: Italian and Jewish Mobilization Against Restrictive Immigration Laws, 1882–1965* (2020) and articles on immigration restriction, US immigration policy, and immigrant mobilization in the *Journal of Policy History*, the *Journal of American Ethnic History*, and the *Social Science History Journal*. She has also co-edited three volumes on different aspects of US immigration history in the twentieth century and a special issue of the *Journal of American History* on the immigration restriction acts of the 1920s. Professor Marinari is president of the Immigration and Ethnic History Society.

ABOUT THE CONTRIBUTORS

JILL C. BENDER is Associate Professor of History at the University of North Carolina–Greensboro. The author of *The 1857 Indian Uprising and the British Empire* (2016), she is currently working on a second book project, *Assisted Emigrants: Irish Female Migration Projects and the British Empire*.

LAUREN BRAUN-STRUMFELS is Associate Professor of History at Cedar Crest College. She is the author of *Partners in Gatekeeping: How Italy Shaped U.S. Immigration Policy over Ten Pivotal Years, 1891–1901* (2023) and co-editor, with Maddalena Marinari and Daniele Fiorentino, of *Managing Migration in Italy and the United States* (2024). Her work has appeared in *Labor* and the *Journal of American Ethnic History*. She is currently writing a book, *The Forgotten Solution to America's Immigration Problem: Italians, Distribution Policy, and the South in the Progressive Era*.

DONNA GABACCIA is Professor Emerita at the University of Toronto. An internationally renowned historian of migration, gender, and food studies, she is the author of *From Sicily to Elizabeth Street: Housing and Social Change among Italian Immigrants, 1880–1930* (1984); *From the Other Side: Women, Gender, and Immigrant Life in the U.S., 1820–1990* (1995); *We Are What We Eat: Ethnic Food and the Making of Americans* (2000); *Foreign Relations: American Immigration in Global Perspective* (2012); and, with Katharine Donato, *Gender and Migration: From the Slavery Era to the Global Age* (2015). Professor Gabaccia is a past president of the Social Science History Association and the Society for the History of the Gilded Age and Progressive Era.

HIDETAKA HIROTA is Associate Professor of History at the University of California, Berkeley. He is the author of *Expelling the Poor:*

Atlantic Seaboard States and the Nineteenth-Century Origins of American Immigration Policy (2017), as well as articles on US immigration history in the *Journal of American History*, the *Journal of American Ethnic History*, and *American Quarterly*.

CIAN T. MCMAHON is Professor of History at the University of Nevada, Las Vegas. He is the author of *The Global Dimensions of Irish Identity: Race, Nation, and the Popular Press, 1840–1880* (2015) and *The Coffin Ship: Life and Death at Sea during the Great Irish Famine* (2021).

GRÁINNE MCEVOY is a historian of US immigration who manages research programming at the Keough-Naughton Institute for Irish Studies at the University of Notre Dame. A graduate of the University of Edinburgh and Trinity College, Dublin, she received her PhD in History from Boston College, where her doctoral research focused on US immigration policy and Catholic social thought.

LINDA REEDER is Professor of History and Women's and Gender Studies at the University of Missouri. She is the author of *Widows in White: Migration and the Transformation of Rural Italian Women* (2003) and *Italy in the Modern World: Society, Culture, and Identity* (2019) and co-editor with Marcelo Borges and Sonia Cancian of *Emotional Landscapes: Love, Gender, and Migration* (2021).

JOAN L. SAVERINO is an independent scholar whose career was in museum education and teaching. Most recently, she was a visiting scholar at the University of Pennsylvania and a research assistant professor at Arcadia University. Her scholarship focuses on material culture, gender, and space and place. Her book manuscript about migrant women's expressive lives from Calabria, Italy, to Appalachia has been accepted into the multicultural folklore series with the University of Mississippi Press.

JOSEPH SCIORRA is Director for Academic and Cultural Programs at the Calandra Italian American Institute, Queens College, CUNY. He researches and publishes on vernacular culture, including religious practices, cultural landscapes, and popular music. He is the author of *Built with Faith: Italian American Imagination and Catholic Material Culture in New York City* (2015) and co-editor with Laura Ruberto of *New Italian Migrations to the United States*, 2 vols. *Vol. 1: Politics and History since 1945* and *Vol. 2: Art and Culture since 1945* (2017).

BERNADETTE WHELAN is Professor Emeritus in the Department of History, University of Limerick, Ireland. She is the author of numerous books on Irish-US relations including, most recently, *De Valera and Roosevelt: Irish and American Diplomacy in Times of Crisis, 1932–1939* (2021), which was awarded the American Conference of Irish Studies Lawrence J. McCaffrey Prize for Books on Irish America, and, with Mary O'Dowd and Gerardine Meaney, *Reading the Irish Woman: Studies in Cultural Encounters and Exchange, 1714–1960* (2013). Her latest book, *Irish First Ladies and First Gentlemen, 1919–2011*, was published in 2024. She is a member of the Royal Irish Academy and co-editor of *Documents on Irish Foreign Policy*, published biannually by the Royal Irish Academy, the Irish Department of Foreign Affairs, and the National Archives of Ireland.

CLARA ZACCAGNINI, an independent scholar, is currently working as a knowledge management consultant on migrants' remittances and diaspora investment at IFAD (International Fund for Agricultural Development) in Rome. She holds a Master's degree in International Studies from Roma Tre University. She is author with Lauren Braun-Strumfels of "Testing the Limits of Italian and US Migration Law: The 1904 Liguria Incident in New Orleans," in *Managing Migration in Italy and the United States*, edited by Lauren Braun-Strumfels, Maddalena Marinari, and Daniele Fiorentino (2024).

INDEX

Page numbers in *italics* indicate Figures and Tables